Come on in

BY JENNY ROSENSTRACH

How to Celebrate Everything
Dinner: The Playbook
Dinner: A Love Story

HOW TO CELEBRATE EVERYTHING

Recipes and Rituals for Birthdays, Holidays,
Family Dinners, and Every Day In Between

JENNY ROSENSTRACH

Photography by Chelsea Cavanaugh
Food Styling by Victoria Granof

BALLANTINE
BOOKS

NEW YORK

Copyright © 2016 by Jenny Rosenstrach

Published in the United States by Ballantine Books,
an imprint of Random House, a division of Penguin
Random House LLC, New York.

BALLANTINE and the HOUSE colophon are registered
trademarks of Penguin Random House LLC.

Salmon and Potatoes with Yogurt Sauce recipe:
Jenny Rosenstrach and Andy Ward, © *Bon
Appétit*, November 2013. Curried Carrots with
Pecans recipe: Jenny Rosenstrach and Andy Ward,
© *Bon Appétit*, December 2013. Portions of
"Vacation Rituals" and "Pick a Country, Any
Country" have appeared in *Bon Appétit*, and have
been reprinted with permission. "Miracle Mashed
Potatoes" appeared in *Real Simple* and has been
reprinted with permission.

Library of Congress Cataloging-in-Publication Data

Names: Rosenstrach, Jenny, author.
Title: How to celebrate everything : recipes and
rituals for birthdays, holidays, family dinners, and
every day in between / Jenny Rosenstrach.
Description: First edition. | New York : Ballantine
Books, 2016. | Includes index. | Description based
on print version record and CIP data provided by
publisher; resource not viewed.
Identifiers: LCCN 2016013191 (print) | LCCN
2016001416 (ebook) | ISBN 9780804176309
(hardback) | ISBN 9780804176316 (E-book)
Subjects: LCSH: Holiday cooking. | Dinners and
dining. | Entertaining. | Families. | BISAC: COOKING
/ Entertaining. | CRAFTS & HOBBIES / Seasonal. |
COOKING / Holiday. | LCGFT: Cookbooks.
Classification: LCC TX739 (print) | LCC TX739.R67
2016 (ebook) | DDC 641.5/68—dc23
LC record available at lccn.loc.gov/2016013191

Printed in China on acid-free paper

randomhousebooks.com

987654321

First Edition

Book design by Kristina DiMatteo

FOR
MOM & DAD,
EMILY & STEVE

♥

Iris's favorite family ritual? Eating a hamburger on her birthday every year. (That's April 12, if you'd like to send a card.)

CONTENTS

INTRODUCTION
PAGE XV
___

Why Rituals?

PART I
HOLIDAYS WE DIDN'T INVENT
PAGE 1
___

"Everything" **2**

Easter Ham **9**

The Edible Gift Ritual (Valentine's Day, Mother's Day, Father's Day) **15**

Fourth of July, aka Cousinland **28**

Halloween Launch Party **37**

On Thanksgiving Traditions **43**

How to Avoid Empty Celebration Syndrome **60**

The Holiday Party **68**

My Dad's Genius Entertaining Trick **77**

Christmas in Virginia **78**

Fancy-Pants Dinner (New Year's Eve) **89**

PART II
OUR FAMILY RITUALS
PAGE 97
___

The Walk to the Farmer's Market **98**

The One-on-One Date **122**

Fruit First Thing **133**

Pickling **135**

Lunch with Dad **143**

The Sleepover Breakfast **146**

Vacation Rituals **156**

Miracle Mashed Potatoes **168**

Après Ski **176**

PART III
BIRTHDAYS
PAGE 185
___

Abby's Birthdaypalooza **186**

Andy's Birthday Breakfasts **196**

Jenny's Mud Cake **199**

Phoebe's Ice Cream Cake **206**

Pick a Country, Any Country **211**

A Sane Parent's Guide to Throwing an At-Home Birthday Party **214**

PART IV
FAMILY DINNERS
PAGE 227
___

Did I Ever Tell You . . . ? **228**

Sunday Dinners **236**

Eating in Front of the TV **258**

After-Dinner Rituals **267**

On Signature Dinners **276**

IN CONCLUSION
PAGE 287
___

Rituals and Holidays Organized by Calendar **289**

Acknowledgments **291**

Index **292**

WHY RITUALS?

"Babies crave routines."

This is what the pediatrician told my husband, Andy, and me on a winter day in 2002, one week after I gave birth to our first daughter, Phoebe. We were unshowered and exhausted, running primarily on new-baby adrenaline, but thirteen years later I can hear those words as though he were standing right in front of me. If I were making a movie of my parenting life, it would be the scene that's revisited throughout the film, fuzzy, sepia-tinted, maybe even in slow motion.

Of course, to a rookie mom and dad, who might've paid a small fortune just to sleep for two straight hours, the concept of a routine seemed laughable. (At that point, the concept of ever watching another twenty-four-minute episode of *The Larry Sanders Show* seemed laughable.) But sure enough, it wasn't long before we'd regained the semblance of a schedule: I'd nurse the baby every three hours; she'd take two naps, a long one in the morning and a short one in the afternoon. Before bedtime, there'd be a rousing rendition of "She'll Be Comin' Round the Mountain" from our Music Together CD, followed by a story in the rocking chair, and a final round of nursing. (Or, as Andy used to call it, "The Knockout Blow.") As soon as Phoebe was safely down for the count, we'd pour ourselves a glass of wine and (*ahhh*) make dinner.

I don't mean to suggest those early days were perfect pictures of order and calm—quite the opposite, in fact, especially after her sister, Abby, showed up twenty months later, bent on upending all notions of twenty-first-century civilized living. But feeding, sleeping, making dinner, sacrificing any shred of dignity in the name of eliciting a giggle—those were the main dots to connect in the course of our days with babies and, later, with toddlers. It was rarely a straight line from one dot to the next, and it rarely resulted in a pretty picture, but the dots were our guides, our goals. Without them, without the routine, there was nothing preventing us from descending into a state of chaos.

Thirteen years later—different dots, different pictures—I find the doctor's advice as resonant as ever. The babies—and in our case, the babies' parents—still crave routines. We like knowing that gym is on Tuesday (wear sneakers) and art is on Thursdays (wear clothes you won't mind ruining). We like knowing that Mom works from home on Wednesdays. We like knowing that allowance comes on Fridays. We like knowing that the school bus will pull up to the corner at eight fifteen sharp and that dinner will

happen around seven o'clock. In short, we like knowing that we have some measure of control over things. (Even though deep down, we also know that this control rides side by side with denial.)

And yet, more than a dozen years into this parenting thing, I'm tempted to amend the doctor's advice a bit. If I were a pediatrician, and not a—ahem—food blogger, this is what I'd tell parents, the rookies and the vets, about my own experience:

Babies crave routines. Families crave rituals.

If routines are about keeping our family from going off the rails, rituals are about infusing those routine days with meaning.

Let's take that morning bus, for instance. Catching it when the girls were in elementary school was never easy. Never! Invariably, with five minutes left on the clock, we'd be turning the house upside down in search of a missing glove or workbook. Every morning we had to remind the girls to pack-your-bag-brush-your-teeth-grab-your-lunch, to *hurry up already* with the slo-mo loop-de-loop shoe tying. (And every morning, I'd wind up screaming *Good Lord! You'd think we didn't do this whole thing yesterday!* Then immediately hate myself.) It was during this seven-year stretch that I developed my superior talent as permission-slip-signing speed-walker.

But once we were finally out the door and safely headed in the right direction, I loved our bus stop ritual. Wow, did I love it. On the way to the pickup corner, we'd walk by a yellowing maple in the fall, a row of exploding magnolia trees in the spring, and thickets of honeysuckle bushes in June. We'd meet up with seven or eight other families, who, all told, counted four dogs (including Iris, our Boston terrier) and almost a dozen kids. As soon as everyone heard the rumbling of the bus as it struggled to make it up the hill, the kids, all wearing giant backpacks that threatened to topple them, would line up on the corner like little robots, knees rising as high as their chests as they took that first step aboard. The parents, some clutching coffee mugs and wearing ski jackets over pajamas, some suited up and ready for their walk to the commuter train, all searched the darkened windows for their kids, waved goodbye like maniacs, then hung around to chat with one another while the dogs tangled leashes and licked each other.

So, you might be thinking, *that sounds a lot like my morning routine*. How does something as mundane as walking to the bus stop qualify as meaningful? How does it get promoted to the status of ritual?

I'll tell you how. Standing out there on that corner year after year, we watched the neighborhood kids sprout before our eyes, evolving from princesses into tomboys and then back again. We laughed at the boys who insisted on wearing shorts on frigid winter days, and at the parents who were powerless to control it. We pretended not to care too much when the kids grew out of kissing us goodbye. We coordinated playdates and dinner parties, shared vacation plans, and swapped Twitter handles. We discussed why the cheese shop in town was closing, when the Halloween parade started, who the new permanent third-grade sub was, and everything else that passed for big news in our small-town New York suburb. On the first and last days of school, at least one person had a camera, and multiple photos were taken of the bus-boarders, even though I knew that, by doing so, we were only setting ourselves up for heartbreak down the road. *Look how teeny you were! That was your first day of first grade! Look at Piper when she was just a puppy! Remember those silver sandals you wore every day?* (Excuse me while I start weeping on my keyboard.)

In other words, the school bus send-off transcended routine because it connected us to something larger. It connected us to our community in a way that, I later realized, would be hard to replicate once there was no more bus to catch. Mostly, though, it connected us as a family. As harried as we felt, as chaotic as the workday ahead of us promised to be, we started off every morning together. From beginning to end, I'd estimate that bus stop ritual lasted under eight minutes each day, but it was pretty much guaranteed that at one point during those eight minutes, a little hand would mindlessly reach up and latch on to mine. (This, in spite of my best Cruella De Vil impersonation only minutes earlier.) That gesture alone put enough fuel in the happy tank to power an entire day at the office.

My family craves rituals. Some of them, like walking to the bus stop, are simple, daily, and downright random. Others, like cooking Thanksgiving dinner with my mother, "Grandma Jody," or baking Christmas cookies with Andy's mom, "Grandma Hubba," are big, huge, once-a-year food-related rituals attached to big, huge, once-a-year holidays. One ritual, family dinner (which is also the subject of my blog, *Dinner: A Love Story*), is so fundamental to the psychological health of our household

The key to creating
and re-creating rituals?
Take lots of notes.
(See page 61.)

ey brought mashed - also
too many
's brussel sprouts a hit
- green salad was finished
pudding pies (2) also a hit
1 gravy package - added
sauce in pan - (add more
2ego Inn)*
stuffing - good
used only elect.   good for turkey
needs adj...   oven

- burns veg
stem: no turkey
no pop up
le solution - r
toes - hit. of ke
- no ricer
lish - Jenny + c
veak - need +
prouts - should
mod sm... ho

year - NYC desserts
Andye pumpkin pie -
broiled asparagus
Jenny's corn bread
Lynn's green salad - not 1
whipped cream - sm.
et pot. casserole -
an bake 12 speeds -
up to 2 hrs.   Ricing
ext for att pecan

Thanksgiving

problem. L

t. - 1 day -

pot. - bo

gus. broil

y sauce (

- Knorr -

- Martha ...

outh

ea

- very good

e (+) at

butter the
on (cut in
quarters)

(2004) at 10 Sout

14' turkey - plenty
mashed potatoes -
sweet pot. - at le
gravy + stuffing from Pau
↳ too watery - next year
Choc. pudding pie + whipp
Cranberry sauce
Jenny - corn bread
Lynn - asparagus & sa

Phil - Tiramisu & (good

sugg. wash turkey
take small bowl +
M.A. - Trader Joe's tu

wrapping
body!)
watch

Dinn

Lynn +

2014 Thanksgiving 6th
- upper 30
- Next year remind Je
for potatoes + mini
sauce 7 and
- All staples: sugar,
cornbread - double check in

Turkey - 14.5' not e
if turkey too lar
try more compact.
sweet pot. - ok - 9 spe
recommended - Jenn

10 South

19 and O

that we think of it as our North Star, something worth organizing our days—maybe even our lives—around.

Whether they're big or small, simple or elaborate, daily or yearly, all our rituals serve the same purpose: They bring comfort, connection, and meaning to our days, days that might otherwise just wind up blurring together. On a daily basis, rituals help me answer the questions that are central to my life as a parent: How do we help our children recognize things that *matter*? How do we teach them to be grateful for everything they have—not the latest Nike Free Runs, but friends and family and community? How do we make days feel special? How do we hold on to moments that are so easily lost in the jam-packed calendar, that disappear behind us like a jet trail?

This book is about the importance of rituals and celebrations in our family, and I hope it serves as a blueprint for starting rituals and optimizing celebrations in yours. For us, it's about waking up on our birthdays to a Big Deal Breakfast (homemade waffles with berries and whipped cream for Abby; sausage-and-egg biscuits for Andy). It's about eating Phoebe-invented butter-fried, cinnamon-dusted pineapple chunks every New Year's Eve and a Jenga-like platter of deluxe nachos every Super Bowl. It's about walking to the farmer's market every Saturday morning from June through November and, season permitting, collecting all the ingredients for a proper tomato sandwich that we will devour for lunch later that afternoon. It's about serving creamy, comforting mashed potatoes after every braces-tightening visit to the orthodontist. It's about the post-dinner concert ritual—laying down a strand of Christmas lights around the perimeter of the upstairs hall to create a "stage," then being treated to "The Dance of the Sugar Plum Fairy," an a capella Taylor Swift ballad, or a Neil Young air guitar solo with a tennis racket. (Wow, do I miss those days.) It's very much about the box of Pop-Tarts Andy throws in the cart as soon as we begin grocery shopping for the vacation rental: The kids aren't allowed to eat Pop-Tarts for breakfast in their regular lives, and the thrill they get from breaking this rule reminds us that the point of vacation is inserting happiness wherever you can, and getting as far away from your daily routine as possible.

Because I recognize that not everyone is going to see the magic in a toaster pastry or in escorting their kids to the school bus before being properly caffeinated, this book is also about celebrating holidays we *didn't* invent. It's about our Easter ham, our Rosh Hashanah challah (yes, both; more on that soon), our Fourth of July festivities, and our big ol' pot of Halloween chili that simmers away while Andy carves pumpkins based on the girls' sketches. It's about family dinners we share, recipes that tell stories, and flavors that are welded to memories and, whenever possible, joy. It's about using the ultimate ritual—family dinner—to remind our kids that they are part of a unit, something bigger than themselves. It's about all the different ways we've found to connect with our kids and parents and grandparents and cousins and aunts and uncles and friends and community through food and rituals—because we are human, and connection is what we humans seem to crave.

If I'm honest with myself, this book is also about denial. Maybe my instinct to ritualize everything is an attempt to convince myself that I have some measure of control over how fast everything is moving, that if I manage to connect all these small happy moments to the larger narrative of our lives—if I make a conscious effort to stop and celebrate as much as possible—then maybe, just maybe, my daughters' childhoods can last forever?

And here you probably thought you picked up a book that would teach you how to roast a Thanksgiving turkey.

(You did, don't worry.)

I am not saying we should throw a party every time our kid burps. What I hope to accomplish, beyond offering up ninety-plus time-tested recipes that have served our family well on just about any special occasion, is to call attention to moments throughout the year that might be the starting points for your own rituals or, at the very least, inspire you to savor the ones you already have in place. Food is at the heart of it for me because we love to cook, but also because it's the draw, the connector, and, in some cases, the starting point for great family stories. Not to mention it's a well-known agent for sealing in memories (see: Proust) so we'd all be crazy not to use it to our advantage.

I've organized *How to Celebrate Everything* into four major ritual groupings: Holidays We Didn't Invent, Our Family Rituals (like the bus stop walk), Birthdays, and Family Dinners. I'm including many of our very specific, personal rituals in this book for two reasons: First, they'll help you get to know the characters in my family, not only Andy, Phoebe, Abby, and me, but the grandparents, aunts, uncles, and cousins,

"THIS BOOK IS ABOUT FAMILY DINNERS WE SHARE, RECIPES THAT TELL STORIES, AND FLAVORS THAT ARE WELDED TO MEMORIES AND, WHENEVER POSSIBLE, JOY."

too. Second, I wanted to make something clear to anyone who has just read this introduction and is asking herself, "Wait, do we have *any* rituals in our family?" Trust me, you do. What I hope to illustrate in the following pages is that rituals don't have to be accompanied by a five-course meal or have an aisle at Hallmark to be special. There can be something memorable in the most ordinary moments of a family's daily routine—even folding the laundry together, even drinking a Coke, even visiting the orthodontist. Once you get in the ritual mindset, you'll see there are endless options for celebrating. You just have to know where to look.

To see rituals and celebrations organized by calendar year, see page 289.

Rituals with Friends and Neighbors

It should come as no surprise to anyone who has read my blog that all the rituals rounded up in this book are attached to recipes—beginning with the bus stop. We loved our morning routine so much that, during those years, we'd host an annual "Bus Stop Social," when school was over, inviting all the families from the corner to attend. Andy and I would call in a big fat order of ribs and baked beans from Corky's BBQ in Memphis, and the rest of the crew would supplement with salads and desserts, potluck style.

I am grateful we did this for many reasons. For the ribs, of course—those are good ribs!—but also because we miraculously had the good sense to know that someday we'd feel nostalgic about all those early mornings. The bus stop social was a way of telling our kids (and their parents) that this mattered, and in the process gave the experience some staying power. I like to think we were beaming a message to our future selves that said, *We are not taking any of this for granted.* None of it. The community, the honeysuckle, the puppies, the hideous pajama pants, the hand-holding. Especially the hand-holding.

I highly recommend creating as many rituals with friends and neighbors as possible, no matter where you are in the parenting game. Beyond the benefits already described, there's comfort in knowing you can count on a potluck dinner across the street every time there's a big snowstorm, or a pot of meatballs across town every Friday night with other new parents, or an end-of-the-season ice-cream party at the soccer coach's house, or a Negroni followed by restaurant-worthy pasta carbonara with your best friends whenever you get that nagging feeling it's been too long. In my mind, that's the best kind of guilt. It's motivating. And it disappears with a single delicious dinner.

"BUS STOP SOCIAL" RIBS

We only order from Corky's for special occasions. Here is the standard recipe we use for ribs on every other weekend of the summer. (For our family of four, we only need two racks. You'll need to adjust accordingly if you're having the whole bus stop over.) I love ribs for entertaining because most of the cooking is done in advance. If this is a potluck, ask your neighbors to bring the side dishes—slaw, baked beans, potato salad, and pie. (If it's not, see Crowd-Pleaser Summer Slaw on page 34, Franks and Beans on page 38, German Potato Salad on page 35, and Triple Berry Summer Pie with Lattice Crust on page 118.) And don't forget napkins. Lots of napkins. If you're doing it right, things will get messy.

SERVES 4 (RECIPE CAN BE DOUBLED OR TRIPLED)

¼ cup brown sugar, packed

3 tablespoons smoked paprika

1 tablespoon regular paprika

2 teaspoons ground cumin

1 teaspoon mustard powder

2 teaspoons kosher salt

1 teaspoon cayenne
   (or to taste if heat is an issue with kids)

2 teaspoons garlic salt

1 teaspoon white pepper or freshly ground black pepper

2 pork rib racks, about 6 pounds total

barbecue sauce, for basting

The best ending to a bus stop social? (Or any summer celebration for that matter?) Triple berry pie. See page 118 for recipe.

- Preheat the oven to 300°F.
- In a medium bowl, whisk together the brown sugar and spices. Smear the rub on the meaty side of the rib racks until coated. Place on a rimmed baking sheet, cover with foil, and bake for 3 hours. Remove and set aside.
- About 30 minutes before the ribs finish roasting, fire up your grill. When the fire is ready (if you are using a charcoal grill, you don't want to put them over a raging fire; let it die down a little until it's about medium heat), grill the ribs for 2 minutes a side to get a little char going. Then brush the meaty side generously with your favorite barbecue sauce. Cook for 5 minutes, flipping every minute or so, being careful not to burn the ribs but getting the sauce nice and caramelized. Remove from the heat, and slice the ribs along the bones on a cutting board.

PASTA NIGHT WITH FRIENDS: CARBONARA

Carbonara is a smart recipe to build a ritual around because, when it's done right, it feels every bit as indulgent as something you'd get in a restaurant, and it's a heck of a lot cheaper. (Plus, what you save on the babysitter, you can put toward a nice Sancerre.) This recipe is based on one our friend Jeff made us, and as simple as it is, it can go to the scrambled-eggs place fast if you're not careful. As far as we can tell, there are two important steps to take to avoid this. First, add a little pasta water to the eggs. This is called tempering, and it helps get the eggs used to the idea of heat slowly rather than all at once (which usually results in scrambling). The other crucial step is to remove the pan from the heat completely before adding the eggs. We set the skillet down on a cutting board before adding them. If you are cooking this for friends for the first time, we recommend a dry run so you're not in panic mode. On the other hand, even if the eggs do scramble, it will still taste delicious.

SERVES 4

1 pound spaghetti

kosher salt

3 tablespoons good-quality olive oil

2 to 3 thick slices pancetta or bacon,
    chopped into lardons or cubes

1 clove garlic, minced (about 1 tablespoon)

4 eggs

¾ cup shredded Pecorino cheese, plus more for serving

freshly ground pepper

• Prepare the spaghetti according to the package directions. (Remember to salt the water!) While the spaghetti cooks, heat the oil in a large deep-sided skillet set over medium heat and fry the pancetta until crisp, about 5 minutes. Lower the heat and add the garlic to the skillet toward the last minute. While everything is cooking, whisk the eggs in a medium bowl.

• Drain the pasta, reserving about ¼ cup of the pasta water. Add the spaghetti to the skillet while it's still a little wet and, using tongs, toss with the garlic and pancetta, adding a tiny drizzle of reserved pasta water to keep it loose and to prevent spaghetti from sticking to the bottom of the pan. Remove the pan from the heat completely. (We set the skillet down on a cutting board on the counter.)

• Vigorously whisk about a tablespoon or two of hot pasta water into the eggs—this is the tempering. Add the eggs to the pasta slowly, tossing until the pasta looks silky and coated but is not drippy and wet. Toss in the ¾ cup of cheese. Serve immediately with more cheese and freshly ground pepper.

CLASSIC NEGRONI

This makes one cocktail. The recipe can be doubled . . . or tripled.
But beware: They're powerful.

SERVES 1

1 ounce gin

1 ounce sweet vermouth

1 ounce Campari

1 orange slice

• Add the gin, vermouth, and Campari to a cocktail shaker with 4 or 5 ice cubes and shake. Pour into a coupe glass straight up, or over ice in a short tumbler or lowball glass. Garnish with the orange slice.

2012 Thanksgiving

Oysters on the half
Turkey - Bell & Ev...
go to N.R.
(next yr. - get...

4th ...
Thanksgiving
7 adults - 6 children

Thanksgiving 2013

2014 Thanksgiving 6th Annual   turkey in 12:20pm
— upper 30's - cold   7 adults, 6 kids

— Next year remind Jenny to bring colander
for potatoes + mini food processor for cranberry
sauce ☐ and

— All staples: sugar, salt, pepper, olive oil
cornbread - double check ingred, but still good

Turkey - 14.5' "not enough" - try + turkey breast; no popup on Trader's turkey
if turkey too large will not fit in oven;
try more compact roaster pan in Tuesday   Brined ok but do B + E Evans next yr.
sweet pot. - ok - 9 spuds - 1/2 pecans on top.
cranberry relish - Jenny + Alison - big hit
neg. trad. cran. sauce - ok but need a bit of leftover
stuffing - hit   J + A's relish
mashed potatoes - beautiful
Gravy - drippings used - but salty alert.   Phil brought
Zabar's gravy - good.
brussel sprouts - excellent - parboil
cauliflower - "
asparagus - do not need next yr.
ward pies - excellent - pumpkin, apple pecan!
choc. pudding - get Jello brand. (not Tempi) - 3?
* co-ordinate stove use/timing bef end of cooking.
no cranberry hands in living room

warming oven worked - esp. for sw. pot. casserole
need 2 gravy boats small
bring food processor / elec. knife
sparkling cider

No detail is too small to qualify for my mom's post-Thanksgiving review. See page 61 for more.

PART I

HOLIDAYS
WE DIDN'T
INVENT

"Everything" / Easter Ham / The Edible Gift /
Fourth of July, aka Cousinland
Halloween Launch Party / On Thanksgiving Traditions
How to Avoid Empty Celebration Syndrome
The Holiday Party / My Dad's Genius Entertaining Trick
Christmas in Virginia
Fancy-Pants Dinner: New Year's Eve

"EVERYTHING"

A few autumns ago, I was attempting to bake challah with then seven-year-old Abby when she asked me a question.

"What am I?" she said, as the two of us tried to braid together three somewhat unwieldy strands of dough. It was the first time I'd ever made my own challah.

"What do you mean?" I replied, knowing full well what she meant. She had been asking versions of the same question a lot lately, and as soon as we had decided to bake the bread, I knew she'd bring it up again.

She continued. "Well, we're making this challah because it's Rosh Hashanah, right? So am I Jewish? Or am I Italian? You always say I'm more Italian than anything, but isn't someone in our family Cuban, too? Is Cuban a religion?"

This conversation was going to be a lot harder than baking the bread. And that's saying something because I'm not a baker. I'm a cook. I was born with a recessive gene in the patience department, which means it can sometimes be difficult for me to follow a recipe whose result hinges on, you know, *following* the recipe. Unlike cooking, where instructions read more like suggestions than mandates to me, baking, with its hyper-specific techniques and ingredient lists (Room temperature eggs? Really?), seem made for the kind of people who revel in detail work, like violin makers or stop-motion animators. The challah recipe, for instance, from my second cousin Ronnie, author of several cookbooks herself, called for warm water, "about 105 degrees." It's the kind of instruction that sends me into a panic spiral.

Compared to Abby's question, though, I loved the scientific, if-this-then-that promise of the recipe. Baking was methodical and a little boring, but at least it was straightforward. The answer to Abby's question was not. If I were to give her the most accurate answer to *"What am I?"* it would go something like this:

"Well, your Papa Ivan, my father, is Jewish. His parents were Russian and Romanian. My mother is one hundred percent Italian; she's Presbyterian but her mother was Catholic. Papa, Daddy's father, was raised Catholic; he was German, English, and Mexican with a little Cuban mixed in, too. Daddy's mom, Grandma Hubba, is half Italian and half a lot of other things—Dutch, German, Scottish—and was raised with no religion. Neither was your dad. Even though I was raised both

**STAR OF DAVID
CHRISTMAS COOKIES**
My life in a nutshell.
(Recipe, page 83)

Presbyterian and Jewish, I was bat mitzvahed in 1983, and my twin brother and I had our after-party at a Japanese steakhouse, where, among other things, a mound of decidedly unkosher shrimp was sent missiling through the air from the hibachi chef to my plate. Your dad and I were married by a Unitarian minister who had once been a rabbi. Your cousins on Dad's side have spent a good number of years matriculating in Catholic schools, while on my side, your cousins are in Hebrew school twice a week, working on their haftarahs. When I was growing up, every Friday night your grandpa would walk in the door with a fresh challah just like this one—and at some point over the weekend, it wouldn't be unusual for me to take two slices of it and put together a bacon-lettuce-and-tomato sandwich with mayo, a sandwich that would've had my kosher grandparents rolling in their graves."

I don't go through all this with Abby, though. Instead, I gave her my cop-out line. "You're everything."

I could tell that she was confused by this answer. I was, too. In fact, I had been working through that confusion for most of my life. My Jewish father and my Presbyterian mother, married in the United Nations chapel in New York in 1968, took a diplomatic approach to raising their three kids with respect to religion: We'd go to Hebrew school and to select services on the High Holy Days, but we'd also go to church on Easter and Christmas Eve or occasionally when my mom was performing in her congregation's choir. I guess the idea was that we would eventually decide which path to take on our own. This dual citizenship didn't bother me at all—especially when the holidays came around and we were allowed to celebrate both Hanukkah *and* Christmas, eat latkes *and* gingerbread cookies. My friends, impressed by the mad dreidel skills I'd picked up at Hebrew school and by my familiarity with all the lyrics in "Hark! The Herald Angels Sing!," would ask: "So what are you? Jewish or Christian?"

"Both," I would say.

Just like "both" can sometimes register as "neither," I worry that telling Abby and her sister, Phoebe, that we are "everything" might register as "nothing." So on this particular day with Abby, I did what I usually do: I focused on the food. For metaphorical purposes, I wished we were making fondue, or something else that required a melting pot, but instead I turned to the challah on the counter in front of us.

"Well, I guess you could say our family is sort of like this bread we're baking for

Aunt Lynn's Rosh Hashanah dinner. It's many ingredients combined and all these strands of dough interwoven, but if you do everything right, it transforms into something whole and meaningful."

"And delicious."

"Yes, that too."

When the challah came out of the oven, it was beautiful. Well, sort of. It was perfectly curvy and golden, but had a bulge in the middle and seemed about 20 percent larger than most of the ones my dad used to bring home on Fridays. Still, we were extremely proud of it. Phoebe, nine years old at the time, walked into the kitchen and decided she couldn't wait until dinner at my sister's. She ripped off a piece at the tip, spread some butter across it, let the butter melt into the sweet, eggy dough, then savored it. I did the same thing, but I studded the top with a few golden raisins, the way I used to as a kid.

I told the girls how a single bite of it beamed me back to my own childhood, to the nights when Papa Ivan would come home from work carrying the loaf that signified Friday, the promise of a weekend. Not only that, I told them, but the recipe we were using had been used by relatives for generations: Legend has it that the bread was first baked by Ronnie's grandmother and that someone once paid her one hundred dollars for it *during the Depression*! Lastly, and perhaps most important, the braided bread that sat before us, even though it looked like it had been mauled by jackals, and even if we didn't have it every Friday night like when I was a kid, would be in the center of a table that my entire family would later share. Maybe we'd make it again next year. Maybe someday they'd make the same recipe with their children before heading off to a family feast, and tell them the same story.

"Amazing, right?" I said. "See how this is not just a loaf of bread? How it connects us to so many other things?"

"Sure, Mom," said Phoebe. "Can I have the butter?"

5

THE $100 CHALLAH

Here is Ronnie's grandmother's one-hundred-dollar recipe. Observant readers will know that the High Holy Days call for a round challah—but this is the one that went for the big bucks, and it is good all year long. I mix golden raisins into the dough because it reminds me of the way I ate it every Friday as a kid—and also because it's delicious. Makes 1 large challah. You can cut the dough in half to make 2 smaller loaves (bake for 22 to 25 minutes) or halve the recipe. (For halved recipes you can use a food processor to mix and knead the dough.)

SERVES 8 TO 10

2 packages active dry yeast

2 cups warm water (about 105°F;
    feels slightly warm to the touch), divided

½ cup sugar, divided

8 cups all-purpose flour, plus more if needed
    for the dough and for the work surface

1 tablespoon kosher salt

5 large eggs

3 tablespoons vegetable oil

½ cup golden raisins (optional)

• In a small bowl, mix the yeast, ½ cup of the warm water, ½ teaspoon of the sugar, and a pinch of the flour. Stir and set aside for about 5 minutes or until the mixture is bubbly.

• While the yeast is activating, place 7½ cups of the flour with the remaining sugar and the salt in the bowl of an electric mixer fitted with a dough hook. Add 4 of the eggs, the vegetable oil, and the remaining 1½ cups warm water. Mix, using the dough hook, until well combined. Add the yeast mixture and the raisins, if using, and blend in thoroughly. Knead for 3 to 4 minutes or until the dough is smooth and elastic. Add the remaining flour as needed to make the dough smooth and soft, but not overly sticky.

• Cover the bowl with a clean kitchen towel and let the dough rise in a warm place for about 1½ hours or until doubled in bulk. Punch the dough down, cover the bowl, and let rise again for about 45 minutes or until doubled in bulk. Remove the dough to a floured surface.

• Cut the dough into 3 or 6 pieces, depending on whether you are going to make a 3- or 6-strand braid. Roll long strands out of each piece. Braid the strands and seal the ends together by pressing on the dough and tucking them under. Place the bread on a lightly greased cookie sheet. Let rise in a warm place for 30 minutes.

• While the dough is in the last rise, preheat the oven to 350°F. Beat the last egg and brush the challah's surface with it. Bake the challah for about 30 minutes or until firm and golden brown.

The whole
reason to make
an apricot-rum
glazed Easter
Ham, in my
opinion? The
leftovers.
Split pea soup,
page 12.

EASTER HAM

My father's mother, Grandma Tillie, didn't attend my parents' wedding. To review, she was Jewish, raised in an Orthodox household by parents who had been born in a Romanian shtetl—and her oldest son marrying a Presbyterian from western Pennsylvania had not exactly been her idea of kosher. Naturally, her wedding-day protest weighed heavily on my father, but once my parents tied the knot and, a year later, had my sister, Lynn, Tillie's boycott all but lifted. (I suppose if anything is powerful enough to disrupt generations of tribal tradition, a new grandchild is it.) And anyway, in spite of my mom's non-Jewish leanings, Tillie loved her. You can't *not* love my mom. She was elected homecoming queen in college, for crying out loud— most likely because she's nice to everybody. *Everybody.* Even to a mother-in-law who was a no-show on her wedding day.

Tillie died two weeks before I was born, and however impressive her strides were on the religious tolerance front, I do always wonder what she would've made of the fifteen-pound ham that arrived on our doorstep every year, just in time for Passover.

It wasn't for Passover, of course. It was for Easter, but, like Christmas and Hanukkah in our house, the two holidays would often blur together. The ham, which would be the anchor of my mom's Easter table, came in a box stamped CATRINO'S MARKET and was accompanied, every year, by the same simple note: "Happy Easter! Love, Albert." Albert was my mom's older brother by twenty-two years. He still lived in the small Pennsylvania town where they had grown up, and he ran the store my grandfather had opened when he moved to America from Italy in 1900. Like my mother, Uncle Albert was a workaholic, hardly ever closing Catrino's Market for vacation or travel, which meant that we only got to see him for weddings and special occasions.

But once a year, at least, we could count on Uncle Albert's ham.

I've never asked my dad how he felt about the ham's arrival—I'm guessing it's something akin to what Woody Allen felt when Annie Hall ordered her pastrami on white bread with mayo—but I can tell you one thing for certain: No one looked forward to that delivery more than I did. I loved Easter dinner, though somehow I don't remember it nearly as clearly as I remember the ham-based leftover meals I'd subsist on for at least a week following the holiday. (Uncle Albert was generous with the portions, so there were *always* leftovers.) For breakfast, I'd chop up some ham bits, fry them in a skillet, letting the fat render, then crack a few eggs on top and scramble in some Parm, salt, and pepper. For lunch, I'd make a sandwich either with ham, pickles, and mustard on a squishy potato roll or (Grandma Tillie: Close your eyes, shut your ears, run the other way!) with ham and mayo on two slices of challah. For dinner, my mom would make split pea soup simmered in a pot with the hock, which was my favorite and, in my humble opinion, the whole reason to serve a ham in the first place. These days, I make that soup all winter and fall, swapping in smoky bacon or ham chunks if I don't have the hock. It's delicious, but, of course, it's never *exactly* the same if it doesn't start with Uncle Albert's delivery.

Uncle Albert died in 1997, the year I got married, so Andy never got to have the true Catrino Passover-Easter (Eastover?) Experience. But we've given the ritual our own spin, trotting out an Albert-inspired ham for our interfaith winter holiday party, where it sits proudly next to a spread of Brisket Sliders (page 70), Potato Latkes (see page 73), and apple sauce. I feel certain both sides of the family would approve.

APRICOT-RUM GLAZED HAM

My mom brushed her ham with mustard and studded the top with cloves, but once we tried a version of this apricot-rum glazed beauty at our friend Adam's house, we never looked back. Sweet and boozy, salty and shiny, it's a showstopper.

SERVES 16 TO 20

> 1 12- to 14-pound whole cured ham (not fresh)
> 4 tablespoons apricot jam
> 4 tablespoons dark rum

• Preheat the oven to 325°F. Using a sharp knife, score the outer skin of the ham in a diamond pattern, about ½ inch deep. Place the ham on a rack in a roasting pan with 1 cup water, and bake for an hour on the oven's lower rack.

• While the ham bakes, make the glaze: Add the jam and rum to a small pot. Set on medium heat and whisk until it reduces by about a third and gets slightly bubbly, about 8 minutes.

• After an hour, remove the ham from the oven and brush on the glaze. Return the ham to the oven for another hour, or until an instant-read thermometer inserted into the thickest part of the ham reads 135°F. While it bakes, baste and glaze with the drippings every 15 to 20 minutes. If the ham starts to burn, tent it with foil.

HAM AND EGGS WITH PARM AND HERBS

Our kids do not like eggs of any kind (how? why?). So alas, eating this for breakfast in the days after Easter, is a family ritual enjoyed by only half the family.

SERVES 2

> 1 tablespoon butter
> 1 generous handful leftover ham,
>   chopped into small pieces (about ½ cup)
> 4 eggs
> 1 tablespoon freshly grated Parmigiano-Reggiano
> freshly ground pepper
> minced fresh chives, for garnish
> sea salt (optional)

• Add the butter to a nonstick skillet over medium heat. When it melts, add the ham, cooking until it's slightly crispy, about 3 minutes. In a small bowl, whisk together the eggs, cheese, and pepper. Add to the pan and mix everything together, scrambling until the eggs are cooked but still slightly wet. (Or however you roll re: egg doneness.) Serve with a sprinkling of chives and flaky sea salt if the ham doesn't add enough saltiness.

HAM SANDWICHES (OR SLIDERS) WITH PICKLED VEGETABLES

For me, this sandwich is all about the finely minced pickled vegetables. To turn the recipe into sliders for a party (see page 70) you'll need the whole ham, not just the leftovers. Slice into small pieces, and serve on a platter alongside forty-eight slider buns and assorted pickles and mustards (whole-grain, hot, Dijon). Have guests serve themselves.

MAKES 4 SANDWICHES

1½ pounds leftover ham (12 to 15 thin slices)

4 potato rolls, preferably Martin's brand

whole-grain mustard

pickled bell peppers, cucumbers, and red onions
   (see page 141), finely minced

• Assemble the ham on the rolls with a small smear of mustard, and top with pickled vegetables.

SPLIT PEA SOUP WITH LEFTOVER HAM AND CHIVE CROUTONS

Usually, when making soups, I advise salting every step of the way, but when briny ham is in the pot, you want to be conservative. If you want to make this with leftover ham (and not the hock), fry about a cup of chopped ham over medium heat for five minutes until crisp, remove, then proceed with the recipe, returning the ham to the pot at the end.

SERVES 4

2 tablespoons butter

1 medium onion, chopped

2 stalks celery, chopped

2 large carrots, chopped (about 1 cup)

kosher salt and freshly ground pepper

leftover ham hock

    (with or without meat still on it)

1¾ cup split peas

2 bay leaves

Chive Croutons (see recipe below)

• In a large stockpot, over medium-low heat, melt the butter. Add the onion, celery, carrots, and pepper and a little salt. Cook for about 8 minutes, until the vegetables are soft.

• Add the ham hock, split peas, bay leaves, and 8 cups of water. Test for saltiness. Add more salt to taste. Bring to a boil, then lower to a simmer, cover, and cook for 1 hour and 15 minutes.

• Remove the ham hock and the bay leaves. Using an immersion blender, puree the soup in the stockpot until it's mostly smooth. Add a little more water if it seems too thick. If there was meat on the bone, pull it off the bone and add back to the soup. Serve with homemade croutons or crusty bread.

Chive Croutons

• Preheat the oven to 325°F. Cut the crusts off two ¾-inch-thick slices of bread, then cut those slices into roughly ¾-inch cubes. In a large bowl, toss the bread cubes with 2 tablespoons olive oil, 2 teaspoons minced fresh chives, and 1 teaspoon garlic salt until every cube is coated in oil. Spread the cubes out in an even layer on a rimmed baking sheet. Sprinkle with salt and pepper. Bake just until the croutons are golden, stirring occasionally, about 15 to 20 minutes.

Remove the meat to a cutting board, carve, and arrange on a platter. Add ‖ or ‖‖ tbs. of warm water to the pot, turn the heat to high, and boil away the water while scraping and loosening all the cooking residue in a pot. Spoon the sauce over the sliced pork and serve. ✤

Great Grandma Turano's Meatball's

Sauce

In olive oil in a large heavy saucepan

Brown:
1 clove → minced garlic
1/4 c. chopped onion →
1/2 c. sliced mushrooms

Add:
salt and pepper to taste → S P
1 can tomato paste + 2 cans water
1 T. ← sugar
1 15 oz can tomato paste & another can of tomato sauce

Heat until sauce begins to bubble, then cover and simmer 30-40 minutes.

In a bowl mix:
3/4 c. Italian bread crumbs
1/4 c. grated Romano or Parmesan
1 [?] lean ground beef
[?] inches fennel seed (important!)
[?] eggs
[?]pped parsley

Rosa's Mud Cake

1 1/4 c. flour
2 c. sugar
3/4 c. cocoa
2 tsp. 1 tsp.
2 eggs → OO
1 c. strong black coffee
1 c. buttermilk
1/2 c.
1 tsp.

(Jeni likes chocolate chips.)

Combine all dry ingredients in large bowl. Add remaining ingredients and beat at medium speed. Dump into a buttered sheet pan and cook in a 350° oven for 30-40 minutes.

Form small meatballs and brown on all sides in a frying pan. Add the balls to the sauce and cook another 15 minutes. Serve with spaghetti.

Grandma Catrino's Biscotti

Cream together 1/2 cup BUTTER, 1 cup sugar, add OOO eggs one at a time. In another bowl, sift together 3 cups plain flour, FLOUR 1/2 tsp. baking powder. Add dry mixture to butter mixture slowly. Stir in 1 tsp. almond extract, 1 Tbl. Anise seed; 1/2 cup chopped pecans or almonds. Flour counter and Knead mixture and work into 3 loaves. Place on a lightly greased cookie sheet and bake at 350° for 15 to 20 minutes until firm and light brown. Cool and cut into strips. For crisper strips, bake strips cup-side down another 10 minutes. ✤ ✤ ✤

THE EDIBLE GIFT

VALENTINE'S DAY, MOTHER'S DAY, FATHER'S DAY

So now that I've established how much I rely on food rituals to impart meaning into the routine, it's time to establish another huge bonus: Food rituals can save you loads of precious time and energy when certain holidays roll around. Specifically holidays that require a gift. For those of you who find yourself stumped on Mother's Day, Father's Day, Valentine's Day, or any day that calls for something more than a spray-painted macaroni card, you'll want to pay attention here. That's because food is *never*—repeat *never*—the wrong answer to any gift-related question that may arise in the course of a family's year of celebrating. Including:

What can I give that's meaningful?

In my case, the answer to that question might be something like Grandma Catrino's biscotti. Like the rest of my grandparents, Grandma Mary Catrino, my mom's mom, died before I was born—long before I was born, in 1950. So what little I know of her, I know from a handful of stories, a framed black-and-white portrait that sits on a dresser in my parents' house, and her almond biscotti. It wasn't until I started my blog in 2010 that I knew this recipe even existed. My mother's niece—and my cousin—Maryanne (rightfully) guessed that I might like to have a copy of Grandma Catrino's biscotti recipe. That Mother's Day, I made a batch for my mom, swapping in pistachios for almonds and adding dried cherries, and tied them up in a cookie tin. They tasted heavenly—but even if they hadn't, the gift would've been a huge win on the sentimental front. They were so much more than something to dunk in a mug of coffee.

My point? When you're stumped for gift ideas, ask yourself: What recipes carry meaning in your family? Which ones qualify as special? Which ones might remind the recipient of something happy? A recipe doesn't necessarily have to be handed down through generations to qualify, either. It can be just as effective to choose a dish or treat that was consumed on a particularly memorable family vacation (Did your dad love lobster rolls in Maine? Surprise him with one for lunch on Father's Day.) or at a birthday or anniversary celebration (Remember that glass of Pinot Noir she ordered at Gramercy Tavern? Buy her a bottle.). Once I baked my dad a homemade version of his favorite discontinued Entenmann's cake (R.I.P., Sour Cream Chocolate Chip Nut Loaf!), and with one bite we were back in our linoleum-tiled 1980s kitchen. I love the gift my friend Jen gave her husband, Ben, on Valentine's Day one year: all the ingredients to make authentic pad thai, the meal they shared when they went out on their first date. She tied up the brown grocery bag with a big red bow, and instead of dining on the customary champagne and chocolate mousse, the two minced lemongrass, whisked tamarind paste, boiled rice noodles, and cracked eggs together, then sat down to toast their history. How sweet is that?

MY GRANDMA CATRINO'S BISCOTTI

This is my mother's mother's recipe, and it's endlessly adaptable. The way it's written here is how it's written on the recipe card sent by my cousin Maryanne. But we often replace the almonds with pistachios, replace the almond extract with vanilla extract, and add dried cherries.

MAKES 30 COOKIES

   3 cups all-purpose flour, plus more for the work surface

   ½ teaspoon kosher salt

   3 tablespoons baking powder

   ½ cup (1 stick) unsalted butter, at room temperature

   1 cup sugar

   3 eggs

   1 teaspoon almond extract

   ½ cup chopped almonds or pecans (raw or roasted)

When is the gift of almond-cherry biscotti more than just a gift of almond-cherry biscotti? When they're made from your great-grandmother's recipe (page 16).

A homemade version of your favorite childhood treat is never going to be a bad idea. Shown here: My best riff on Entenmann's Sour Cream Chocolate Chip Nut Loaf.

Dad

- Preheat the oven to 350°F.
- In a large bowl, sift (or whisk) together the flour, salt, and baking powder. In the bowl of an electric mixer, cream together the butter and sugar until light and fluffy, about 4 minutes. Add the eggs, one at a time.
- Add the flour mixture to the butter-sugar-egg mixture slowly so you don't overload the mixer. Stir in the almond extract and nuts.
- Place the dough on a floured surface and knead, working into 3 equal-size rounded loaves measuring about 9 by 3½ inches. Place on a lightly greased cookie sheet and bake for 30 to 35 minutes, until firm and light brown. Cool and cut into strips. For crispier strips, bake another 10 minutes.

SOUR CREAM CHOCOLATE CHIP NUT LOAF

At any point during the 1980s, you could've opened the middle pantry drawer in our kitchen and discovered a treasure trove of baked goods from our supermarket's Entenmann's display: fudge-frosted doughnuts, mini chocolate chip cookies, thick-glazed cupcakes. My father had—and still has—an epic sweet tooth that deserves a three-hundred-page volume all to itself. The king of the drawer, though, was the Sour Cream Chocolate Chip Nut Loaf, because it only made rare appearances at the supermarket, and, much to our dismay, eventually disappeared from shelves across the country. (We never did find out why.) My father and I were the biggest fans of the loaf, and in the twenty-five years since I've seen it, I don't think I've ever walked by the Entenmann's section without secretly hoping I'll spy one amid the doughnut holes and crumb cakes. Until then, I have this homemade version, which comes about as close as you can get.

MAKES 1 LOAF

butter, for greasing the pan

Cinnamon Sugar

¼ cup sugar
¾ teaspoon ground cinnamon

Batter

2 eggs

⅔ cup sugar

½ teaspoon pure vanilla extract

1½ cups all-purpose flour

1¼ teaspoons baking powder

1¼ teaspoons baking soda

1 teaspoon salt

½ cup (1 stick) butter, melted

1⅓ cups sour cream

¾ cup semisweet chocolate chips

⅓ cup roughly chopped walnuts

- Preheat the oven to 375°F. Butter a 9 by 5-inch standard loaf pan.
- Make the cinnamon sugar: In a small bowl, mix together the sugar and cinnamon.
- Make the batter: In a large bowl, using an electric mixer at medium speed, beat the eggs until frothy, about 3 minutes. Add the sugar and vanilla, beating until smooth. In a medium bowl, whisk together the flour, baking powder, baking soda, and salt.
- Add the melted butter and the sour cream to the egg-and-sugar mixture; beat until well combined. At low speed, add the dry mixture to the wet mixture a spoonful at a time, beating just until smooth. Fold in the chocolate chips.
- Spread half of the batter in the prepared pan and sprinkle evenly with about two-thirds of the cinnamon sugar. Sprinkle with the walnuts. Top with the remaining batter, spreading evenly. (This cake rises considerably, so be sure the batter is at least ¾ inch below the rim of the pan.) Sprinkle with the remaining cinnamon sugar.
- Bake for 45 to 50 minutes or until a knife or skewer inserted in the center comes out clean.

"FOOD IS NEVER—REPEAT NEVER—THE WRONG ANSWER TO ANY GIFT-RELATED QUESTION."

That all sounds great, but what can I give that won't require a lot of . . . uh . . . work?

On the other hand, a food gift doesn't have to be homemade to be meaningful. For as long as I can remember, my father has had a few store-bought treats—nougaty halvah, cinnamon marbled babka, detecting a theme here?—that qualify as Kryptonite Foods, as in, foods he is *powerless* to resist when they are set before him. So in the weeks leading up to Father's Day, I never walk by a Jewish or Middle Eastern specialty store without checking out the offerings, since I know halvah or a babka is going to be a slam dunk every time. For my mom, I can say the same thing about a dozen beautiful fresh eggs, procured at my local farmer's market for six bucks, a price that would curl her toes. My mother-in-law will practically weep with gratitude whenever we pick up her special bottle of olive oil (it's called Madre Sicilia; she hails from Sicily, get it?); for my father-in-law it's a Zagnut bar, the toasted coconut candy bar he ate on the Jersey Shore as a kid. My Kryptonite? That would be the dark chocolate–covered marzipan acorns from Li-Lac, the legendary candy store in New York City. If that box shows up on Mother's Day or Valentine's Day or Any Day, I call the day a huge success.

But I don't want to spend money on lobsters and fancy chocolates. What can I give that's not expensive?

If you do have time to make something in your own kitchen—no matter what it is—it's safe to say that anything homemade is going to be received with deep appreciation. Now is the time to ask yourself: Am I known for making anything particularly well? Do I have a *signature* baked good or dish? (Once you have a signature baked good, you are set on the gift front.) As you'll read about on page 136, I'm fond of gifting Andy's homemade pickles—a win-win considering I don't do any of the work there— but I've also had great success with homemade barbecue sauce (which takes under ten minutes to put together) for Father's Day, Maida Heatter's Mexican Chocolate Icebox Cookies (definitely worth googling) for Mother's Day, and homemade granola for Valentine's Day.

I should note here that I don't expect much on Valentine's Day from Andy. (My Hallmark-hating high school boyfriend turned me into a cynic about the holiday long before it was cool to be one.) But I think you'll agree that cynicism has no place in a house where two little girls still come home from school and spend hours— or at least many *many* minutes—combing through their doily-festooned classmate Valentines, ranking their favorites, separating out important ones from boys and best friends. So for them, it's all about hearts: heart-shaped pancakes, heart-shaped toast with strawberry jam, and, if I'm feeling supermom-ish, a heart-shaped cake that requires no fancy equipment, just one 9-inch square pan and one 9-inch round one. I learned that trick from a circa 1950s housekeeping magazine. (Good ideas never go out of style.)

OUR FAVORITE GRANOLA

This works particularly well as a thank-you gift for the mom or dad who has been pulling way more of his or her fair share on carpool duty.

MAKES 5½ TO 6 CUPS

1 large egg white, lightly beaten

3 cups old-fashioned rolled oats

1 cup raw sliced almonds

¾ cup pure maple syrup

½ cup good-quality olive oil or coconut oil

½ cup light brown sugar, packed

1 teaspoon pure vanilla extract

½ teaspoon kosher salt

½ teaspoon ground cinnamon

1 cup dried cherries

• Preheat the oven to 300°F. Line an 11 by 13-inch rimmed baking sheet with foil. In a large bowl, toss together the egg white, oats, nuts, maple syrup, olive oil, brown sugar, vanilla, salt, and cinnamon. Spread the granola onto the baking sheet in an even layer and bake, tossing occasionally, until golden, 35 to 40 minutes. Let cool. Toss in the cherries.

• For gifts: When completely cool, add the granola to Mason jars or cellophane bags. (Tie bags and lids with butcher's twine or ribbons.) If you're keeping the granola for yourself—and I wouldn't blame you if you do—serve with yogurt or milk, and fresh berries.

HEART CAKE
No fancy heart mold required for this
Valentine's Day special. Just use
one 9-inch square pan and one 9-inch
round pan, then cut and assemble as
shown. (Rosa's Mud Cake is pictured,
but it works with any cake recipe.)

But Valentine's Day/Mother's Day/Father's Day is tomorrow. I don't have time to go shopping for food gifts or ingredients. What now?

If there is one recipe every parent (human?) should have in his or her arsenal, it should be this one: the humble snickerdoodle. Why? Well, for starters, there's no tastier or more classic cookie out there—sweet and buttery, cakey and still somehow airy. I can't think of a single person on earth who wouldn't be thrilled to receive a bag of these as a gift. I also think this recipe is crucial to know because I'd be willing to bet that nine out of ten times you have all the ingredients on hand to bake a few dozen of them at a moment's notice. (Go ahead, check your pantry right now, I'll wait.)

Once you discover the Snickerdoodle Solution, you'll see it comes in handy for just about every occasion, not just when you are looking for something to bake and give. I can't tell you how many times this cookie has saved me on bake-sale or in-class party days—on those days when I wasn't smart enough to volunteer to bring the beverage. (Note to parents: Always volunteer to bring the beverages!) It's also a good rainy-day recipe to make with the kids.

SNICKERDOODLES

Not accustomed to adding sea salt to your cinnamon sugar? In this recipe it's the key.

MAKES 3½ DOZEN

Dough

2¾ cups all-purpose flour

1 teaspoon baking soda

½ teaspoon kosher salt

1 cup (2 sticks) unsalted butter, softened

1½ cups sugar

2 eggs

1 teaspoon pure vanilla extract

Cinnamon sugar

3 tablespoons sugar

1 tablespoon ground cinnamon

¼ teaspoon sea salt

• In a large bowl, whisk together the flour, baking soda, and salt.

• In the bowl of a standing mixer (or using a large bowl with a hand mixer), cream together the butter and sugar until light and fluffy, about 1 minute. Blend in the eggs and vanilla until combined.

• Gradually add the dry mixture to the wet mixture until it's all blended. Wrap the dough in parchment paper, shaping into a large disk, and chill for 1 hour in the freezer.

• Preheat the oven to 400°F. Remove the dough from the freezer and form balls of dough the size of small walnuts.

• Roll the balls in the cinnamon sugar mixture. Place on a cookie sheet 2 inches apart and bake for 8 to 10 minutes. Cool on a rack.

What can I give that is thoughtful, but doesn't require a lot of . . . thought?

This is where the *ritual* part of the ritual gift becomes crucial. The answer to the above question, of course, is instituting an Annual Gift Ritual, where you give the same thing, or a version of the same thing, year after year. I am such a sucker for this ritual—not only because those gifts tell stories and connect us to celebrations past, and all that good stuff, but because they save a ton of think work if you're on the giving end. It's thoughtful giving on autopilot.

A few examples: Andy's uncle Julian used to give his aunt Patty a cordial glass every year on her birthday. No two were the same, some were new, some were vintage, but he had an eye for that stuff, and when he broke out a bottle of Sauternes or dessert wine, it was always amazing to see how beautiful each tiny glass looked next to the others. Then there's Uncle Mike (yes, it's practically law that uncles are the best gift-givers), who buys a few cases of wine every Christmas, then divvies them all up for his brothers and nephews. In exchange for the wine, we have our own mini annual gift ritual—we give Uncle Mike whatever cookbook seems to be the cookbook of the moment. (We've presented him with *Canal House Cooks Every Day*, *The Zuni Cafe Cookbook*, *Jerusalem*, and *The New York Times Cookbook*, to name a few.)

The best thing about this ritual is that you can start any time with any item. Just take note of a gift that is received particularly well and, if possible, see if there's any kind of twist you can give it the next year. For instance: Let's say your father-in-law really enjoys a gin and tonic. I'm guessing he would love to receive a special bottle of gin every year for Father's Day. Maybe one year it's that small-batch stuff from the Berkshires; the next, it's the botanical one you discovered in California. Once an Annual Gift Ritual is established, you'll see that options present themselves everywhere, all year long. If you're worried that this might seem un-creative and, after a while, tiresome, to that I say, do it anyway! Why *not* go with what makes the recipient happy? Why not go with what works? Remember: *It's not being lazy, it's respecting tradition.*

FOURTH OF JULY, AKA COUSINLAND

When I was growing up, summer camp happened in front of my house, on the small dead-end street where two dozen of the neighborhood kids congregated every afternoon to play epic games of hopscotch, running bases, kickball, capture the flag, and boxball (or "foursquare" to those who didn't grow up in the Northeast). When it got hot, we sat in the shade of our dogwood tree, broke out a lawn sprinkler, or raided my parents' freezer, which was always good for a ream of Fla-Vor-Ice. If it was raining, we'd write plays or perform versions of stories we already knew, once even setting up chairs in our neighbor's backyard, hand-drawing every program, and inviting the parents to a special post-dinner showing of Rumpelstiltskin. It's possible that my feet never saw a pair of shoes in July or August. When I'd finally climb into a bathtub at the end of the day, I remember the water turning gray, dirt shed from a day of seventies-style fun.

Don't worry, this is not another essay bemoaning our current state of over-scheduled, oversupervised children or pining for the lost art of an old-fashioned, analog summer. As much as I wish I were the person who could put a moratorium on organized activities and camps and just fling open the front door shouting, "Be home in time for dinner!" there is the small problem that I have to work, and having a huge chunk of guaranteed kid-free time every day is crucial to, you know, paying a mortgage. So instead, I fill my daughters' days with tennis lessons . . . or soccer clinics . . . or pottery class . . . or farm camp. They have plenty of unstructured time *after* camp, I tell myself. It's scheduled right there in the daily iCalendar between "hammock swinging" and "daydreaming."

I'm kidding. Sort of.

However miserable I am at under-scheduling the girls, I take solace in the fact that there's usually one long weekend in the summer when they are free: the Fourth of July. Every year, my sister hosts at her beach house in Long Island, and though her neighborhood out there isn't exactly teeming with filthy kickball-playing stage performers in terry-cloth shorts, it doesn't matter. We bring our own mayhem: The

Cousins. My brother has one son, Nathan. My sister has two daughters, Amanda and Alison, and one son, Owen. Between the four of them, plus Abby and Phoebe (and two poorly trained dogs), their ages span five years. If you met each of these kids individually, you'd probably really like them and even comment on how "smiley" and "friendly" they are. But if you met them together, all at once, you wouldn't have time to say anything because you'd be too busy hatching your escape plan trying to get as far away from them as possible. I'm not a scientist, so I don't know what it is exactly, but some kind of chemical reaction occurs when they get together. They are no longer of the civilized world. It's like they are beamed to Cousinland, a place where it's not enough to just listen to music; they have to stand on tables and scream the lyrics in unison. In Cousinland, they don't walk; they sprint. They don't ask; they take. They don't talk; they shout. Once, when my nephews and nieces arrived at my parents' house to meet our family for dinner, another guest, who was seated at the table, said that as soon as they entered it sounded like an alarm had gone off.

If you think I disapprove of this mayhem, you've got me all wrong. I couldn't love it more. On my iPhone, I have a two-year-old video of my daughters and nieces screaming and dancing to Taylor Swift, and I watch it whenever I feel like my heart needs a hit of happiness. If these kids have any inhibitions or worries in the world—and they do, because as I write this, four of them are in middle school—those worries evaporate in Cousinland. In Cousinland, they are stripped down to their best selves, and there is no judging. In Cousinland, if there is fighting (and there is, and it's loud), within the hour everyone's outside assembling s'mores together or digging into a slice of pie. They are developing their own rituals, too, playing heated games of soccer and baseball in the backyard and performing original plays that they work on for hours. (Owen once delivered an Oscar-worthy interpretation of the word "and" in a play called "Red, White, *and* Blue"—the three colors had already been taken by his older cousins.) The parents spend large swaths of the afternoon without laying eyes on them and—get this—*the kids are fine.* Better than fine. They have the time of their lives.

This whole cousin thing is not unique to my side of the family, of course. The same thing happens when we get together with Sophia, Aidan, and Luca, the girls' cousins from Andy's side. And from everything I've observed, I'm pretty sure the phenomenon is common across Cousinlands around the world.

FOURTH OF JULY CHICKEN
There's no such thing as one dish that every kid likes, but your odds are about as good as they're gonna get with this sweet-and-smoky grilled Picnic Chicken (page 32). We serve it with German Potato Salad (page 35) and Crowd-Pleaser Summer Slaw (page 34).

With the kids out of the way, those who are so inclined have nothing but time on their hands to dream up ways in which to feed a dozen and a half dinner guests before sending them off to the fireworks display. In case you haven't gathered by now, Andy and I are so inclined. It's a lot of people to cook for, especially when you factor kids' varied palates into the equation,* but there are two reasons we don't generally freak out about it: 1) My sister's house has a kitchen roomy enough to accommodate several cooks at once. So while the rest of the house is in Cousinland, the cooks are in heaven. 2) The night almost always ends with a s'more.

---

* No pasta, no red meat, no fish, no beans, no rice, no creamy salad dressings, no eggs, no salad, no mayo-based anything, no greens unless it's iceberg, no pork unless it's in a dumpling, no chicken unless it's white meat, no avocado unless it's guacamole, no shellfish unless it's shrimp, no ice cream unless it's chocolate.

PICNIC CHICKEN

Abby would swim across an ocean if this chicken were waiting for her on the opposite shore. The recipe is from the café at Stone Barns Center for Food and Agriculture (home to Dan Barber's farm-to-table mecca, Blue Hill at Stone Barns) in Tarrytown, New York, which, as luck would have it, is only a twenty-minute drive from our house. Last year, I convinced the chefs there to give me the recipe, which, I will say, is an excellent thing to have in your Fourth of July (and make-ahead) arsenal. The marinade makes enough for four pounds of chicken, which serves about six. The café only sells drumsticks that have been baked, but we think it's also delicious with thighs on the grill. Both techniques follow.

SERVES 6

½ cup soy sauce

juice from ½ orange (about ¼ cup),
    plus ½ orange cut into wedges

juice from 2 small lemons
    (about ¼ cup)

2 tablespoons honey

2 cloves garlic, minced

1 tablespoon mild smoked paprika

2 teaspoons ground cumin

½ cup good-quality olive oil

kosher salt and freshly ground pepper

4 pounds chicken legs and thighs

• Place soy sauce, orange juice, lemon juice, honey, garlic, paprika, and cumin in a blender. Puree for 30 seconds on high.

• With the motor running, slowly add the oil. Season well with salt and pepper. Add the chicken and marinade to a large zip-top plastic bag and marinate for 24 hours in the refrigerator.

To bake:

• Preheat the oven to 400°F. Remove the chicken from the marinade, discarding the marinade, and place in a single layer in a roasting pan or on a rimmed baking sheet along with the orange wedges. Roast for 40 to 45 minutes, flipping halfway through, until nicely browned and cooked through. Serve hot, at room temp, or cold.

To grill:

• Make a medium-hot fire in a charcoal grill, preheat a gas grill to medium, or set a stovetop grill pan over medium-high heat. Add the chicken pieces in batches, flipping frequently, until lacquered and cooked through, about 10 minutes total for thighs, 12 minutes total for legs. During the last 3 minutes of cooking, add the orange wedges and grill, flipping frequently.

• Remove the chicken and oranges to a serving platter, squeezing one of the orange wedges all over the chicken pieces.

CROWD-PLEASER SUMMER SLAW

I'm always amazed by how much kids love this as a side dish, even though it's not your typical mayo-based picnic slaw. It's Asian inspired and goes with just about anything we're eating for dinner all summer—actually all year—long. I usually toss in the dressing about an hour before serving. That way the flavors get to meld, but the cabbage retains its crunch. Crucial!

SERVES 8 TO 10

Dressing

⅓ cup rice wine vinegar

1 tablespoon light brown sugar, loosely packed

2 teaspoons fish sauce (or soy sauce)

2 tablespoons fresh lime juice (from about ½ large lime)

2 teaspoons finely minced peeled fresh ginger

1 teaspoon Sriracha sauce (optional)

⅔ cup neutral oil such as grapeseed or sunflower seed
(but olive oil is okay in a pinch)

Salad

1 medium head of red cabbage, shredded with a mandoline
or as fine as you can manage (about 8 cups)

1 cup shredded baby spinach

½ cup chopped scallions, white and light green parts only

½ cup chopped fresh cilantro leaves

⅓ cup chopped fresh mint leaves

• In a large bowl, whisk together all of the dressing ingredients. Add the salad ingredients and toss until combined.

GERMAN POTATO SALAD

*I've been a sucker for this potato salad ever since I was a kid, when my dad
would bring home a plastic pint of the sweet-and-bacony stuff from our local deli.
I only recently had the courage to go up against that food memory and re-create
it in my own kitchen. Nailed it.*

SERVES 8 TO 10

3 pounds unpeeled small firm potatoes
(red, white, Yukon Gold), quartered

5 bacon slices

⅓ cup white wine vinegar

1 heaping tablespoon whole-grain mustard

1 tablespoon sugar

kosher salt and freshly ground pepper

⅓ cup good-quality olive oil

2 tablespoons chopped fresh dill

1 bunch of scallions, white and light green parts only,
chopped (about ¼ cup)

• Add the potatoes to a large pot, cover with water, and generously salt the water. Bring
to a boil and boil gently, until a knife slides through the potatoes easily, about 15 minutes.

• While the potatoes are boiling, fry the bacon in a skillet until cooked. Drain on paper
towels, reserving 2 tablespoons of the bacon grease. Crumble the bacon. Add the grease
to a large bowl and let cool slightly. Whisk in the vinegar, mustard, sugar, salt and pepper,
and olive oil.

• When the potatoes have finished cooking, drain, then immediately toss them in the
dressing in the large bowl to allow them to absorb the dressing. Add the bacon crumbles,
dill, and scallions, tossing to combine.

NOTE: Other ideas for a Fourth of July
grill-out: Phoebe's Hatch Burgers (page 130),
Grilled Soy-Glazed Pork Chops (page 246),
and Grilled Halloumi and Asparagus with Pesto
(page 248).

The secret to a
good pre—Trick
or Treat party:
Franks and Beans
(page 38) for
the kids, bourbon
for the parents.

HALLOWEEN
LAUNCH PARTY

There was a solid stretch of years where you could ask my girls, "What are you going to be for Halloween?" and they'd have an answer for you, even if it wasn't October. Even if it was July or August or *November*. As soon as the last mini Butterfinger was down the hatch, they'd start plotting whether to be Hermione or Vampire Cheerleader or Jellyfish or Little Orphan Annie or Tintin next year.

Halloween is still huge for them, don't get me wrong, but probably more so for those Butterfingers than for the dressing-up part. If the girls are growing up, though, it doesn't mean Andy and I are moving on. We are usually one of the first on our block to hang the ghost on the front door and plant the flashing eyeballs in the bushes, and on the actual day itself, we usually take off work to attend whatever parade is happening at school or in town—and to prep for our annual Halloween Launch Party.

Our house happens to be centrally located on a block that prides itself on being prime trick-or-treating real estate. Our neighbors get majorly into it: Down the street, Fran and Bob serve hot cider and popcorn in their driveway. Up the block, Jane, a professional actress, turns her garage into a witch's cave, presides over a chuffing cauldron, and makes unsuspecting trick-or-treaters place their hands in bowls of spaghetti "brains." Across the street, our neighbors pump out spooky music from speakers and smoke from a smoke machine. (So effective, we once overheard parents of trick-or-treaters wonder if they should call the fire department.) All this is awesome for many obvious reasons, but mostly because it means that the girls, the girls' friends, and the girls' parents want to kick off the night in the center of all the action, namely, our house. (Hello, Halloween photo ops!)

This means, of course, that we have an excuse to feed them all: the witches, the Cinderellas, and the LeBrons, and the parents of the witches, the Cinderellas, and the LeBrons. If you get spooked just thinking about taking this on, fear not. I find that Halloween entertaining is relatively stress-free because almost no one cares what you serve as long as it can be eaten quickly to make time for pictures. I rarely even set the table, opting instead to make a big pot of something flavorful and cozy like chili or franks and beans, leave it on the stovetop, and tell people to grab a bowl and serve themselves. Also key: On average, the launch party lasts about a half hour—just long enough for the kids to consume something somewhat healthy (read: not Milk Duds) and the grown-ups to consume something somewhat alcoholic (read: bourbon), before we send them out into the streets.

FRANKS AND BEANS

The baked beans part of this recipe comes from my friend and recipe developer, Victoria Granof. The "franks part"? That comes straight from my daughters.

MAKES 8 TO 10 HALF-CUP PORTIONS

1 pound dried navy or great northern beans

1 small onion, chopped

½ cup pure maple syrup

¼ cup ketchup

2 tablespoons apple cider vinegar

2 tablespoons light brown sugar, packed

2 tablespoons spicy brown mustard

2 tablespoons molasses

2 teaspoons kosher salt

¼ teaspoon freshly ground pepper

1 thick strip bacon

5 to 6 cups boiling water

3 good-quality hot dogs, sliced into rounds

• In a large pot, cover the beans with water. Bring to a boil and simmer until tender, about 1 hour. Drain. Return the pot to the stovetop.

• Preheat the oven to 300°F. In the large pot, over low heat, combine all of the ingredients except the boiling water and the hot dogs. Stir in the cooked beans.

• Add just enough of the boiling water to the pot to cover everything. Cover the pot with aluminum foil, then cover the foil with the lid. Bake for 5 hours, adding more warm

"SOMETIMES
THE SWEETEST—
IF MOST
UNLIKELY—RITUALS
HAPPEN
BY ACCIDENT."

water as necessary to keep the beans submerged. Uncover completely for the last 30 minutes to brown the top. During the last 10 minutes of cooking, stir in the hot dog slices until warmed through.

CHICKEN CHORIZO CHILI

This recipe is super versatile—you can replace the chicken sausage with pork sausage, and use black beans or pinto beans instead of white. We set up the toppings on the side of the stovetop and have everyone help themselves. The recipe can be halved for a regular old weeknight dinner.

SERVES 12 TO 15

2 pounds chicken chorizo sausage
    (about 6 links), casings removed

3 tablespoons good-quality olive oil

2 cups chopped onion
    (from about 3 small yellow onions)

4 cloves garlic, minced

kosher salt and freshly ground pepper

2 tablespoons dried oregano

7 tablespoons chili powder

1½ teaspoons ground cinnamon

¼ cup red wine

2 28-ounce cans diced tomatoes

1 28-ounce can tomato puree

1 mildly spicy dried chile pepper (such as guajillo)

3 bay leaves

2 15-ounce cans small white beans, rinsed

assorted toppings, such as shredded cheddar,
    chopped avocado, chopped cilantro,
    and sour cream

• In a large Dutch oven (this works in my 5¾-quart pot, but if you have a slightly larger one, that would be better) over medium-high heat, brown the sausage in the olive oil for about 3 minutes, breaking it up with a fork as it cooks. (It does not have to cook all the way through.) Remove to a bowl with a slotted spoon.

• Lower the heat to medium, then add the onion and garlic to the pot with salt and pepper. Cook for about 5 minutes, until the onions are soft and golden from the chorizo juice. Stir in the oregano, chili powder, and cinnamon and allow the spices to get a little toasty, about 1 minute. Add the wine, tomatoes, tomato puree, chile pepper, bay leaves, and cooked chorizo. Stir until well blended.

• Cover the pot, leaving the lid slightly ajar, and cook at a lazy simmer for 30 minutes to 2 hours (the longer the better), stirring occasionally. Add the beans and warm through. Discard the bay leaves. Serve with assorted toppings.

I'd so much rather eat my Thanksgiving dinner on Phoebe's melamine make-a-plate (circa 2007) than on fancy china. If only we had a set of 12.

ON THANKSGIVING TRADITIONS

A few Thanksgivings ago, I decided I was going to do the unthinkable, and in retrospect, the unconscionable: I was going to make a chocolate pudding pie for dessert . . . *from scratch.*

Chocolate Pudding Pie was sacred territory that had been claimed decades ago by the matriarch of the family, my mother. Dating back to the early 1980s (there's the operative phrase), it was practically law: Mom would make two chocolate pudding pies for Thanksgiving. And every year, in her pregame holiday shopping cart, you could count on finding all the ingredients needed to make that happen: two Keebler Ready Crust graham cracker pie crusts, two chocolate Jell-O pudding packets, one gallon of whole milk. It would take her roughly ten minutes to boil the milk and stir in the powder, unwrap the plastic from the ready-made crusts, and pour the pudding into the pie shells. She'd cover her pies with plastic wrap when the pudding was still slightly warm, which often led to a little watery discoloration on top of the filling. If that sounds unappetizing, trust me, it wasn't. My mom's chocolate pudding pie could do no wrong, for the very reason that it was my mom's chocolate pudding pie. On the big night, there the two pies would sit, in their aluminum dishes, among homemade Thanksgiving pie royalty—bourbon pecan, pumpkin, maple buttermilk, deep-dish apple—and always, *always* be the first to disappear.

So why did I decide to go head-to-head with it and make my own from-scratch pudding pie on that Thanksgiving back in 2011? Because it was 2011, not 1981. Because the whole food movement thing had happened. (Michael Pollan ring a bell here?) Because I was the author of two cookbooks by that point and wrote a column for *Bon Appétit* and thought maybe a chocolate pie on Thanksgiving should be made with Valrhona and not disodium phosphate. In short, because I'm an idiot.

It's not that my pie went untouched exactly. My family ate the from-scratch pie—topped beautifully, I might add, with a mess of freshly whipped cream—but they ate it after the premier pies were gone, and even as they did so, they were skeptical. Especially the nieces and nephews. *Why,* they all asked me, *would I want to mess with*

KING OF ALL PIES
You can try to top
my mom's chocolate
pudding pie with
a fancy from-scratch
version, but you
will lose.

tradition? *What* exactly was the problem with my mother's world-renowned pies? Who cares what Michael Pollan eats at his Thanksgiving table? (And by the way, who *is* Michael Pollan?) This is our Thanksgiving table, and it's the only one that matters.

Okay, they didn't exactly say that. But that was how I read the situation. Especially when Abby decided to taste a bite of my pie and my mom's pie, one after the other, blindfolded, to see which one she liked better. The result was hardly shocking: Nostalgia wins over Valrhona every time. I got over it.

I have to admit, I was a little wary of the whole experiment myself, even as I scraped that silky, rich chocolate pudding into its buttery homemade shell. I was wary about stepping on my mom's toes (even though she thought the whole thing was hilarious), wary of my own food-snobbiness, and, worst of all, wary that my pie would actually win over all those taste buds, marking the end of my mom's pie reign, and the end of a tradition that dated back to a time when I had Duran Duran posters on my bedroom walls. Because making the same thing year in and year out, though boring and routinized any other time of the year, is what Thanksgiving is all about. (I mean, isn't that why the entire *country* is still making essentially the same menu that appeared in Plymouth four hundred years ago?) On a random Sunday in October, sure, I'll mess around with some miso in the Brussels sprouts. Or harissa on a roast chicken. I'll tweak or change up the ingredients associated with many of the other recipes in this chapter. But on the last Thursday of November—well, I learned my lesson: Tradition rules the day.

MOM'S CHOCOLATE PUDDING PIE

I'm not gonna lie: It's a good one.

SERVES 8

• Pick up one Keebler Ready Crust graham cracker crust (or two or three if you are serving many fans of the famous recipe) and follow the instructions on the label. You'll also need instant pudding and whole milk.

MY CHOCOLATE PUDDING PIE

I'm including this recipe here just in case you are the one launching the chocolate pudding pie tradition at your table and do not have to tussle with pie ghosts of Thanksgivings past.

SERVES 8

Crust

1½ packages honey graham crackers (13 to 14 crackers)

10 tablespoons unsalted butter, melted

5 tablespoons sugar

Filling

2 cups whole milk

2 egg yolks

⅔ cup sugar

4 tablespoons unsweetened cocoa powder

2 tablespoons cornstarch

½ teaspoon kosher salt

2 teaspoons pure vanilla extract

Make the Crust

• Preheat the oven to 350°F. In a food processor fitted with a metal blade, process the honey graham crackers until they resemble fine crumbs. Add the melted butter and sugar and pulse to combine until the crust just comes together and slightly holds a shape when pinched between two fingers. Using your fingers, firmly press the mixture into a 9-inch pie dish. Bake for 10 minutes. Cool.

Make the Pudding

• In a medium bowl, whisk together the milk and yolks. In a heavy medium saucepan, whisk together the sugar, cocoa, cornstarch, and salt. Whisk in the milk mixture until thoroughly combined, then turn on the heat to medium. Cook, whisking constantly, until the pudding thickens and comes to a boil, about 5 minutes. Continue boiling for 1 more minute, whisking constantly so it stays smooth. Remove the pudding from the heat and add the vanilla. Cool for 10 minutes.

• Pour the pudding into the prepared crust. Allow the pie to cool, then cover with foil or plastic wrap and chill for at least 6 hours (and up to 24). Serve topped with freshly whipped cream (see page 59).

My from-scratch chocolate pudding pie should fit in beautifully on your Thanksgiving dessert spread—provided no one in your family has any sentimental attachment to Jell-O Chocolate Pudding like mine.

THANKSGIVING DINNER

Mom's Herb-Roasted Turkey with Gravy
"Confetti" Brussels Sprouts with Bacon and Raisins
Sausage and Apple Stuffing / Cranberry Relish
Potato Gratin with Gruyère

MOM'S HERB-ROASTED TURKEY WITH GRAVY

Figuring out how much turkey to serve is such a complicated proposition—even my mom's famous notes (which you'll read about on page 61) are all over the place because it's so hard to track which of her seven grandchildren has decided she no longer likes turkey, or is not eating meat that year, or is in the middle of a growth spurt so has consumed twice his or her regular portion size. If I am to learn anything from the notes, however, it's that a fourteen-and-a-half-pound turkey consistently serves eight to ten typical eaters without leftovers. This recipe accommodates all size turkeys, though, as long as you time the roasting accordingly once the heat is turned down.

SERVES 8 TO 10 (WITHOUT LEFTOVERS)

½ cup (1 stick) unsalted butter

1 teaspoon chopped fresh rosemary leaves

2 tablespoons fresh thyme leaves,
    plus 4 thyme sprigs for the roasting pan

2 tablespoons chopped fresh sage leaves

2 large onions, 1 roughly chopped, 1 quartered

3 carrots, peeled and roughly chopped (about 1¼ cups)

2 stalks celery, roughly chopped (about 1 cup)

5 to 6 cups chicken stock, preferably homemade,
    kept warm on the stovetop while the turkey roasts

juice from 1 large orange (about ⅓ cup)

1 13- to 16-pound turkey, giblets and neck removed,
    patted dry inside and out, at room temperature

kosher salt and freshly ground pepper

- Preheat the oven to 425°F.
- Melt the butter in a small saucepan. Remove from heat and mix in the chopped herbs. Set aside.
- Add the chopped onions, carrots, celery, and the thyme sprigs to a large roasting pan. Stir in about ¾ cup of the hot stock along with the juice from the orange. Place a rack inside the roasting dish (on top of the vegetables), and place the turkey on top, stuffing the cavity with the quartered onion. Tuck the wings tightly underneath the bird, trussing the turkey legs with twine if the cavity feels too exposed. Brush herb butter all over the surface of the bird. Generously salt and pepper the skin and place the entire thing in the oven on a low rack.
- After 30 minutes, baste with turkey juices and tent with foil; reduce heat to 325°F.
- Here's a good rule of thumb I learned from food writer (and Thanksgiving master) Sam Sifton: From this point, at this temperature, the turkey will cook 15 minutes per pound, or until a meat thermometer inserted into the thigh reads 165°F; set a timer accordingly.
- Baste the turkey every 30 minutes with its own juices, supplementing with hot broth from the stovetop if the vegetables look like they are drying up.
- Remove the foil for the last half hour of roasting and brush with any remaining herb butter. (You'll need to warm up the butter on low heat.) When a thermometer stuck in the turkey's thigh reads 165°F, and when the skin has reached the golden, burnished color that will invite admiration, transfer to a cutting board and let rest for 30 minutes before carving.
- Meanwhile, strain the pan juices into a medium saucepan for the gravy.

GRAVY

Gravy is one of those nonrecipe recipes that seem to come out different every time. If you start with the pan juices, though, it's hard to go wrong.

SERVES 8 TO 10 (DRIZZLING PORTIONS)

> pan juices
> reserved hot stock from turkey recipe
> 3 to 6 tablespoons all-purpose flour
> 3 tablespoons unsalted butter
> kosher salt and freshly ground pepper

- You should have 1½ to 2 cups of pan juices in the medium saucepan, but if you don't, add a little reserved stock. Skim a little of the turkey fat off the top. Turn the heat to medium low, then cook, whisking constantly, adding alternating tablespoons of flour and butter until it reaches what you consider desired gravy consistency. We like ours on the thinner end, but do what makes you happy. Taste constantly and add salt and pepper accordingly.
- Arrange the turkey on your most beautiful platter and serve with gravy on the side.

"CONFETTI" BRUSSELS SPROUTS WITH BACON AND RAISINS

Unlike most Thanksgiving dishes, this one comes together fast and at the very end. So unless you enjoy the adrenaline rush that results from an eleventh-hour panic, make sure you have all your ingredients premeasured and your skillet and serving platter ready to go.

SERVES 8

3 thick slices bacon

2 tablespoons good-quality olive oil

2 medium shallots, finely chopped

kosher salt and freshly ground pepper

8 cups (about 2 pounds) Brussels sprouts, preshredded
or shredded with the shredding disk of a food processor

1 clove garlic, minced

2 tablespoons unsalted butter

⅔ cup chicken stock, preferably homemade

¼ cup apple cider vinegar

½ cup golden raisins

- Over medium heat, fry the bacon in a very large skillet until crispy. Remove the bacon and chop into small pieces. Add 1 tablespoon of the olive oil, the shallots, and salt and pepper and cook until the shallots soften slightly, about 2 minutes. Add the Brussels sprouts, garlic, and remaining olive oil. (It will feel like there are too many sprouts in the pan, but don't worry, they will wilt.) Stir for about 2 minutes, then stir in the butter. Add the chicken stock and cook for another 2 to 3 minutes until heated through. Remove from the heat and stir in the vinegar, bacon pieces, and raisins. Serve in a deep-dish platter.

TURKEY ACCORDING TO MOM:
SEVEN THINGS TO REMEMBER WHEN ROASTING A BIRD

On Thanksgiving day, Andy and I are in the kitchen from morning until night
chopping onions, baking pies, shredding Brussels sprouts, mashing potatoes—but one thing we're
rarely doing is attending to the turkey. That's my mom's domain, and, in fact, the first time
I ever attempted to roast one myself was on a warm October day in 2015, when I was testing her turkey
recipe for this book. After studying a decade's worth of my mother's notes (see page 61)
and after a marathon coaching session with Mom over the phone, though, I was ready.
Here are a few things I learned from the master to get there.

— 1 —
Always have a pot of hot stock* on the stove while the turkey is roasting.

"It's your assistant, your friend," she says. You'll use it for basting and later for adjusting the gravy if it's too thick. One year, I took homemade stock to Thanksgiving, which earned me the accolade "superb" in Mom's notes.

— 2 —
Pay attention to how the skin burnishes.

"Yes, it's important that it tastes good, but most important is that everyone admires it!" To that end, "make it tight," be sure the wings are tucked under. "You don't want to have black skinny pointy things sticking out at everyone." In other words: Watch your bird vigilantly at the end, when the foil is lifted.

— 3 —
Don't panic; be flexible.

"Every time I make our Thanksgiving turkey it's like the first time I've ever made one."

— 4 —
Understand your own oven.

Know how hot your oven gets, and if the temperature is accurate. When I suggest calibrating the oven, she says, "Oh, just buy one of those thermometers for three dollars and fifty cents that you stick inside."

— 5 —
Baste every thirty minutes and season.

My mom uses a store-bought poultry seasoning mix that comes in a yellowy-orange packet and that's "as old as I am," in her words, but I found using fresh herbs and the turkey's pan juices sufficed.

— 6 —
Don't trust the pop-up thermometers.

Look at the juices. When they run clear, it's a good sign of doneness.

— 7 —
Always put an onion in the cavity of the bird. Always.

"Even when it's not a Thanksgiving turkey!"

---

* Homemade Stock: In a large pot add chicken bones, halved onion, carrots, parsley, salt and pepper, and a Parmesan rind. Cover with water and simmer for 2 to 3 hours. Strain and store in an air-tight container.

SAUSAGE AND APPLE STUFFING

This is as classic as classic gets. I know I've said this already, but it bears repeating: Using homemade stock takes this from good to great. (Homemade stock instructions are on the bottom of page 52).

SERVES 8

4 tablespoons unsalted butter

2 small onions, chopped

4 stalks celery, chopped

6 sage leaves, chopped

kosher salt and freshly ground pepper to taste

2 links sweet Italian sausage, casings removed

2 loaves French or Italian bread,
    cut into ½-inch cubes and left out for an hour or two
    to get slightly stale (about 12 cups total)

1 cup chicken stock, preferably homemade

1 bunch of parsley, chopped

2 eggs, lightly beaten

1 apple, peeled, chopped into chunks

- Preheat the oven to 400°F.
- Heat butter in a large, deep skillet over medium heat. Add onions, celery, sage, and salt and pepper. Cook until the vegetables are soft, about 15 minutes. Transfer to a bowl and let cool. While it cools, cook the sausage in the same skillet over medium heat, breaking up the meat with a fork.
- Once the meat is cooked, add to the onion mixture in the bowl, along with bread cubes, chicken stock, parsley, eggs, and apple. Add the mixture to a baking dish, cover with foil, and bake for 30 minutes. Remove the foil; bake until golden, about 20 more minutes.

CRANBERRY RELISH

When this dish, inspired by a Bon Appétit *recipe, debuted at our 2012 Thanksgiving table, my mom was skeptical. (Then again, she's skeptical of most new things. Including, but definitely not limited to: syrup that's not Aunt Jemima, designer labels, machines that fly, text messaging, farmer's markets, miso.) "You don't cook the cranberries?" No, I explained. It was more of a relish and less of a sauce, a nice hit of brightness amid all the buttery richness. She gave clearance for my niece Alison and me to try it but, just in case, also served her own alongside. The 2012 notes say, "Cranberry newcomer this year," without any editorializing, but underneath, I noticed she also wrote, "Next year, make both again." Translation: Not quite ready to make the switch, but didn't hate it either. Victory!*

SERVES 8

4 cups (about 1 16-ounce bag) fresh or
   completely thawed frozen cranberries
1 cup fresh pineapple, roughly chopped
3 oranges, sectioned (supremed) and chopped,
   plus their juices
⅓ cup sugar
1 teaspoon minced peeled fresh ginger
¼ cup minced red onion
¼ cup chopped fresh mint leaves

• In the bowl of a food processer, pulse the cranberries and pineapple until roughly chopped. Transfer to a large bowl and stir in the remaining ingredients. Cover and chill up to 24 hours before serving.

2012 Thanksgiving - 4th ann.
perfect weather
Oysters on the halfshell
Turkey -
6th Annual turkey in 12:20 pm
2014 Thanksgiving
- upper 30's - cold   7 adults, 6 kids
1. run colander,

2011 Thanksgiving
temp: 60° - 7 adults; 6 keds
- year of the Pie
- 14' turkey

Sweet

cranb

2004 at 10 Sout

14' turkey - plenty
mashed patatoes -
sweet pot.   - at le
gravy + stuffing from Pau
↳ too watery - next year
choc. pudding pie + whipp
cranberry sauce
Jennp - corn bread
Lynn - asparagus + sa

Phil - Tiramisu + c

sugg. wash turkey a
take small bowl +
M.A. - Trader Joe's turk

POTATO GRATIN WITH GRUYÈRE

The important thing here is the instruction to make sure the milk comes "almost to the top" of the layered potatoes. Don't panic when you see the milk browning on the edges; the flavor that results is delicious. (Just make sure the browning is in fact brown and not black.) This can be made in advance, then reheated at 350°F, covered in foil, for 20 minutes. (Bring to room temperature first.)

SERVES 6 TO 8

1 large clove garlic, halved

3 tablespoons unsalted butter

2½ to 3 pounds Yukon Gold potatoes
   (enough to fill a 9 by 13-inch baking dish),
   peeled and sliced as thin as possible
   (a mandoline is helpful here)

2½ cups whole milk

kosher salt and freshly ground pepper

½ cup grated Gruyère cheese

• Preheat the oven to 400°F. Rub the garlic halves all over a 9 by 13-inch baking dish, followed by 1 tablespoon of the butter. Layer the potatoes in the dish, overlapping as you go.

• In a medium saucepan, heat the milk until warm. Remove from the heat and whisk in the salt and pepper to taste. Pour all over the potatoes. The milk should come almost all the way to the top of the potatoes; you don't want them to be submerged. Cut the remaining butter into dots and sprinkle over the potatoes along with the Gruyère and more salt and pepper. Bake until the potatoes are golden and the milk has been absorbed, 45 to 50 minutes.

JACKPOT
These potatoes are
so simple—as good
on a Tuesday night
as they are on
Thanksgiving.

HOMEMADE WHIPPED CREAM
More, please.

TAG-TEAM WHIPPED CREAM

Andy's aunt Patty was one of the first people I ever met who knew how to cook. I mean *really* cook, as though every recipe was an opportunity to learn and every dinner was a chance to impress the large parties she'd regularly amass at her dining room table. The first time I ever sat at one of those dining room tables, she served us "Pork in Milk," the classic Marcella Hazan recipe that calls for braising a pork loin in little more than whole milk for two hours, and that struck me as *amazing* in its brazen un-kosher-ness. Aunt Patty's cooking was legendary when Andy was a kid, too. This is how he remembered it on my blog a few years ago: "She'd get up at five A.M., run six or seven miles, come home, make a big pot of coffee, and start making the gooiest, butteriest challah French toast I'd ever seen. (At holiday time, she made it with eggnog. And she always added a dash of vanilla, a tradition we've continued.) She'd clean up breakfast and start in on lunch: maybe a wild rice salad with scallions and cranberries, maybe some egg salad sandwiches with onion and celery, maybe some chicken Milanese (pounded flat and dredged in cornflakes crumbs). Then she'd clean up lunch and start in on dinner. She'd stuff roasts with egg and pancetta and marinate butterflied legs of lamb in great big plastic tubs; she'd make fresh ricotta cheesecakes and tiramisu with home-baked lady fingers; and she would always, always turn down any offers of help. 'Cooking is my therapy,' she'd say, tossing another pot onto the pile in the sink."

The one thing she would let us do, though, was whip the cream for whatever elaborate confection was on the menu. The first time she handed me a whisk and a chilled metal mixing bowl containing cream (plus a little powdered sugar and maybe vanilla extract), I was sitting at her antique-linen-covered dining room table, I was about twenty-one years old, and I was confused. I'm not entirely sure I had put together the idea that whipped cream was *cream that had been whipped.*

"Did you just fall off the turnip truck or something?" she said. "Jenny! Whip the cream!" She gave me a little demo. *Whisk in a circular motion to get the air into the cream. Don't whisk side to side. It's all in the wrist. Circular.* As soon as my wrist looked like it was tiring, she ordered me to pass the bowl to the next person at the table, who would take over. By the time it made its way around—*Stop as soon as stiff peaks form or else you've got butter*—we had freshly whipped cream. I was relatively new to the family, but I remember thinking to myself that this was the way I wanted to whip cream for the rest of my life: No spray can. No electric mixer. A whisk, and a bowl, and a tag-teaming family of whippers.

I haven't completely stood by this vow, but we've communally whipped cream often enough to call it ritual, and often enough to remind us, again and again, that it doesn't take much to spark a treasured, time-honored tradition.

BASIC RECIPE FOR WHIPPED CREAM

• In a medium metal mixing bowl, preferably chilled, whisk together 8 ounces heavy whipping cream, 1 teaspoon powdered sugar, and ¼ teaspoon pure vanilla extract until stiff peaks form. Makes enough to generously decorate one 9-inch pie.

HOW TO AVOID EMPTY CELEBRATION SYNDROME

On Thanksgiving, more than any other big annual occasion, I worry that I'm at risk for Empty Celebration Syndrome—you know, ECS, that feeling you get when you go to a wedding or a party, and even though the menu is perfect, the guest list is well considered, and the festivities take place around tables that are festooned with flowers, you just can't shake the feeling that something is . . . missing? This dilemma is almost always solved with a heartfelt toast, but that is easier said than done, especially if the toast-giver fears public speaking and has been known to go completely blank when standing before hundreds of guests, even though she had practiced in front of the mirror a dozen times a day for seven days straight. For example.

At Thanksgiving, though, we're all at risk for a different kind of emptiness. It's the one that settles in after you spend a week or two exchanging emails with your siblings and parents about schedules and driving and shopping; coordinating who is bringing the wine, who is in charge of the starters, who is baking which pies, whether you are going with mashed potatoes or scalloped potatoes (remember, with most Thanksgiving menu questions, the answer is usually: "both"). Then on the Day Of, it's like you're trapped in some kind of kitchen version of Mario Kart, trying to get to the finish line, even as culinary missiles fly at you from all sides—the oven's busted again, someone stole the platter you put *right there* for the Brussels sprouts, the cauliflower is not browning, the stuffing is dry, the turkey . . . Oh God, the turkey! You expend all that energy—emotional and physical—finally making it to the table unscathed, and then you, what, eat? An hour later, there won't be a whole lot to show for what went into the feast beyond the untouched pile of Brussels sprouts on your toddler's (or your uncle's) plate and the stack of Tupperwared leftovers. (Not that I'm in any way dismissing those Tupperwared leftovers.) So the fridge is packed full of leftovers, but you feel empty, like you never had a real moment to give thanks on Thanksgiving.

Obviously there's not a whole lot you can do in terms of getting the high-energy toddlers to grasp the concept of sitting down, let alone the concept of gratitude. But for the rest of us, there are a few things we can do that help alleviate at least some of the symptoms of ECS. You probably don't need me to tell you that it's never a bad idea to simply go around the table and ask all present to announce one thing they are thankful for. If this is what you do, no need to read any farther. It doesn't get purer or more effective than that. But if you are in the market for new ways to impart meaning to family occasions—and these can work well beyond Thanksgiving—here are a few ideas.

1. Take Notes

I like to think that the reason why Thanksgiving doesn't completely spiral into chaos in our house is because of my mother's post-feast recording ritual. Every year, on the morning after Thanksgiving, she grabs a legal pad and starts taking detailed post-feast notes in perfect cursive: Date, menu, number and names of attendees, temperature, who cooked what, who bought what and from where, what she needs more of next year, what she needs less of, what worked, what didn't. What makes her system awesome is not just that it reminds us that a 16.3-pound turkey provided more than enough for the thirteen of us in 2013, or that the sweet potato casserole that same year was "a hit." She takes the time to note that my then nine-year-old niece requested fewer pecans in the casserole next time around and that my then eleven-year-old niece was the one spearheading the new cranberry recipe with me, sectioning the oranges and chopping the mint. In that way, it's more like a diary than anything else.

Of course, I look to the notes to see how I can improve my own performance next year, too. I was pleased to see I had done a couple things right in 2011: I provided "superb" homemade stock for the gravy and my buttermilk pie was "a winner." But it's not all gold stars. In the mashed potatoes department—my department—she always notes "too much." (Personally, I don't think this is possible.) In 2009, the stuffing was "not moist enough," but at least Mom was nice enough to blame Martha Stewart, instead of the person who executed Martha Stewart's recipe. Sometimes, much to our delight, she forgets that other people besides her are reading these notes, as was the case when I discovered a crushing "B-" next to Andy's 2008 homemade bourbon-pecan pie. Needless to say, she was mortified, but he was *thrilled* to have something to lord over her for every Thanksgiving thereafter. (He also upped his pie game considerably, eventually earning his pie "keeper" status.)

The takeaway here is not only that there is a blueprint for next year, but that there is a written record to immortalize each Thanksgiving and connect it to Thanksgivings past and future. For that effort, even Andy would admit she's earned an A+.

2. Make a Mad Lib

This was Andy's invention, and it takes the "What are you thankful for" ritual to the next level. He creates a template like the one you see on the opposite page and asks the kids to fill them out before sitting down to feast. Not because he wants to turn the table into school, but because it makes them think a little more about what they're going to say and—here's the best part—we get to keep them in the Thanksgiving file for all eternity. Note: This template works well for any holiday or occasion when it's important to you that the kids express gratitude, but when you know they don't necessarily know where to start. On the other hand, it works for grown-ups, too. I think my most favorite Mad Lib was the one filled out by Papa Ivan (my dad), where his answers to "What are you most thankful for" were 1) Grandchildren 2) Own Children 3) See Above.

3. Say Something

For as long as I can remember, if someone is graduating, getting married, celebrating a birthday or anniversary, or marking any other major milestone, my father-in-law, Steve, has written a poem to commemorate the occasion. And when I say poem, I'm not talking about the kind of thing one hears at a wedding, read in unison by two drunk groomsmen written on a piece of toilet paper. I'm talking masterfully crafted four-line stanzas—usually about a dozen of them—written in unrelenting iambic pentameter. The first time I ever heard one was at Andy's college graduation in 1994. We were sitting on the town green, surrounded by Andy's parents, brother, aunt, and

THANKSGIVING
MAD LIB TEMPLATE

I know assignments like this can seem _____,
but I also realize they're _____ because
_____. So I, who go by my given name, _____
_____, hereby promise to take this as seriously as
possible and to fill it out in the true spirit of the day, which is one
of giving thanks and acknowledging both the people we love and depend
on, and the fortunate life we lead.

On this Thanksgiving, 20____, I am thankful for the following things
(which, by the way, can be things on your plate, friends you have
made and who support you, parents and relatives and siblings [hint,
hint], pets, trips you've taken, gifts you've received, things made
from chocolate, feelings you've had about the general awesomeness of
the universe, constellations, trees, goals you've scored, things that
occur in nature, etc., etc.). In other words, please think before you
fill these in:

One, _____.

Two, _____.

And, most of all, three: _____.

By signing this document, I swear that I tried my hardest to fill
it out accurately and that I also realize how _____
and _____ my parents, grandparents, and aunts and
uncles probably feel to have me in their lives.

Signed, _____

uncle, finishing up a dinner picnic on one of those lovely late spring New England nights, when Steve removed an eight-by-eleven manila folder from his bag and said he had a few words. I would later recognize that folder as a Pavlovian cue for *Something good is about to happen.*

But on that occasion, I had no idea what I was in for. To give you an example, here's a stanza about Andy defending his honors thesis in front of a panel of professors:

> But Amherst dons are cotton candy
> How they gasped when they saw Andy,
> Put in his thumb, pulled out the plum,
> So he could leave here magna cum.

And another that made me think that maybe this was a family worth marrying into:

> Who brought him back when he was down,
> Who really turned his world around
> That bluest chip of New York stock,
> The Lady Jenny Rosenstrach

As I type this, I'm not even referring to the framed, signed original copy of the poem, which is hanging in our office twenty-some-odd years later. I don't have to because I memorized it, along with the one he wrote for our wedding in Brooklyn Heights with views of the downtown skyline:

> October's moon, Manhattan's lights,
> Love's fireworks ignite the Heights,
> As bride and groom set sail aboard
> The Love Boat Rosenstrach and Ward

And how we found each other in spite of the fact that I grew up in a suburb of New York and Andy grew up in Virginia:

> Who would've thought a Larchmont lass,
> In racquet sports who ranks world class,

would find a love so sweet and fine,
Below the Mason-Dixon Line.

Then there's the one he wrote for Phoebe's second birthday, only a few weeks after a skunk snuck into *our house:*

See her dance the hokey-pokey!
Hear her sing the karaoke!
What badge of honor does she wear?
"Survivor of the Great Skunk Scare."

And, for Abby, in response to an exhausting first year with her:

In truth if we were keeping score
She'd eat and sleep a little more
and in the process liberate
Her parents from their Zombie state

There's a lot to love about these poems. How funny they are. How he presents the most mundane details of our daily lives in such a formal, romantic style. And there's the writing. Steve was a speechwriter in Washington, D.C., for a good part of his career, and not incidentally was the man who crafted Lloyd Bentsen's famous "Senator, you're no Jack Kennedy" retort to Dan Quayle in the 1988 vice presidential debate. (How could he write a live retort, you ask? As you might expect, when one is working on a presidential campaign, the teams entertain every possible issue that might arise in the course of the evening, and they knew that the youthful Dan Quayle was going to compare himself to the youthful Kennedy.) But when Steve wasn't writing political comebacks for speeches, he was weaving family jokes into poems to commemorate major milestones.

I can't tell you how much pleasure the family has gleaned from these poems, which Andy's mom, Emily, compiled in a binder a few years ago for their fiftieth anniversary party, and which serves as a kind of memoir in verse. When you are the recipient of one (as I was for my fortieth birthday), you feel as though you've been anointed.

From Steve, and from his poems, I learned an important lesson in celebrating: You can bake the best double fudge frosted birthday cake; you can pick up a filet mignon from the best butcher; but without a few thoughtful words to commemorate the occasion, to give the celebrants a moment of reflection, it's going to fall short.

This moment of reflection does not have to happen in verse or iambic pentameter. Let me repeat: *This moment of reflection does not have to happen in verse or iambic pentameter.* When it comes to toasts—at a wedding, at a dinner party, at a Thanksgiving table— while elegance and lyricism are certainly a welcome bonus for the listeners, they're secondary to the simple act of taking a moment to express yourself in a true and genuine way.

Perhaps the most emotional toast I can remember wasn't even spoken aloud. It happened at my father's Passover table years ago, way before there were any grandchildren around to instigate spontaneous riots and wince at the parsley dipped in saltwater. I can't remember exactly why, but it had been a while since the Seder had been held at my father's dining room table, in his home, and he started by saying how grateful he was that we were all there. Then he went on to tell us how meaningful Passover was for him because he could so vividly picture his own father leading the Seder at his childhood table in the Bronx so many decades earlier. My father didn't make it very far into this toast before he became too overwhelmed by the memory to speak—it remains one of the few times I've seen him cry. But he didn't have to say anything else; he didn't have to finish. We all got it.

A Birthday Poem For Phoebe

The poet's challenge? To compose
An ode befitting Phoebe Rose.
Tune in while Papa serenades
Our Princess of the Palisades.

What can we say, what can we do
To mark her birthday number two?
For Phoebe we'll work overtime
To catch her magic in a rhyme.

Ms Phoebe's in the cat bird's seat.
She dwells in Bellair's master suite
Where she can watch the Hudson flow
And catch the New York skyline's glow.

You've seen her face, seen the dimple
In the pages of Real Simple.
What lights the stars in dark night skies?
The twinkle in our Phoebe's eyes.

See her dance the hokey-pokey!
Hear her sing the karaoke!
What badge of honor does she wear?
"Survivor of the Great Skunk Scare."

Accustomed to the center stage,
With charm and grace she turned the page,
The new star in our fairytale:
Big Sister to Miss Abigail.

With her flair for the dramatic,
Charm and presence charismatic –
How could it be, do you suppose
That we were blessed with Phoebe Rose?

Strike up a tune that we all know –
Sing one more round of "Trot Old Joe"
Then clap and cheer, hip-hip hooray!
To Phoebe on her special day.

Love,
Papa

Papa's poem for Phoebe's second birthday still hangs on her bedroom wall.

THE HOLIDAY PARTY

The first thing I pictured when our real estate broker escorted my family of three (almost four; Abby was on the way) through the house we now own was the annual holiday party. Not family dinners. Not what I would do with extra closet space. Not, perhaps, a one-and-a-half-year-old Phoebe on the backyard swing set. No. I pictured the holiday party we'd already been hosting in our various five-hundred- to seven-hundred-square-foot Brooklyn apartments every year for nearly a decade. I knew the charcuterie board and brisket sliders would be on a long table at the south end of the house, the bar and the Christmas tree would be in the living room, and the stuffed grape leaves and hummus—wait, could you find that stuff in the suburbs?— would be on the other side of the room, next to the menorah.

What I didn't envision was the absolute chaos that would ensue at this party a few months later, not long after we'd moved in. Even though I had an almost fully gestated Abby in my belly during the initial walk-through, I had somehow overlooked the fact that she'd be around for the party, too. Wanting to eat. Wanting to be changed. Wanting to be heard. And she was the easy one. Phoebe was in her terrible twos, and even though we hired the daughter of a neighbor to come watch her at the party, she wouldn't let go of my leg, seemingly determined not to let her parents have a single conversation without interruption. Which was actually fine, because we had told other parents to bring their two-, three-, and four-year-olds as well, so instead of a grown-up, candle-lit, bourbon-fueled, Christmas-light-twinkling holiday party, it became one giant ode to the unfinished conversation.

That holiday party was our last for a while. Which was too bad, because until that point in our lives, it had been the highlight of our holiday. Sure, it was a lot of work planning it, but it was the fun kind of work. We'd spend hours coming up with menu ideas, assembling individual bruschettas and stuffed mushrooms, stringing Christmas lights around door frames, making playlists, shopping for dried sausage, cheese, and many jars of Dijon, whole-grain, sweet, and hot mustards. (We took to heart what Martha Stewart wrote in her famous hors d'oeuvres book: You want a lot of mustards to "create a feeling of bounty.") In Brooklyn, when it was just the two of us (and then for a short time, the three of us), we never minded how much planning was involved. Besides the fact that we were really into cooking, we felt every drop of sweat paid off as soon as the party started: We loved seeing our friends, catching up with people we'd been meaning to see all year, and we'd live off the high for days. But once our kids—and our guests' kids—entered the equation, we couldn't figure out a way to make it work in an all-inclusive way that wasn't completely stressful. The only payoff we'd have at the end of the night, it seemed, was a bounty of mustard-smeared dishes to clean.

When the next December rolled around, our first party-less December in a decade, I remember sitting on the couch with Andy post–bedtime routine, about to queue up an episode of *Lost*, and saying, "How happy are you that you don't have to make a hundred smoked salmon toasts this week?" I think his only response was something like *"Ahhhhhhhhh."*

But the truth is, I felt a little empty. That's the thing about rituals—a good one can be addictive, and without it, whatever you're celebrating can feel like you're just going through the motions. I depended on that party to check in with old friends and new—some of whom I saw only once a year. Every time one of them got in touch to find out if we had set a date for our party, I thought about changing my mind—but then I'd remember Phoebe doing her best impression of a barnacle on my velvet-panted leg, and Andy's *"Ahhhh,"* and I'd snap back to reality. "Maybe next year," I'd say, and really mean it.

"Next year" finally came four years later. Toddlerhood was behind us, and we felt ready to take on holiday entertaining again—but a somewhat altered version of it. We figured we'd work our way up to the big party, starting with a small dinner for five or six guests. If they had children, we'd invite them, feed them with our kids, then plant them in front of *The Incredibles,* while the grown-ups feasted on their coq au vin and champagne. Because we didn't have as many mouths to feed as we had for previous holiday celebrations, we were able to justify a few splurges—poor man's caviar, rosé champagne, that truffley Pecorino from the local cheese shop that I coveted all year long. The feast would be just festive enough to signify the holidays, but would end early enough to get the kids (and their tired parents) to bed at a decent hour. It was perfect.

Gradually, we upped the ante. When the girls were old enough to shepherd the visiting kids to their bedrooms to organize a game of Twister and stream a movie on

Netflix, we went from small dinner party to medium-size, inviting seven or eight friends and embracing an elaborate three- or four-course menu. A year or two later, we graduated to an official cocktail party, but instead of inviting everyone we knew, as we used to do in Brooklyn, we decided to keep the guest list "themed"—only locals, only work friends, only family. This way, it was easy to keep the number to twenty, the magic number in our house. (What the brokers don't tell you on a walk-through: It's a fine line between "good energy" and "utter freaking mayhem" when your house is small.) We didn't mention kids on the invitation—we wanted our guests to decide. Either way, there would be enough food, usually in the form of "interfaith sliders"— filled with brisket or ham—or make-ahead flatbread pizzas, and crudités. Big or small, it didn't matter. It just felt good to be back in the game.

INTERFAITH SLIDERS (BRISKET & HAM)

This brisket recipe makes enough for forty-eight small party sliders, but if you want to skip the rolls, it also yields enough meat for six to eight proper dinner portions.

1 3½- to 4-pound first-cut brisket,
   generously salted and peppered
½ cup plus 3 tablespoons good-quality olive oil
1 medium onion, roughly chopped
1 2-inch piece of fresh ginger, peeled and roughly chopped
3 cloves garlic
¼ cup brown sugar, packed
¼ cup Dijon mustard
½ cup red wine
¾ cup ketchup
⅓ cup balsamic vinegar
½ cup chicken or beef stock
4 sprigs fresh thyme
4 dozen small challah rolls or slider buns
freshly grated horseradish, for garnish
pickles, for garnish

SLIDER, SCHLIDER
Mini brisket sandwiches sit side by side with ham for a little interfaith inspiration.

• Preheat the oven to 325°F. In a large pot or Dutch oven set over medium-high heat, brown the brisket in 3 tablespoons of the olive oil, about 5 minutes a side. Remove to a roasting pan, fat side up.

• Place the onion, ginger, garlic, brown sugar, mustard, wine, ketchup, vinegar, stock, and remaining ½ cup oil in the bowl of a food processor and process until smooth. Pour the sauce on top of the brisket and add the thyme. The brisket should fit somewhat snugly in the roaster and be mostly immersed in the liquid. Cover tightly with foil. Bake for 2 hours. Turn the brisket over and bake uncovered for 1 more hour or until fork-tender. Cool, cover the brisket, and refrigerate overnight.

• When ready to serve, preheat the oven to 350°F. Remove the brisket from the pan to a cutting board and remove as much fat as you can before slicing the meat against the grain into thin pieces. Add the meat back to pan, cover with foil, and heat in the oven for 20 minutes.

• Remove the meat to a shallow bowl and pour the sauce into a warmed dish. Serve with slider buns, freshly grated horseradish, and pickles, and let guests help themselves.

HAM SLIDERS

(SEE PAGE 12)

POTATO LATKES WITH FIXIN'S

It's a good thing these latkes are always greeted by gasps of unadulterated glee— from both kids and grown-ups—because I've never found a way to make them that isn't messy and a little laborious. This method, which uses onion powder instead of the standard shredded onion, comes close, but if you're serving them at a party, definitely make them ahead of time, then reheat, covered with foil, at 300°F for 20 minutes. I like setting out some sample combos—latke with smoked salmon and capers, latke with caviar and sour cream—to get people started.

THIS RECIPE MAKES 18 TO 20 SMALL-MEDIUM PANCAKES, WHICH IS JUST ABOUT RIGHT FOR A FAMILY OF FOUR CELEBRATING HANUKKAH. FOR A PARTY, DOUBLE OR TRIPLE AS NEEDED.

3 large russet potatoes, washed and peeled (about 6 cups)

1 teaspoon onion powder

1 egg, lightly beaten

4 tablespoons all-purpose flour

½ teaspoon baking powder

2 teaspoons kosher salt

vegetable oil (a lot, or at least enough to maintain
about ½ inch in the pan)

Assorted toppings: smoked salmon, sour cream,
chopped fresh dill, capers, freshly grated horseradish,
chunky applesauce, minced red onion, caviar

• Grate the potatoes in a food processor, using the shredding disk. Add to a colander and rinse with cold water. Press down to remove as much liquid as possible, then transfer the potatoes to a dish towel and wrap, squeezing so every last drop of moisture is extracted. Add to a large mixing bowl with the onion powder, egg, flour, baking powder, and salt. In a large skillet in about ¼ inch of vegetable oil over medium-high heat, fry ¼-cup dollops of the potato mixture, flattening with a spoon, for about 4 minutes a side. Remove to a paper-towel-lined platter, then place in a baking dish, covered with foil, to keep warm.

• Serve with various toppings.

PARTY LATKES

I mean, seriously—what else do you need on a holiday spread besides potato pancakes with all the trimmings? Shown here: latkes with apple sauce, sour cream, capers, red onion, smoked salmon, paddlefish caviar, freshly grated horseradish.

MY DAD'S GENIUS ENTERTAINING TRICK

No matter how early I got out of bed when I was a kid, I would come down to a set breakfast table. Even during the school week. Even in the winter, when my alarm would go off in the pitch black. Even when I was the first one up on Christmas morning, I could expect to flip on the kitchen light and see five placemats, five plates, five juice glasses, five forks, knives, and spoons. This was not Santa's elves at work. It was my dad, who had set the breakfast table the night before, after dinner, after the dishwasher cycle. After we had all retired to our bedrooms to do whatever it was we did before teenagers holed up in the dark texting their friends. When my friend Jenny called me at night, the first thing she always asked was, "Did Ivan set the table yet?"

We made endless fun of him for his obsessive habit—and yet, there I was, a few years ago, with our holiday table all ready to go (sans the fresh flowers) a full week and a half before any guest would walk through my white-Christmas-light-framed doorway. The truth is, that dinner was the first (and only) Christmas dinner Andy and I had ever hosted (it's always at Andy's parents' house, see page 78), and I was overwhelmed by all that had to go into feeding ten adults and six children. I found that hosting the holiday dinner wasn't like the rest of the season's chaos—much of which could be done in advance and usually one-clicked while waiting for the chicken to finish roasting. When I sat down and looked at my dinner to-do list, it was a lot of last-minute shopping and stressing, and the only thing I could think of to do to feel more in control was . . . set the table.

Don't knock it until you try it! I can't believe how good it felt to have that part of the event under control. So much so that now I do it before almost any occasion that merits the Dining Room Table treatment. Phoebe's Secret Agent Party birthday table was set at least three days ahead of time, and when Andy came home from work that night and saw it, he looked at me as if I had nine heads. Just like we all used to look at Dad.

CHRISTMAS IN VIRGINIA

My in-laws downsized in 2013. They had lived in a townhouse on a lake in northern Virginia for almost thirty years and decided it was time to try out apartment life in the middle of their bustling town. It made sense—they could walk to everything and didn't have to climb three wooden flights to get to their bedroom. I had been visiting them at their townhouse for twenty of those years when Andy, the girls, and I headed down from New York to help them in the final days of their packing, to help them decide what to keep, what to toss, what to hand off to Andy and his brother, Tony. I was only there for a weekend of what was a long and emotional process for Emily and Steve, but all I had to do was watch Andy spend a few hours combing through boxes in the basement to rethink our entire relationship to the stuff in our life, and the *acquisition* of stuff in our life. Harder to bear than rummaging through soccer trophies, adverb-laden college papers, and Elton John albums was the heaviness of leaving behind so many memories. In these situations, no matter how often I tell myself it's about new beginnings, it's brutal, this moving-on business. The kids walked out of the house with weighted hearts, too, and we kept reminding them how lucky we were that it was so hard to leave. It means we had nothing but happy memories there, we told them. Wouldn't it be worse if we could just walk right out feeling happy? Or worse, without feeling anything at all?

I knew their house was special as soon as I first stepped into it in January 1993, a few months after Andy and I started dating. Everywhere I looked I saw evidence of a life well lived: shelf after shelf of family albums, row after row of hardcovers, wall after wall of their collections—of everything from antique maps to Indian beaded curios to tramp art frames to *objets* from the Middle East, where they had been stationed when Steve was in the Foreign Service in the late 1960s and early 1970s. Inside a kitchen pantry door was a bulletin board with a rotating assembly of photographs: pictures of Andy and his brother at various graduations, shots from the family's world travels, vintage photos of aunts and uncles, grandparents and cousins. The door was a work in progress, evolving over the years until it became overrun by the exploits of their

☆

Christmas Dinner, December 25, 2014 (14)
Hubba, Papa Doc, Tony, Trish, Mike*, Earl, Doug,
Jenny, Andy, Sophia, Aidan, Luca, Phoebe, Abby, Iris
                                    * Mike got sick ☹

Menu: Caviar + creme fraiche on potato chips
       Cheese + crackers w/ olives
       Sybil's Salad
       Curried Carrots w/ Pecans
       Filet w/ Cranberry Sauce
       Bouche du Noel

Notes * 8 lbs of filet was more than enough
         we had about 2 lbs left over
       * 10 Idaho potatoes for 14 people was
         enough if you don't want leftovers
       * Next year, make everything ahead
         of time + keep in LOUNGE warming
         oven so we can minimize the
         up + down with the elevator
       * Don't forget sponges
       * More carrots

five grandchildren. I had never seen a house like this before. In every corner, there was a nod to their history. It was what a house should be but often isn't—a celebration of a family's life and its many phases.

I loved visiting that house. When I wasn't wandering the halls contemplating the collection of vintage milkshake blenders that reminded Steve of his days working as a "soda jerk" on the Jersey Shore in the 1950s, or admiring the 150-year-old box crafted entirely of matchsticks, I was using the treadmill in the basement or taking a nap in the guest bedroom, the one with the ironed sheets and hospital corners. I used to joke that spending a weekend in their house was like staying in a boutique hotel. We had our own floor and bathroom and woke up to fruit salad in glass bowls every morning.

The girls had other things in mind, though. As soon as they'd walk into their grandparents' house, they'd head straight to the basement. There, Abby would unearth the large box containing Emily's childhood dollhouse, complete with original figurines and 1940s furniture, and spend whatever free time she could in that teeny wallpapered world. Phoebe would beeline for her dad's old record collection, a treasure trove of Donald Duck and Looney Tunes and Sesame Street LPs. Anticipating Phoebe's arrival, a record player would have already been set up on the floor, where she'd sit for hours, Indian-style, listening and laughing to the audio adventures of Uncle Scrooge, Hiawatha, and Bugs Bunny.

Is it any wonder that the girls begged to visit Hubba and Papa whenever possible? And why saying goodbye to the house on that cold March day was so hard?

Abby, who gets more attached to rituals and memories than most people (maybe even more than her mother), had an especially hard time grasping how Christmas would ever happen again, given that every memory she had of the holiday, every Christmas ritual revisited year after year, took place inside that house. We had been celebrating it there for as long as she could remember.

I'm guessing I'm not the first parent to say that rituals associated with the holidays hold a special power over my kids. On the five-hour drive from New York to Virginia, even now as middle schoolers, Phoebe and Abby always tick off everything they can't wait to do upon arrival: ice skating at the rink in town, the epic four- or five-course Christmas Eve feast at their uncle Mike's house in Washington, D.C., the visit to the United States Botanic Garden to see the elaborate holiday train show, the once-a-year filet that gets trotted out for the centerpiece at Christmas dinner. Opening presents to Frank Sinatra while snacking on stollen. The dollhouse and record player, of course, too, but those can wait. There are more pressing things when it's holiday time, like baking Christmas cookies with Hubba.

The recipe for those cookies is handwritten on a grease-stained index card that Hubba has been using for thirty years. Usually, she makes the dough ahead of time so the girls can get right to the fun stuff: shaping the dough into Christmas trees, reindeer, and bells, mixing food coloring into little mugs of icing, and smearing it artlessly all over the cookies once they're baked. Every year, we take the same photo of the girls standing next to Hubba at the counter—in the early years, standing on step stools—hard at work. If we turned these shots into a flip book, I'd see my daughters grow up before my eyes.

The whole family goes crazy over Hubba's cookies, gorging on them in between skating and napping, cooking and gift-wrapping, but we always save some for the sampler plate the girls leave by the fireplace on Christmas Eve. The two or three iced sugar cookies sit alongside a few baby carrots, a glass of milk for Rudolph, and a can of Bud for Santa. (The parents and grandparents are only too happy to partake in the name of Keeping the Santa Dream Alive.)

Naturally, the first time we visited Hubba and Steve in their new apartment, the first thing the girls noticed was what was missing: a fireplace. Neither of them believed in Santa by that point in their lives, but it didn't matter. It was what they were going to miss: the cookies and milk for Rudolph, the beer for Santa, *the ritual*.

It turns out, though, that rituals don't require much more than a certain commitment to the right spirit and the presence of close friends and family in order to be meaningful. Rudolph got his cookies and Santa got his bottle of Budweiser, which we left on the coffee table in the living room. (We're pretty sure they came in via the patio.) We had our traditional Christmas dinner, filet of beef and all, even though Andy's parents had to rent out some communal space in the apartment building in order to fit everyone. But we fit everyone. Everyone was there. And it tasted exactly like Christmas.

HUBBA'S CHRISTMAS COOKIES

Every Christmas Eve, we leave a plate of these cookies, carrots, some milk, and a can of Bud by the fireplace. In the morning, most of the carrots, milk, and beer remain, but the cookies? Santa's no dummy.

MAKES ABOUT 3 DOZEN COOKIES

2¾ cups flour, plus more for rolling the dough

1 teaspoon baking powder

1 teaspoon kosher salt

¾ cup (1½ sticks) unsalted butter, softened

1 cup sugar

2 eggs

1 teaspoon pure vanilla extract

- In a large bowl, whisk together the flour, baking powder, and salt. In another large bowl, using a mixer, blend together the butter, sugar, eggs, and vanilla until light and fluffy.
- Slowly beat the flour mixture into the butter mixture. Form the dough into a disk, wrap in wax paper, and chill in the fridge until firm, at least 1 hour.
- Preheat the oven to 350°F. Roll out the dough on a floured surface until it's about ¼ inch thick. Using your favorite cookie cutters, make cookies and place them on cookie sheets. Bake for 8 to 10 minutes until golden edges barely start forming.

Frosting

- Blend together 4 tablespoons (½ stick) butter, 4 cups powdered sugar, ¼ cup heated milk, and 1 teaspoon pure vanilla extract. Separate into bowls and add two or three drops of food coloring to each. Spread on the cooled cookies and top with sprinkles and sugar crystals. The frosting will be gooey at first but will harden after spread. If the frosting hardens in the bowl, just stir with a whisk to loosen it. Apply liberally.

COOKIE PARTY!
Want to feel like
you've done the
holidays right?
Follow Hubba's lead:
Bake the cookies,
make the frosting,
set out the cookie
cutters (Jewish
stars and dreidls,
too, natch), then
invite a few kids
over to decorate
and watch *Elf*.

CHRISTMAS DINNER

Cranberry-Marinated Beef Tenderloin
Curried Carrots with Pecans / Sybil's Salad
Horseradish Mashed Potatoes (see page 175)

CRANBERRY-MARINATED BEEF TENDERLOIN

Christmas Dinner is the one meal all year long when our family sits down to beef tenderloin—the price of which shocks me every time I spy it stuck on the butcher paper. The thing is, though, even if tenderloin were as affordable as chicken, I love the idea of saving a special recipe for a special dinner year in and year out. In that way, it tastes like Christmas and nothing else.

SERVES 8 TO 10

1 4-pound beef tenderloin
1 cup dried cranberries
1 cup cranberry juice
3 tablespoons fresh orange juice
1 cup red wine
2 tablespoons soy sauce
¼ teaspoon kosher salt
1 teaspoon freshly ground pepper
3 cloves garlic, crushed
1 sprig fresh rosemary
1 tablespoon all-purpose flour, plus 1 teaspoon
2 tablespoons unsalted butter

• In a large zip-top plastic bag, combine the tenderloin, cranberries, cranberry juice, orange juice, wine, soy sauce, salt, pepper, garlic, and rosemary. Seal and marinate in the refrigerator for 24 hours.

• Preheat the oven to 500°F. Place the tenderloin in a broiler pan and lightly pat it dry. Reserve the marinade, removing rosemary and garlic. Place the tenderloin in the oven and immediately reduce the oven temperature to 350°F. Bake for 40 minutes (start watching it at 30 minutes) until the thickest part reads 125°F (rare) on a meat thermometer. Broil for 2 or 3 minutes, until brown on top. Remove and let sit 15 minutes.

• In a medium pot over medium heat, whisk the flour and the reserved marinade to combine. Bring to a boil, then cook, stirring constantly, for 8 minutes or until thick. Stir in the butter until melted. Serve warm with the tenderloin.

CURRIED CARROTS WITH PECANS

In addition to being a holiday-worthy side dish, this recipe, modified from Emily's old Silver Palate Cookbook, *holds the distinct honor of being the one that turned Abby into a cooked-carrot lover.*

SERVES 8 TO 10

kosher salt

½ cup pecans

2½ pounds carrots, peeled and cut into 2-inch pieces

½ cup (1 stick) unsalted butter

1 tablespoon curry powder

2 tablespoons light brown sugar, packed

2 tablespoons fresh lemon juice

freshly ground pepper

2 tablespoons chopped fresh chives

• Preheat the oven to 325°F. Bring a large pot of salted water to a boil.

• Spread out the pecans on a small rimmed baking sheet and toast, tossing occasionally, until fragrant and slightly darker, 4 to 6 minutes; let cool. Coarsely chop and set aside. Working in 2 batches, cook the carrots in the boiling water until tender, 6 to 8 minutes per batch. Using a slotted spoon, transfer to a bowl of ice water. Drain the carrots and pat dry.

• Melt the butter in a large Dutch oven over medium-high heat. Add the curry powder and cook, stirring frequently, until fragrant, about 30 seconds. Reduce the heat to medium, add the carrots and brown sugar, and cook, tossing occasionally, until the carrots are coated and heated through, 8 to 10 minutes. Add the lemon juice and toss gently to combine. Season with salt and pepper. Serve the carrots topped with the chives and reserved pecans.

SYBIL'S SALAD

There was a period in the late 1990s when this salad—discovered by Emily and Steve's best friend, Sybil—seemed to make an appearance on the menu for everything from bridal shower brunches to book club dinners. Naturally, it found its way to the holiday table around the same time—and there it stayed, for going on twenty years now. Sybil's original recipe calls for watercress and toasted pine nuts, but we've swapped in arugula and candied walnuts with happy results.

SERVES 8 TO 10

1 bunch of Boston or Bibb lettuce, rinsed and torn

1 bunch of arugula, rinsed and torn

2 pears, peeled and chopped into bite-size pieces

1 cup candied walnuts, roughly chopped

½ cup chopped scallions, white and light green parts only (2 bunches)

4 ounces good-quality blue cheese, crumbled

Dressing

½ cup good-quality olive oil

¼ cup white wine vinegar

1 teaspoon fresh lemon juice

1 clove garlic, finely minced

kosher salt and freshly ground pepper

• In a large bowl, combine all of the salad ingredients. In a small bowl, whisk together the ingredients for the dressing. When it's time to serve, drizzle the salad with the dressing and toss.

HORSERADISH MASHED POTATOES

(SEE PAGE 175)

FANCY-PANTS DINNER

New Year's Eve

This might sound odd coming from a food writer (or from anyone, actually), but half the china place settings we received for our wedding still have their price tags on them—and we got married when Bill Clinton was president. There's a good reason for this. Sort of: Though I am always cooking china-worthy holiday meals, I am rarely cooking china-worthy holiday meals in my own house. With few exceptions over the years, I'm at my sister's for Thanksgiving, my in-laws' for Christmas, or my parents' for Easter or Passover. Being in this position, I realize, means I get off easy; I don't have to think about houseguests or clean towels in the bathrooms or niggling details like, *Do we need to pick up more Scotch for Uncle Bob?*

Because of this, when we *do* bust out the fancy stuff, I can't help but feel as though we're playing house, like we're not actual grown-ups with two middle schoolers and a mortgage. Maybe that's because we are, on some level, pretending. We're not formal entertainers. For dinner parties, we prefer the kitchen table and short wineglasses over the dining room and crystal stemware. (A convenient philosophy, since we don't actually *own* crystal stemware.) Sometimes it can be hard to distinguish a meal we make for guests from the ones we make for the family on a typical weekend night. (I mean, really, is anyone ever going to be unhappy about spaghetti and meatballs or grilled fish tacos?) About a decade ago, my mother-in-law gave me a box of the most beautiful antique table linens, most of which are in a box on the bottom shelf of a closet, still waiting for their close-up.

Perhaps this is how we arrived at our New Year's Eve ritual, an honest-to-goodness multicourse Fancy Feast, born from the notion that at least once a year, we should have an excuse to dig out our china and linens and go *off*. When we are only feeding our immediate family, versus a gaggle of relatives, we can afford to get all Eloise with the evening: passed hors d'oeuvres, bubbly drinks, place cards, lobsters, and (finally!) four place settings of wedding china: salad plate, dinner plate, and even the tea cups, which we use for chocolate mousse or sloppy brownie sundaes. (Okay, so maybe it's not *all* refined eating.) The kids love it because it feels special, and we love

Caviar and
crème fraîche
on supermarket
potato chips.
I dare you to
eat just one.

A NEW YEAR'S EVE FANCY-PANTS FEAST

Sparkling Cider
for the girls

Champagne
for the grown-ups

Fussy Finger Food
(including Caviar on
Potato Chips)

New Year's Eve Lobsters
with Champagne Butter
(page 93)

Horseradish
Mashed Potatoes
(see page 175)

Beet and Blood Orange Salad
with Pistachios
(page 94)

Tea Cup Brownie Sundaes
(page 95)

it because, while we're splurging a little, we're not succumbing to an overpriced prix fixe. Here are a few things we serve.

FUSSY FINGER FOOD

Caviar on Potato Chips

Before you roll your eyes—Caviar? For *kids*?—we are not talking special reserve Ossetra here. We're talking American paddlefish caviar you can find at better supermarkets, that will set you back about fifteen bucks. Serve it on kettle-cooked potato chips (chips: they're the easier, saltier blinis) and a dollop of sour cream or crème fraîche, and you'll feel like you've kicked off the night right. If the kids pass on the fish eggs, they can stick with the chips—more of the good stuff left for you.

Truffle Popcorn

At the Inn at Little Washington, in Washington, Virginia, chef Patrick O'Connell is famous for grating a whole truffle over a batch of warm popcorn, which is both appalling and off-the-hook delicious. We go with the poor man's version: good-quality popcorn (we like Rancho Gordo) salted and drizzled with a little truffle oil.

Phoebe's Fried Pineapple

I can't remember how long ago this started, but I can tell you one thing: We're in deep with this ritual, and I don't see it stopping. Phoebe must've been five or six, just tall enough to reach the stovetop, when, in a flash of culinary inspiration, she decided she wanted to fry pineapple chunks in butter, then sprinkle them with cinnamon. Where she got this idea from, we have no idea, but we do know that our job is to encourage her participation and reinforce the pride that inevitably results. It's okay if you skip this particular starter on your New Year's Eve menu, but I highly advise trying out at least one thing that's kid-made and truly random.

Warm Artichoke Dip (with or without crab)

A good way to decide if an hors d'oeuvre is New Year's Eve worthy? If you can easily envision it on a party spread in the 1950s. This dip is a classic, made more classic with the addition with lump crab meat if you're up for it. In a medium bowl, mix together one 14-ounce can artichoke hearts (completely drained, then chopped), ⅓ cup Hellmann's mayonnaise, 1 cup shredded mozzarella cheese, ½ cup freshly grated Parmigiano-Reggiano, 1 teaspoon Worcestershire sauce, 2 teaspoons fresh lemon juice, and 4 ounces lump crab meat (drained and patted completely dry), if using. Bake at 400°F for 20 minutes until golden and bubbly. Let cool slightly, then serve warm with baked pita chips or crusty bread.

NEW YEAR'S EVE LOBSTERS WITH CHAMPAGNE BUTTER

We favor steaming (instead of boiling) because it results in a more tender lobster. You don't need to have a special pot for it, you just need a large one (or two if you are cooking a lot of lobsters; make sure they fit comfortably) that can be tightly fitted with a lid. A steamer rack keeps the lobsters from getting charred on the bottom of the pot, but it's not crucial. If you don't have one, use a vegetable steamer instead.

SERVES 4

kosher salt

4 lobsters (we usually buy four 1¼-pounders)

6 tablespoons (¾ stick) butter

1 tablespoon champagne (optional—in fact, I'm not really sure
   what this adds except that the kids get a real kick out of it)

1 tablespoon fresh lemon juice

• Put 2 inches of salted water in the bottom of the pot. (You want the salinity to be roughly equal to the sea.) Set a steamer rack inside and bring the water to a rolling boil over high heat. Add the live lobsters one at a time, cover the pot, and start timing (see the table below). Halfway through, lift the lid (careful—the steam is hot) and shift the lobsters around so they cook evenly. Shell the lobsters and arrange the meat on a New Year's Eve-worthy platter, wedding china encouraged, but not required.

• To make champagne butter: Melt the butter in a small saucepan. Stir in the champagne, if using, and the lemon juice. Serve in a small bowl alongside the shelled lobsters. When eating, save the best (the tail) for last.

Note:
Lobster Weight Steam Time
(no matter how many are in the pot)
• 1 pound: 10 minutes
• 1¼ pounds: 12 minutes
• 1½ pounds: 14 minutes
• 1¾ pounds: 16 minutes
• 2 pounds: 18 minutes

BEET AND BLOOD ORANGE SALAD WITH PISTACHIOS

There is a lot of peeling and shelling for this seemingly simple salad, but I promise you it's worth it. If you decided to take some store-bought shortcuts—preshelled pistachios, presliced oranges, or those shrink-wrapped precooked beets, which are actually pretty good—I wouldn't blame you. Also, if you are making this in advance, don't toss in the oranges until a few minutes before you serve. That way, they don't turn completely pink from the beet juice.

SERVES 4

7 whole medium beets, unpeeled

2 tablespoons red wine vinegar

¼ cup good-quality olive oil

½ teaspoon honey

kosher salt and freshly ground pepper

2 blood oranges (or regular oranges),
    sectioned or supremed

⅓ cup pistachios

6 fresh mint leaves, minced

2 tablespoons minced fresh cilantro leaves

⅓ cup crumbled feta cheese

1 tablespoon minced scallions (about 3 scallions)

- Preheat the oven to 425°F.
- Wrap the beets in 2 foil packets and roast for 45 minutes or until a knife slips through them fairly easily. Let cool, then peel and chop them into 1-inch chunks. (You should have about 3 cups.) In a medium bowl, whisk together the vinegar, olive oil, honey, and salt and pepper to taste. Add the oranges, pistachios, mint, cilantro, feta, and scallions and toss.

TEA CUP BROWNIE SUNDAES

No, that is not a mistake: This brownie recipe calls for salted *butter, not unsalted. I find this somehow enhances the chocolate factor—not to mention contrasts beautifully with cool, creamy ice cream. If you like your brownies on the fudgier side, reduce the flour to ½ cup.*

SERVES 16

½ cup (1 stick) salted butter,
    plus more for greasing the baking dish
1¼ cups sugar
¾ cup unsweetened cocoa powder
1 teaspoon pure vanilla extract
2 eggs
⅔ cup all-purpose flour
assorted sundae toppings: ice cream,
    whipped cream (see page 59), fudge sauce,
    caramel, sprinkles, maraschino cherries

• Preheat the oven to 325°F. Grease a 9-inch square baking dish with a pat of butter. Melt the ½ cup butter in a small saucepan over medium-low heat. Let cool slightly. In a medium bowl, whisk the sugar and cocoa powder to combine. Slowly whisk the butter into the dry ingredients just until combined. Whisk in the vanilla and eggs, beating to blend after each addition. Stir in the flour until just combined, then spread the batter into the baking dish. (It will be thick.) Bake for 25 to 30 minutes, until the top begins to crack. Cool on a wire rack, then cut into squares that fit your tea cups. Top with the desired sundae fixings.

PART II

OUR FAMILY RITUALS

The Walk to the Farmer's Market
The One-on-One Date / Fruit First Thing
Pickling / Lunch with Dad
The Sleepover Breakfast / Vacation Rituals
Miracle Mashed Potatoes / Après Ski

THE WALK TO THE FARMER'S MARKET

Like many parents, we learned the value of a good bribe early on. As soon as the girls were old enough to understand the concept of *if-this-then-that,* we were promising them a Teletubbies video if they stopped crying, or an extra bedtime story if they changed into their pjs quickly, or a Mallomar if they tried a bite of broccoli. Essentially doing everything you are told not to do by anyone out there purporting to be an expert in parenting.

I do, however, credit our finely honed bribery skills with cultivating one of my most favorite family rituals: taking a walk.

As in: Girls, if we all walk to town, we can stop by the bakery for a cupcake. Or, if we take a stroll after dinner, we can come back to have brownies for dessert. Or, if we hike around the pond, we can order one of those homemade bologna sandwiches from the farm café at the end of the trail. Or, if we hike up Bear Mountain, we can have a picnic at the summit. Or, if we walk over the Brooklyn Bridge from Brooklyn to Manhattan, we can reward ourselves with those soup dumplings at the Oriental Garden in Chinatown.

Surely I'm not the only one out there who has discovered this magical strategy?

I'm not necessarily saying the girls are unable to appreciate the value of a 150-year-old historical landmark, or the beauty of a lilac-infused amble into town on a summer morning, or the singular rush you earn from making it to the summit of a 1,200-foot mountain. They do. (At least, I think they do.) But you don't have to be an expert in child psychology to realize that a family walk is going to be a little more *marketable* when there's some kind of treat at the end of it. Maybe I inherited this gene from my always-on-the-move mother, but I've always enjoyed a stroll more when we have a destination or a *purpose,* here defined as a hot chocolate, a Shake Shack burger, soup dumplings, picnic chicken, spider rolls, kettle corn, strawberry milkshakes, double chocolate chip ice cream, hot dogs, samosas, *carnitas,* scallion pancakes, Belgian waffles, warm onion bagels with cream cheese, or cider doughnuts.

Cider doughnuts! I owe so much to those crispy-doughy, sometimes still-warm

**ROAST MARKET
VEGETABLES**
When in doubt,
toss your loot
with olive oil,
salt, and pepper,
and roast at
400°F. Shown
here: Carrots and
fennel, soon to
be combined with
quinoa, feta,
and herbs
(page 117).

little lovelies they sell at our farmer's market. Every Saturday morning, you'll find our daughters under a vendor's tent, clutching a few bucks in their fingers and hotly debating whether to go with the cinnamon-dusted or the old-fashioned. Our local market is held in a library parking lot that overlooks the Hudson River, and since we first moved more than a decade ago, we've used it as an excuse to peel the kids away from Saturday morning *Dora* (or *Backyardigans* or *iCarly* or, these days, *Glee*), get them dressed, grab our dog, Iris, and walk a mile down the hill to check out the offerings. As much as I like to think the girls look forward to this because it's family time, because they get to enjoy a beautiful spring day after a long New York winter, or because they inevitably run into friends or teammates and maybe even get to feel that swell of community pride like we do . . . I'm no fool. I know it comes down to the doughnuts.

I have no problem with this at all. In fact, I am a big believer in anything that creates an aura of excitement around good food for kids, particularly *shopping* for good food, and our market is definitely not lacking in either the excitement factor or the food incentives. Besides the cider doughnuts, there is the crepe table, the breakfast burrito stand, the pickler, the old-fashioned ice-cream cart, the honey stick man, and the pizza truck whose daily special is conceived that morning based on what they've plucked from the vendors surrounding them. And no, in case you're wondering, nine A.M. is not too early to eat a full-on wood-fired margherita pie if you are eleven years old. Or if you are forty.

Andy and I have our own favorite foods at the market, which we procure like lions on the hunt: The lacinato kale, from the Ulster County farmers, that we will shred and toss with herby homemade ranch dressing or a pomegranate vinaigrette; the sweet Italian sausages, from the guy in the northeast corner of the lot, that we will crumble into lentils for a quick healthy dinner. The Hudson Valley duck breast from Sullivan County that Andy grills and serves with a cherry-peach relish. The peaches, which we will mix with berries and turn into a cobbler. The fish (Oh man, the fish! Lemon sole, gray sole, sea trout, flounder, littlenecks, sea bass, striped bass), most of which has been swimming off the coast of Long Island only hours before it's wrapped up for us.

A lot of our go-tos, as you'd expect, change with the season. In the spring, we seek out the tiny red-through-and-through strawberries that we will whirl with almond milk for a "liquid breakfast" or sprinkle with sugar and top with freshly whipped cream for dessert. For the six minutes in April that ramps are in season, we make like good little food fetishists and transform our bunches into pesto, roast them with olive oil, salt, and pepper, or throw them on top of pizzas. In the summer, when we're feeling ambitious, we'll lug home raspberries, blueberries, and blackberries to bake Abby's favorite: a triple-berry pie with a lattice-top crust. We always hit the vendor who sells the amazing summer spinach and rainbow chard, both of which are so reliably the best versions of themselves that they never need anything more than a quick sauté in olive oil, garlic, and salt and pepper to win over even the most stalwart green-ophobe.

If it's the first weekend of the month—especially in June, July, and August—I'll stock up on my favorite chutney from the Bombay Emerald vendors, and mix it into smashed roasted potatoes or serve it with grilled fish or chicken topped with spicy yogurt and cilantro. If it's tomato season, we take that sh*t seriously and do a full round of the market, examining the heirloom situation *very* carefully before deciding where to plunk our cash. Is the color deep? Is the weight hefty? Is it charmingly misshapen? Will these golden cherry tomatoes last the walk home or be mindlessly popped into little mouths like so many peanut M&Ms? Whatever the haul, it's best if we get enough to last at least a couple of days. I love nothing more than serving a bunch of multisize, multicolored tomatoes alongside a ball of gooey, milky burrata, a baguette, sea salt, and a generous drizzle of olive oil. It works as a starter for outdoor entertaining or—the best—for a no-cook, no-meat summer family dinner.

Wait, I take that back. There's one thing I love more: the tomato sandwich. Not the bacon-lettuce-and-tomato sandwich; not the grilled-cheese-and-tomato sandwich; not the tomato-mozzarella-and-basil sandwich. The tomato sandwich. Period. It is a thing of simple, summery, kid-friendly beauty, and one of my great regrets is that I went the first thirty years of my life without knowing it existed. The sandwich requires only four ingredients—white bread, mayo, tomato, sea salt—but it begins and ends with the tomato. If we can't track down a sweet, juicy heirloom, it fails. Because the stakes are so high, the whole family is deployed for duty at the market—holding, smelling, comparing. If the right one is procured, the next purchase is the boule of country white bread, then the one-mile walk home, where a jar of Hellmann's awaits our return. If that is not the ultimate incentive, I don't know what is.

"I LIKE TO THINK THE GIRLS LOOK FORWARD TO THE FARMER'S MARKET BECAUSE IT'S QUALITY FAMILY TIME, BUT I'M NO FOOL. I KNOW IT COMES DOWN TO THE DOUGHNUTS."

THE TOMATO SANDWICH

It's not a sandwich. It's a religion.

THE TOMATO SANDWICH

There are times for whole wheat bread; this is not one of them. The recipe will yield four open-face sandwiches, but I can't promise you'll want to stop at one per person.

SERVES 4

> 4 slices thick country white bread
>
> Hellmann's mayonnaise (no other mayo will do, except *maybe* Duke's)
>
> 3 to 5 tomatoes of various shapes, colors, and varieties, sliced
>
> sea salt

• Toast the bread. Lightly coat each slice with mayo, but—this is crucial—be sure to do this while the toast is still warm. You want the mayo to get melty. Now, arrange 2 or 3 slices of tomato on top of the toast. Let the kids pick the colors, mixing red, yellow, and green; heirloom, Jersey, and beefsteak—whatever. Sprinkle with salt.

GRILLED DUCK BREAST WITH CHERRY-PEACH RELISH

We credit the girls' first babysitter, Devika, with launching Phoebe's duck obsession. On special occasions, Devika would bring us a stash of her famous, one-hundred-ingredient duck curry, which Phoebe would scoop up with the accompanying homemade roti. We tend to go simpler, grilling a breast we buy from a Hudson Valley market vendor, and serving it with a summery, fruity relish to cut its richness.

SERVES 4

> **Cherry-Peach Relish**
>
> ½ cup dried pitted cherries
>   (such as Montmorency cherries)
>
> ½ cup red wine
>
> 1 cup peaches, peeled and chopped
>   into medium dice (from about 2 medium-size peaches)
>
> 1 teaspoon finely minced fresh ginger
>
> 1 tablespoon sherry vinegar (or red wine vinegar)
>
> 2 teaspoons sugar
>
> 1 teaspoon fresh lemon juice
>
> ¼ cup water

Duck

1½-pound duck breast, scored in a diamond pattern
   on the fatty side if necessary
kosher salt and freshly ground pepper

• *For Relish:* In a bowl, soak the dried cherries in just enough red wine to cover for 3 hours. When ready to make the relish, place the cherries and the wine in a medium saucepan and add the peaches, ginger, sherry vinegar, sugar, lemon juice, and the water. Bring to a boil, then simmer over low heat until the liquid is thick and mostly evaporated, 12 to 15 minutes. Let cool and store in the refrigerator if you are not using right away. (It will keep for 2 to 3 days.)

• *For duck:* Make a fire in a charcoal grill or preheat a gas grill for indirect heat. If using a charcoal grill, move the coals to one side of the grill and let them burn down to medium heat.

• Season the duck with salt and pepper, then cook it, skin side up, for 8 minutes on the side of the grill that is not directly over the heat, so you render some of the fat over indirect heat and it drips right off. (There is so much fat on the skin that you have to be careful it doesn't start a fire and burn the duck to a crisp.) Flip the duck and grill it skin side down (again over indirect heat; you do not want big flames) for another 5 to 8 minutes. After that, move the duck to direct heat, flipping it every minute or so, until it has a nice burnished (not burned) color on the skin side. The duck should cook for a total of about 15 minutes. Let sit for 10 minutes, then slice. Serve with Cherry-Peach Relish.

GRILLED FISH WITH BLENDER SAUCE

Our favorite thing to do with grilled fish from the farmer's market is serve it with a vibrant blender sauce. For one, a fresh fish deserves a fresh sauce. For two, why turn on the stovetop or the oven in the summer if you don't have to? I've provided recipes that make ⅓ cup of salsa verde and 1½ cups of tomato coulis, both of which can also be made in a food processor. Try one sauce this week and the other next week, and see which your family likes best.

SERVES 4

Fish

1¼ pounds firm local grilling fish (in our neck of the woods
    that means striped bass, black bass, and occasionally swordfish),
    cut into four 5-ounce fillets

good-quality olive oil

kosher salt and freshly ground pepper

squeeze of fresh lemon juice

Blender Sauce Option 1: Salsa Verde

1 cup fresh flat-leaf parsley, cilantro, or mint leaves, or a combination of all three

⅓ cup good-quality olive oil

¼ cup roughly chopped scallions, white and light green parts only
    (from about 1 bunch)

1 tablespoon capers, rinsed and drained

¼ teaspoon kosher salt

freshly ground pepper

1½ teaspoons fresh lemon juice

pinch of red pepper flakes (optional)

Blender Sauce Option 2: Tomato Coulis

about 2 cups fresh grape tomatoes (red or yellow or both)

¼ cup good-quality olive oil

1 tablespoon red wine vinegar

3 fresh basil leaves

1 tablespoon chopped scallions, white and light green parts only

squeeze of Sriracha sauce

kosher salt and freshly ground pepper

- Make a fire in a charcoal grill or preheat a gas grill to medium.
- Meanwhile, on a plate or in a zip-top plastic bag, marinate the fish in olive oil, salt and pepper, and lemon juice. (Add the lemon only about 5 minutes before you grill.) Once the grill is medium hot, grill the fillets for 4 to 5 minutes per side, depending on thickness. Remove to a platter.
- Place the ingredients for the salsa verde or the tomato coulis in a blender and process until emulsified. Drizzle the sauce over the fish and serve.

GRILLED SMASHED POTATOES WITH CHUTNEY

Listen to the potatoes as they're grilling: If they sound really sizzly, move the packets around a little or check to make sure they're not burning.

SERVES 4

>about 4 medium Yukon Gold potatoes, washed and unpeeled,
>   cut into medium chunks (3 cups)
>2 to 3 tablespoons good-quality olive oil
>kosher salt and freshly ground pepper
>3 tablespoons plum or pomegranate chutney (or your favorite kind)
>chopped fresh cilantro leaves or chives, for garnish
>plain whole-milk yogurt, for garnish (optional)

- Make a fire in a charcoal grill or preheat a gas grill to medium.
- Divide the potatoes among 3 sheets of aluminum foil. Drizzle with the olive oil, season with salt and pepper, and wrap completely. Place them on a grill grate for 30 minutes. Move the foil packets around every now and then to ensure even cooking. Dump the cooked potatoes into a bowl and toss with the chutney, smashing slightly just until the skins break. Top with the herbs and with yogurt, if desired.

KALE SALAD WITH POMEGRANATES

This is one of those rare salads that seems to work for every meal: with burgers on a Tuesday night after soccer practice, with grilled shrimp when doing penance for a week of gorging on vacation, or with a roasted leg of lamb on a Saturday night when a bunch of friends come over for dinner and we bust out the cloth napkins. It's often met with some skepticism—adults: "You just eat it raw?"; kids: "What is this stuff?"—until they taste it and ask for the recipe. Note: It calls for pomegranate molasses, but if you don't have that, or you can't find it, you can substitute agave or a pinch or two of sugar.

SERVES 4

Vinaigrette

½ teaspoon Dijon mustard

⅓ cup good-quality olive oil

¼ cup white balsamic vinegar

1½ teaspoons pomegranate molasses

1 teaspoon Sriracha sauce

kosher salt and freshly ground pepper

juice from ¼ lime (about 1 teaspoon)

Salad

1 bunch of lacinato (also called Tuscan) kale, stems removed,
    leaves cut into ¼-inch ribbons (about 4 cups)

½ cup pomegranate seeds, from 1 small pomegranate

2 tablespoons finely minced red onion

handful of finely chopped fresh herbs such as dill, cilantro,
    or flat-leaf parsley (or any combo of the three)

sea salt and freshly ground pepper

• In a jar or measuring cup, whisk together all of the vinaigrette ingredients until emulsified. Toss the vinaigrette in a large bowl with the kale, pomegranate seeds, onion, and herbs, then sprinkle the whole thing with salt and pepper.

I can't exactly
explain why
this is, but as
soon as I eat
shredded kale
salads like these,
I feel smarter.

Strawberry-Almond
Milkshakes power
Phoebe through
homework hour.
They also make
a pretty tasty
breakfast.

STRAWBERRY–ALMOND MILKSHAKES

It goes without saying that this tastes best when we track down the freshest strawberries we can find at the market. It works for breakfast or as an energizing midafternoon snack.

SERVES 1

strawberries
almond milk

• There are no measurements for this smoothie. I find it much easier to simply fill a drinking glass with strawberries. Don't pack them in—just lightly pile them together. Then pour the almond milk into the same glass until it's about two-thirds full, allowing the milk to sneak into whatever gaps remain between the berries. Dump the whole thing into a blender, whirl on high, and pour back into the glass. Perfect every time.

PIZZA WITH RAMPS AND TALEGGIO

Here, ramps are paired with Taleggio, a slightly runny, slightly stinky, extremely tasty Italian cheese, on our version of a pizza we had once at New York's Il Buco. After her first bite, Phoebe pronounced it her "favorite pizza EVER." Of course, she had just returned from soccer practice—i.e., she was starving and pretty indiscriminating— so she might've said that about anything we put in front of her. If you don't have access to ramps, try this with scallions, fennel, or garlic scapes.

SERVES 4 TO 6

1 bunch of ramps, washed and trimmed at their root ends

2 tablespoons olive oil, plus more for brushing the dough

kosher salt and freshly ground pepper

1 16-ounce ball store-bought pizza dough

½ cup freshly grated Parmigiano-Reggiano, plus more for sprinkling

4 ounces Taleggio cheese

¼ teaspoon garlic powder

snipped fresh chives, for serving

- Preheat the oven to 375°F.

- On a rimmed baking sheet, toss the ramps with the olive oil and sprinkle with salt and pepper. Roast for 25 minutes, tossing with tongs now and then to make sure they cook evenly. When they have finished roasting, remove, then increase the oven temperature to 450°F.

- Meanwhile, place the pizza dough in the center of a lightly oiled cookie sheet. Using your fingers, stretch it out to the sides of the pan as much as possible. (The goal is to get the crust as thin as possible). Distribute the ½ cup Parm all over the dough, then distribute dollops of the Taleggio, leaving a 1-inch border around the rim. Evenly sprinkle the garlic powder over the cheeses. Brush the rim with olive oil and bake for 10 to 15 minutes (start checking after 10), until the cheese is bubbling and the crust is golden and crispy. Remove from the oven and top with the ramps, chives, and more Parm.

"I AM A BIG BELIEVER IN ANYTHING THAT CREATES AN AURA OF EXCITEMENT AROUND GOOD FOOD FOR KIDS."

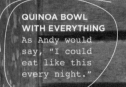

**QUINOA BOWL
WITH EVERYTHING**
As Andy would
say, "I could
eat like this
every night."

QUINOA SALAD WITH ROAST VEGETABLES, FETA, AND HERBS

If you have ever found yourself in that most familiar of circumstances—i.e., staring at your farmer's market bounty without a clue how to use it—remember this golden rule: When in doubt, quinoa. This salad, for instance, was invented on the fly, on a night before we were traveling and wanted to use up every last bit of our CSA loot. (Being part of a CSA, which stands for Community Supported Agriculture, means we get a box of produce every other week in exchange for investing in the farm where it grew.) We had just a small amount of each vegetable—a few carrots, a beet or two, a tiny fennel bulb, little herb bouquets—but it was all easily stretched into a vegetarian dinner by tossing with quinoa and a good vinaigrette. (Note: If you have quinoa haters in the house, you might consider the other golden rule: When in doubt, quesadillas.)

SERVES 4 TO 6

5 to 6 medium-large carrots, washed, peeled,
   and halved lengthwise if on the thicker side

½ small fennel bulb, cored and sliced into thin rounds, about ¼ inch thick

4 tablespoons good-quality olive oil, divided

½ teaspoon ground coriander

kosher salt and freshly ground pepper

5 to 6 beets, any color, ends trimmed, wrapped in foil

1 small onion, sliced (about 1¾ cup)

1 cup quinoa

1 tablespoon butter

1 cup crumbled feta cheese

3 tablespoons pepitas or pistachios

⅔ cup Basic Vinaigrette (recipe follows)

2 tablespoons chopped fresh mint leaves

2 tablespoons chopped fresh flat-leaf parsley

• Preheat the oven to 400°F. Line a roasting pan with foil.

• In the prepared pan, toss the carrots and fennel with 2 tablespoons of the olive oil, the coriander, and salt and pepper. Place in the oven along with the foil-wrapped beets, and roast until the carrots are tender, golden, and lacquered but not burned, and the fennel is tender, about 30 minutes. Keep the beets in for another 20 to 30 minutes, or until a knife easily slips through one. Allow to cool, then peel and quarter.

- Meanwhile, in a medium skillet cook the onion in the remaining 2 tablespoons olive oil over low heat until caramelized and brown (but not burned), about 25 minutes. While it cooks, bring 2 cups water to a boil in a medium pot. Add the quinoa, stir, and cover with a tight-fitting lid. Reduce the heat and cook for 13 to 15 minutes, until all of the water has been absorbed. Fluff with a fork and remove to a bowl. Toss in the butter right away. Let cool.
- In a large bowl, toss the quinoa, carrots, beets, fennel, onion, feta, pepitas, and vinaigrette. Top with the herbs and season with salt and pepper.

Basic Vinaigrette
MAKES ⅔ CUP

2 teaspoons Dijon mustard

¼ cup white balsamic vinegar (or red wine or apple cider vinegar)

1 tablespoon minced shallot

2 teaspoons fresh lemon juice

¼ teaspoon sugar

kosher salt and freshly ground pepper

⅓ cup good-quality olive oil

- Add the mustard, vinegar, shallot, lemon juice, sugar, and salt and pepper to a small jar and shake vigorously. (Or whisk together in a small bowl.) Add the olive oil and shake or whisk again until emulsified.

TRIPLE BERRY SUMMER PIE WITH LATTICE CRUST

Making pie with a lattice top is one of those things—along with French braiding and paper doll-making—that has earned me big points in the Fun Mom column with the girls. The truth is, lattice tops are much simpler than they look (sketching, coloring, and cutting hundreds of miniature paper dolls are another story), but if you aren't up for it, the pie is just as delicious with a regular old top crust, too. Note: It's a good idea to taste the berries before you toss them with the sugar. If they are extra tart, you might think about upping the sugar to ½ cup.

SERVES 8

TRIPLE BERRY PIE
The ultimate farmer's
market reward.

Yes, I'm crimping the edge with an old key

2 9-inch pie crusts (bottom and top), homemade or store-bought

6 cups combination of blueberries, blackberries, and raspberries

⅓ cup sugar

¼ cup cornstarch

2 tablespoons fresh lemon juice

¼ teaspoon ground cinnamon

all-purpose flour, for the work surface

1 tablespoon chilled unsalted butter, cut into small pieces

1 egg, lightly beaten

turbinado sugar, for sprinkling (optional)

ice cream, for serving

- Preheat the oven to 425°F. Line a pie dish with the bottom crust.
- In a large bowl, combine the berries, sugar, cornstarch, lemon juice, and cinnamon, tossing to coat the fruit completely. Add the berry mixture to the pie dish.
- Lay the top crust on a floured surface. Using a sharp knife, slice the dough into 7 strips of even width as shown in photo 1 on page 120.
- Make the lattice top: Lay 3 dough strips across the pie in the same direction (photo 2).
- Peel back the middle strip almost all the way to the left. Lay down 1 strip, top to bottom, along the left side of the pie, perpendicular to other strips, then place the middle strip back on top of it (photo 3).
- Repeat with the right side (photo 4), then one more time all the way to the left and all the way to the right (photo 5).
- Pinch all dough strips to the edge, pulling up the overhang if there is any, and, using a fork (or the head of a key!), crimp the circumference of the pie (photos 6 and 7). Tuck the pieces of butter into the exposed filling. Brush the lattice top with the beaten egg and sprinkle with turbinado sugar, if using.
- Bake at 425°F for 15 minutes. Turn down the heat to 350°F and bake for another 45 minutes, or until the crust is golden brown and the filling is bubbly. It's not a bad idea to place a sheet of foil on the rack below the pie, just in case that bubbling gets enthusiastic. Serve warm with ice cream.

THE ONE-ON-ONE DATE

In February 2003, a week after we celebrated Phoebe's first birthday, I took a pregnancy test. It was almost on a whim: Andy and I knew we wanted more kids, but since we were still getting used to life with Phoebe, we hadn't really discussed when the right time might be for baby number two. (And anyway, I was wary of the whole concept of "the right time," since it had been relatively hard to get pregnant with Phoebe in the first place.) But I felt a little . . . *off* . . . and without even telling Andy what I was about to do, I grabbed the First Response box from the medicine cabinet—oh good, I had one from way back when—took the test, then brushed my teeth, practically forgetting about it. When I picked up the stick a few minutes later, it took me a second to process what I was looking at. I pulled the box from the trash to double-check the reference pictures. Two pink lines = pregnant. Oh God. I was pregnant.

I had three responses to this. The first, obviously, was shock, tinged with euphoria. The second: real estate panic. Our tiny Brooklyn apartment was already too small for our family, and we aren't the types who end up in "city living" columns featuring creative solutions to crib space. Where was this mysterious new little family member going to sleep? The only available space seemed to be smack-dab in the middle of the living room.

My third response: Maybe I should tell Andy.

I walked into living room where he was sitting with Phoebe and handed him the little stick with the huge news.

Perhaps reassuringly, Andy didn't immediately think about real estate. But I will never forget what he said to me soon after he caught his breath.

He looked at our newly mobile one-year-old booking across the living room and said, "Poor Phoebe. She had so little time to be an only child."

There was an undercurrent of wistfulness when he said it, but now that we know our daughters so well—daughters who are, in fact, polar opposites—it veers more toward the hilarious. The birth of any sibling in any family is going to rock a kid's world, but the birth of Abby seemed to rock the universe. There's always been an electricity around our second daughter. When she enters the house, picture a calm and steady Richter scale needle suddenly recording wild reverberations. As she once said to me when she was nine, "I'm glad I'm not awake when I'm sleeping because I'd be so *bored.*" Abby is only happy when she's moving. She's a nonstop burning fireball of energy.

Phoebe has her own special energy—the Buddhist kind that inspires a dog to instinctively curl up next to her on a couch, where she will sit for hours at a stretch reading or listening to podcasts. I'll leave it to the evolutionists to figure out whether her personality is in direct response to her younger sister's, a necessary adaptation taken to maintain the equilibrium of the house. But one thing is for sure: We rely on Phoebe's calm to be the antidote to Abby's rowdiness, just like we rely on Abby to bring her magical mojo to the family formula.

What I find fascinating, though, is how different the energy in the house is when they're in the rare position of only child, or when they are one-on-one with Mom or Dad instead of two-on-two, fighting for the last cider doughnut, the TV remote, or, maybe more to the point, their parents' attention.

I first discovered the power of the one-on-one date when the girls were in pre-school. Phoebe's class was in the morning and Abby's was in the afternoon, which made me crazy on the days I was working from home. When I complained about this to another mother-of-two at school, I remember she said, "Oh, that happened to me last year, but it ended up being *great* because I got to spend quality time with each of them *individually.*"

When she said this to me, I'm afraid that quality time with the kids was much lower on my list of priorities than catching up on some sleep, taking an uninterrupted shower, getting through a single article in *The New York Times,* or, as mentioned above, *working;* but I pretended to see the wisdom in this, lest I come off as anything but the most devoted mother of all. Eventually, though, I came around to the schedule—not because I was getting so much quality time with each girl, but because it allowed me to do things I wouldn't necessarily be able to do with two kids in tow. (It should be noted that here is yet another instance where I gain a whole new respect for families whose parent-to-child ratio exceeds 1:1.) For example, when it was just Phoebe, I could take her to the diner for pancakes because she was old enough to sit in a restaurant without repeatedly sliding under the table to play peekaboo with her napkin like her sister, or testing (and retesting) gravity by dropping sugar packets to the floor. When it was just Abby, I could go grocery shopping because I didn't have to schlep along a stroller to accommodate the kid who didn't fit in the cart seat. (Anyone who doesn't think that grocery shopping with your kid counts as quality time, please see me after class.)

Fast-forward almost ten years to the summer they each spent a week at sleepaway camp. Different camps, different weeks. The best part of the setup for us—besides the letters, of course; is there anything better than a handwritten letter from camp?—was the time we got to spend with the sister left behind. I hadn't planned it this way, but giving each of them a week of only-child-dom meant, obviously, that we only had to account for the interests and tastes of a single kid all week long. When Abby wanted spaghetti with pesto, we didn't have to make a separate baguette with pesto and mozzarella for pasta-hating Phoebe. When Phoebe requested Hatch burgers, we didn't have to do a special turkey-burger version for Abby—who was (and remains) in a no-red-meat phase. The novelty extended beyond the dinner table, too. I couldn't believe how easy it was to agree on a movie or a Saturday activity when we only had to negotiate with one daughter instead of two. The girls loved it, too—maybe a little *too* much.

The one-on-one date can have other benefits as well. A good friend of mine—I'll call him Josh—whose daughter is in middle school—I'll call her Addie—went through a phase when he worried Addie was "slipping away from him." After reassuring Josh that I could relate to this concern, and that this concern, in fact, informed almost every day of my life since becoming a mother, he told me he was starting to carve out more one-on-one time with Addie: hikes, dinners, and walks without her younger brother tagging along. In those situations, he said, he can engage more, and Addie is more willing to open up about her life than she is when the whole family is, for instance, gunning down the highway to a soccer game.

My friend Jay, father to three grown children, took this idea one step farther, inviting each of his kids on a father-child trip for their sixth birthday. It was a family tradition: Jay would hand them a map of the United States, locate their hometown (in Bergen County, New Jersey), then the two of them would look at all the possible cities they could visit on a short flight or drive. (Though adventure was the name of the game, Jay would never be too disappointed if his kid picked a place like St. Louis, where there was a grandparent and free room and board.) We stole this ritual shamelessly and without remorse from his family, and I strongly suggest you do the same. When Phoebe turned six, Andy took her to Skaneateles, a postcard-ready

Why does it not strike me in the least bit strange that Abby's most favorite food (gnocchi or anything in the pasta family) is one that Phoebe has steadfastly refused to eat for a decade? Here, Homemade Gnocchi with Basil and Cheese, Abby's choice for dinner on nights when her sister is out (page 129).

small town in New York's Finger Lakes region. They went for boat rides, spent a lazy afternoon in the local bookstore, walked in the woods, and ate fried fish, baked beans, and strawberry sundaes from a place called Doug's Fish Fry that blew Phoebe's mind. Two years later, Andy and Abby road-tripped to Philadelphia, where the guiding principle of the weekend was "Your Wish is My Command." Whatever Abby wanted to do, they did. That meant tracking down her favorite food group (anything Japanese), pretending to be a weatherman in front of a green screen at the Franklin Institute science museum, and swimming in the hotel pool at ten o'clock at night. That was six years ago, and she can still tell you every detail about the trip like it happened yesterday. So can Andy.

Sometimes we take the one-on-one ritual on family vacations, splitting into two teams and spending a chunk of the day apart. This might not sound like the most radical concept to you, but for us, it was revolutionary. We had always thought of vacation, and especially summer vacation, as something synonymous with family togetherness. The opposite of our real-world, divide-and-conquer existence, where we are pin-balling all over the county in two cars, shepherding the girls to their various athletic, musical, and balletic commitments, texting logistics (and scores!) until we can regroup at home. But a few summers ago, when we were lucky enough to spend a week in Paris at a friend's apartment, we decided to split up for a few hours. Andy would take seven-year-old Abby to the patisserie near Luxembourg Gardens, the one with the macarons she had been ogling in the window all week; I would take nine-year-old Phoebe to a little café in the sixth arrondissement, where I had sat with Andy ten years earlier, right after we were married but before we had kids. Phoebe was fascinated by this chapter in my life—"What did you guys do all day?" Answer: "I have no idea!"—and over a croissant and a café crème, without any interruptions from her sister, one-to-one, eye-to-eye, we had our first heart-to-heart of the trip.

One-on-One Recipes

Though it's certainly nice to have one-on-one dates on vacation or in foreign cities, the best kind usually just happen right at the family dinner table. On nights when, by chance, you are feeding only one of your kids, think about the foods that he or she never gets to eat because a sibling mounts a full-throttle protest. For us, that's burgers for Phoebe and any kind of pasta dinner for Abby, particularly gnocchi. It feels special because it's homemade, but doesn't require breaking out a pasta maker.

ABBY'S HOMEMADE GNOCCHI WITH BASIL AND CHEESE

When the pasta is homemade, you don't want to overpower it with a big sauce. Butter, cheese, and fresh basil will be all you need. Feel free to swap in a few sage leaves for the basil.

SERVES 6 TO 8

2½ pounds unpeeled russet potatoes
(about 3 large)
1½ cups all-purpose flour
1 egg, lightly beaten
kosher salt
2 tablespoons unsalted butter
½ cup freshly grated Parmigiano-Reggiano,
plus more if desired
8 fresh basil leaves, thinly sliced
freshly ground pepper

• Place the whole potatoes (skins on) in a saucepan with water to cover. Bring to a boil, reduce to a simmer, and cook until the potatoes are tender when pierced with a knife, about 40 minutes.

• Drain the potatoes and peel while still hot with a paring knife (use a pot holder to hold them). Pass the potatoes through a potato ricer (or mash with a potato masher or large fork) into a large bowl. Let cool completely.

• Make a well in the center of the potatoes and sprinkle all over with almost all the flour, reserving about ¼ cup. Pour the egg into the center of the well and whisk it into the potatoes and flour like you're making pasta. Add 1½ teaspoons salt. With your hands, work the dough and knead until it becomes smooth but not elastic, dusting with extra flour if it becomes too sticky, about 4 minutes. Do not overwork.

- Divide into 8 pieces. Roll one piece at a time into a rope ½ inch in diameter, cutting the rope into ½-inch lengths with the side of a fork. Arrange in a single layer on a very lightly flour-dusted baking sheet. (Press the tines of the fork into each piece lightly if you want the little ridged design.)
- Bring a large pot of salted water to a boil. In batches, add a few handfuls of gnocchi and cook until most have floated to the top, about 2 minutes. When the gnocchi are done, gently remove them with a slotted spoon to individual bowls, dividing the butter, cheese, and basil evenly among the portions and tossing. (I usually do everything in 2 batches.)
- Top with salt and pepper and more cheese, if desired.

PHOEBE'S HATCH BURGERS

These burgers are named for the chiles that hail from Hatch, New Mexico. We use Santa Fe Olé brand, which comes in a jar; but you can find green chiles in the Mexican aisle of most supermarkets. I first had a version of one at an Umami Burger in Santa Monica. (And later, a blog reader sent me a recipe for it.) I think the waiter knew I was a rookie when I asked for ketchup and mustard on the side. "You want to eat this exactly as it's served," he said. He was right.

SERVES 4

1¼ pounds ground beef

2 teaspoons soy sauce

kosher salt and freshly ground pepper

4 slices American cheese (preferably white, not orange)

4 hamburger buns

4 heaping tablespoons roasted green Hatch chiles

- In a large bowl, use your hands to gently mix the ground beef with the soy sauce and season with salt and pepper, then form 4 loosely packed patties. In a large deep skillet (or on a medium-hot grill), cook the patties over medium heat, until cooked rare or medium rare, about 3 minutes a side. During the last minute of cooking, top each with a slice of cheese, cover the skillet (or grill), and cook until the cheese melts. Slide the burgers onto hamburger buns, and top with chiles.

"ANDY LOOKED
AT OUR NEWLY
MOBILE
ONE-YEAR-OLD
AND SAID
'POOR PHOEBE,
SHE HAD SO LITTLE
TIME TO BE
AN ONLY CHILD.'"

FRUIT FIRST THING

When Phoebe went away to sleepaway camp for two weeks, she did all the things kids do at sleepaway camp: She paddle-boarded in the lake, slept in an open-air cabin, competed in color wars, roasted marshmallows in bonfires after dinner, complained about that dinner (and lunch and breakfast), and wrote her parents letters during her free time summarizing it all. Wow, were those some good letters! Though, as anyone who sends their kid away to camp knows, it doesn't take much for a letter to qualify as "good"—regardless of the contents, it's hugely terrifying, I mean *satisfying*, to know that they can survive without us, and can even have the wherewithal to put pen to paper.

One letter in particular was my favorite, though. It read, in part:

"I eat fruit before breakfast. I seriously think that if I don't, my brain will get confused."

In the same letter, there were tales of sunrise swims in the lake, coed dances on the dock, and an overnight adventure where she camped deep in the woods, in a sleeping bag on open ground. Let's just say, I'm glad I didn't know about that last one until it was over.

Somehow, though, it was the breakfast detail that captivated me.

Until that point, every morning of Phoebe's eleven-year-old life, with very few exceptions, began with fruit. I remember her as a baby, banging on the high-chair tray for some cut-up strawberries. I remember her as a toddler, eating a banana in front of Elmo, then one day, miraculously, grabbing the whole banana from her mother's hands and feeding it to herself. I remember her as a kindergartner, first grader, second grader, and beyond, shoveling pineapple chunks and pomegranate seeds into her mouth before her bagel, before we sent her off to school, otherwise known as a land far far away, where brains were filled with knowledge and bellies were filled with sour cream and onion potato chips. It felt so good knowing we got at least a little healthy stuff into her body—and her sister's body—before whatever followed.

As parents, we all try to instill healthy habits, try to make smart decisions for our kids at home, so that someday they can hopefully make smart decisions for themselves, when we're not around force-feeding them watermelon cubes . . . or broccoli . . . or, for that matter, advice on friends and camp cabin politics. So often it feels like the day-to-day advice dispensed is just background noise—*wear layers, eat something before practice, wash your hands, say please and thank you, clear your plate, use a napkin, just try your hardest, look both ways, call when you get there, look him in the eye, don't fill up before dinner, stand up straight, be kind, squeeze the tube from the bottom up, don't forget to floss, it's hot, drink water*—but here was hard evidence, *in writing*, that at least some of that advice was . . . could it be? . . . getting through. She was making smart decisions, taking care of herself in the big wide world without me. As long as I didn't think about it too hard, that was a pretty great thing.

PICKLING

Every now and then when there's a particularly busy Saturday and Sunday on the books, I'll take a moment on Friday afternoon to email Andy the weekend's master schedule down to the hour. I do this not only because any self-respecting control freak would do the same, but because I want to avoid him asking me all weekend long, "What time do we have to be at Abby's game? What time is Phoebe's party again? When are the Vales coming over?" and then a few hours later, "What time do we have to be at Abby's game? What time is Phoebe's party again? When are the Vales coming over?" Sometimes I'll even toss in a little handyman wish-list item between the parties and the games. I'll never forget Andy's friend Will emailing one Saturday afternoon and saying, "It's one o'clock EST, and if all is going according to plan, right now you are assembling some patio furniture." Unbeknownst to me, Andy had forwarded the master schedule to Will, who spent a decade in the Special Forces and is a man who can appreciate a well-run ship.

Andy's response to the master schedule is usually along the lines of, "Oh dear Lord." Or "When is our next free weekend?"

I don't know why he pretends to be so put upon—there's literally nothing he enjoys more than sitting outside and watching the girls play sports. (Shuttling them to a laser-tag birthday party and hanging out in a windowless mall for two hours awaiting its end is another story.) And also, it's not exactly like he would be *relaxing* if there were nothing planned. This is something you need to know about him. Andy's not the best at sitting still—especially on a weekend. Which is why there's a high level of probability that on a lazy weekend afternoon, he will at some point run a few errands and come home bearing a sixteen-pack of canning jars (procured at the local hardware store) and five pounds of vegetables including but not limited to: cucumbers, cauliflower, carrots, beets, and cabbage.

"Yup," he'll say as soon as he sees me. "We're pickling."

While I'm catching up on my book club reading or nodding off in the sunroom off the kitchen (i.e., they don't call it a lazy afternoon for nuthin'), I'll watch Andy climb upstairs and down between the kitchen and basement to fetch his gear: lobster pot, jar tongs, ginormous jugs of white vinegar left over from the last pickling session.

Pretty soon, he's mobilized a few li'l assistants; pots are boiling; and there's an assembly line of sterilized jars across the counter like a giant science experiment. The kids, aproned and wearing serious faces, weigh in on important questions such as "Do we slice our cucumbers into sandwich pickles or do we cut them into spears for snacking pickles?" My sole contribution to this project is shouting something along the lines of, "Make extra jars of cabbage. You know it's my favorite."

Something else you should know about Andy: He does not wear wool caps in the middle of the summer, or sport an ironic waxed 'stache. He's about as far away from today's hipster artisanal DIY-er as you can imagine, and he came by his love of pickling honestly: Our friend Kendra joined us for dinner one night a few years ago and, instead of bringing the customary bottle of wine, showed up with a bushel of cucumbers and a few gallons of white vinegar. It was the best host gift ever. By the time the night was over, we had a dozen jars of pickles lined up on a basement shelf, and Andy had a new obsession.

The best thing about Andy's pickling ritual is that we always end up with way more jars than we know what to do with, so all year long, we can hand out pickles to party hosts and birthday celebrants. It's especially convenient when we're headed to someone's house for dinner, or at the end of the school year or during holiday season when it just feels wrong to show up empty-handed to the last karate/gymnastics/piano/ cello lesson of the year, the open house party at the neighbors', or the conference-room office grab-bag party. Other smart uses: teacher gift, coach gift, holiday gift, Father's Day or Mother's Day gift, coworker gift. In other words, we are giving them away constantly—but I always make sure there's a stash left over for us.

DILL PICKLED VEGETABLES

Here is a version of the magical recipe Kendra showed up with. I promise,
once you have a jar of these in the fridge you'll find endless ways to use them.
See page 142 for some suggestions.

MAKES SIX 20-OUNCE JARS

10 cups distilled white vinegar

15 cloves garlic, peeled and halved

9 cups water

¾ cup kosher salt

4 to 5 pounds pickling vegetables, such as kirby cucumbers, cauliflower,
   shredded red cabbage, carrots (sliced into coins), beets (peeled and sliced),
   green beans, wax beans, bean sprouts, bell peppers, radishes, ramps,
   chiles (such as Fresno or jalapeño)

⅓ cup peppercorns

6 dried mild chiles such as guajillo

1 bunch of fresh dill

Equipment

1 small saucepan

1 lobster pot

1 large stainless-steel pasta pot

6 20-ounce canning jars, the kind you can find
   at the local hardware store

• In a small saucepan, bring 1 cup of the vinegar to boil. Turn off the heat and add the garlic to the saucepan. Let stand for 1 minute, then strain and set the garlic aside.

• Fill a lobster pot to an inch or two from the top with water and bring to a boil. In another pot—which must be stainless steel—combine the remaining 9 cups vinegar with the water and the salt. This is the brine. Stir until the salt is dissolved and bring the brine to a boil.

• While you're waiting for both pots to boil, prepare the vegetables. If you are making cucumber spears, make sure they are sliced small enough to fit into the jars; if they don't, trim the ends so that they stand about ½ inch from the top of the jar.

• Once the water in the lobster pot is boiling, submerge the jars completely—with the open tops facing up, letting them fill slowly with water—and sterilize for a few minutes. (Warning: Do this very carefully and if the kids are helping, make sure they are standing

137

Andy was so into pickling that for his birthday one year, I asked my friend Gina Triplett, the amazing illustrator, to design a pretend logo for him. I get such a kick slapping those labels onto jars and handing them out all year long. (P.S. Redwing? Long story.)

My number one way to
enjoy the fruits
of our pickling labor
(see #1 page 142)

back when you submerge the jars—the hot water can splash up.) Then, using jar tongs, tip each jar to empty the water, remove from the pot, and set on the counter. (Do not empty the lobster pot yet; you'll need this boiling water in a minute.) Into each jar, put some of the garlic cloves, peppercorns, one dried chile, and a handful of dill. Fill each jar with vegetables until good and snug. Then take the jar tops—which come in two pieces, the flat disk and the rim—and place them in the boiling water in the lobster pot for 2 minutes. Remove with tongs and place in a clean bowl. Keep the water boiling in the pot.

• Ladle boiling brine from the stainless-steel pot and fill the jars to ¼ inch from the top. Place the jar tops on the jars and close the lids, then turn the jars over on the counter to ensure a good seal. Now, place all the sealed jars—full of vegetables in brine—back into the water in the lobster pot and boil for 10 minutes. (NOTE: You may need to take a little of the boiling water out of the pot before doing this, since the full jars displace a lot of liquid.)

• Remove the jars and let them sit for an hour or two, until the tops have all depressed (which means they have sealed, and which means, when you open them later, they will make a pop). Put them somewhere cool, and wait 2 weeks, if you can bear it.

Quick Pickles

Don't want to deal with tongs and lobster pots and sterilizing and waiting? Have some market vegetables that are on their last legs? Want to have your nap and eat your pickles, too? Quick pickling is the way to go. The general formula is: Add pickling vegetables (shredded cabbage, wax beans, quartered radishes, peppers) to a clean 14- to 16-ounce jar. In a small pot, simmer ½ cup water, ½ cup vinegar, 2 tablespoons sugar, and 1 tablespoon kosher salt until the sugar has dissolved, about 3 minutes. Let cool slightly, then pour the pickling mixture over the vegetables. Let cool, seal, then refrigerate. The pickles will be ready within twenty-four hours and keep up to two weeks, refrigerated.

I like this method because it lets you improvise from one jar to the next, and by improvise I mean it lets you use whatever vegetables and vinegar you have at the ready. A few shown in the photo on page 139: cucumber slices with rice wine vinegar, one smashed garlic clove, a sprig of dill, and a few black peppercorns; halved radishes with red wine vinegar, whole dried chile pepper, and a few coriander seeds; shredded cabbage with cider vinegar, garlic, and whole dried chile pepper; and purple cauliflower with white vinegar, one smashed garlic clove, black peppercorns, and one whole dried chile pepper.

10 USES
FOR PICKLED VEGETABLES

— 1 —

Rye Finn Crisps + smoked trout
+ pickled cabbage =
Perfect throw-together lunch.

— 2 —

Slice and use for cheeseburgers
all summer long.

— 3 —

Mix chopped pickled
cucumbers into chicken or egg salad
for sandwiches.

— 4 —

Baguette + butter + ham + pickles =
Pretend we're catching a train
at the Gare du Nord.

— 5 —

Toss pickled bean sprouts into
sweet hoisin-based stir-fries.

— 6 —

Make Cubanos: In a panini maker,
press together slices of pork,
Swiss cheese, mustard, and pickles on a
baguette. (Or just skip the pork.)

— 7 —

Toss fresh chopped sweet raw
sugar snap peas with pickled cabbage,
cilantro, a tiny bit of diced
red onion, olive oil, salt, and pepper.

— 8 —

Use pickled cauliflower, carrots,
beans, and wax beans for starters
when you have people over,
or on the holiday party spread
(see page 68).

— 9 —

Steal Abby's favorite salad:
Bibb lettuce, pickled beets,
scallions, buttermilk ranch dressing.

— 10 —

Add a shot of leftover brine
to your martini.

LUNCH WITH DAD

When I picture my dad, I almost always picture him standing outside somewhere, hands on hips, chin tilted up slightly, looking around to get the lay of the land. He's not admiring the scenery, though—even if he's on a beach with his whole family, the mighty Atlantic stretched out before him, he's not looking at the ocean or the sunset. He couldn't care less about the light dancing on the dunes. He's looking around because he's doing a head count.

Three kids, two sons-in-law, six grandchildren, two dogs. When he's accounted for them all and made sure everyone is safe or within rescue distance, he relaxes. A few minutes later, he'll start over. Chin tilts up, hands on hips, head nodding as he counts *1-2-3-4*. Sometimes, I'll just sit in my beach chair watching him for entertainment.

He's always been like this. When I was a kid, he'd walk in the house, and the first thing he'd ask my mom was, "Where's Phil? Where's Lynn? Where's Jen?" referring to my brother, my sister, and me. When we make plans to travel, the first question is, "When are you leaving?" and the second is, "When are you coming back?" (followed soon after by "What airline?" and "What flight number?").

He likes to know where everyone is, but, more to the point, he likes us to be nearby. If he could get away with planting a GPS chip in his grandchildren, he'd probably consider it. I always think of that scene in *Father of the Bride* when Steve Martin is waiting for his daughter's flight to return from Europe and he says to a coworker, "You have kids . . . you understand. It's better when they're on the ground." That's my father. (Okay, fine, it's me, too.)

Dad definitely did not complain when Phil, Lynn, and I all somehow ended up moving back to New York City after college, a quick drive from my parents' suburban house, the one where we grew up, and the one they still live in today. And if that wasn't close enough for my dad, there was that two- or three-year stretch in the mid- to late nineties when my sister, my dad, and I all worked within eight blocks of one another on Third Avenue in midtown Manhattan. (Lynn was on Thirty-Ninth Street, I was on Forty-Fifth, and right up the road was Dad, on Forty-Seventh.) During the phase when most of my newly graduated friends were volunteering for NGOs or backpacking through Prague or toiling away at entry-level jobs in distant cities, we were only blocks away from our father twelve hours a day, five days a week. Among other things, this made it easy for him to keep track of us. Especially since he could bribe his two barely-making-rent daughters with free lunches any day of the week. Those lunches kicked off a tradition with my dad that remains intact today.

Our lunches were rarely fancy, but no matter where we were going, the destination was almost always driven by a particular dish or dessert that my father wanted us to try. My dad is a food lover of the first order and is not afraid to walk an extra block or two for what he wants. At Fiftieth and Third there was (and still is) Ess-a-Bagel, where the bagels were as big as life preservers and were always just out of the oven. There was the minestrone at the cubbyhole-size Italian place on Second Avenue between Forty-Ninth and Fiftieth, where every storefront was a restaurant with a special lunch menu. Then there was our favorite: the oyster-cracker-topped Manhattan clam chowder at the Oyster Bar in Grand Central Terminal.

It was at the Oyster Bar's snaky, S-shaped counter that I most vividly remember the three of us hashing out our jobs and our futures. My sister was heading to business school, and I was working for a cable TV company and thinking about heading to business school. At the time, it seemed like the clock was already ticking—if we didn't figure out what we wanted to do before we turned thirty, that was it: We'd missed our window of opportunity. In between slurps of his chowder, my dad would offer some long-game perspective and whatever guidance he could, such as, a New York–area business school, no matter which one we were talking about, would be a much better choice than any other possible one we'd think to apply to out of state. It did not come as a surprise to us that his favorites usually ended up being between fifteen and thirty miles from his front doorstep.

Over the next decade, of course, a lot changed. We all got married and had kids. Dad, who had been in market research for most of his career, started working from home more, eventually working his way toward retirement. I changed jobs a few times, hopping from magazine to magazine. My sister and I moved to the suburbs while my brother stayed on the Upper West Side. All of this happened within easy driving distance from my parents, and—hey, look at that!—within easy-lunch-date distance from my dad.

Now, we eat all around the county, hitting my favorite childhood pizzerias for salad pizzas and Dr Peppers, or the prepared food department of Balducci's to sample my dad's favorite chili. We rejoiced when a Smashburger opened in a strip mall exactly halfway between the two towns we live in. One Friday, we ate at a disappointing grilled-chicken-Caesar-salad kind of joint, redeemed only when he made me walk across town to sample the quiche at a new French place in town. "Another time," he told me, "we'll come here first and have the fish soup." My dad has always had his food obsessions. That has never changed.

What *has* changed is the conversation. When he isn't talking about the cholesterol in the quiche lorraine or the short-story collection he's reading for a continuing ed class he's taking through the local high school, he's telling stories about his own childhood growing up in the Bronx. Stories, I'm embarrassed to say, I should know by this point in our lives. He's talked about his frugal grandfather Max and his generous grandmother Betty. About Mrs. Mitchell, the sixth-grade teacher who saw something special in him and sent him to a school for smart kids. He talks a lot about basketball—my dad was a big high school star in the Bronx—and about his rivals, whose names I Google as soon as I get home. There was the ski trip he took in the Alps when he was younger, where he boarded a chairlift to the top of an expert trail to impress a girl but ended up sliding down the mountain on his butt instead. He talks a lot about his own father, who worked as a furrier in the fashion district and who died in 1960—passing away, like all my grandparents, before I was born.

I try to hold on to as much as I can from these conversations, usually by repeating them to my own kids, who love nothing more than picturing their grandfather sliding down a mountain on his rear. The older we get, the more I realize how valuable even the most ordinary story is, and the more I realize how crucial it is for me to pass on these stories to my own children. Both of whom, by the way, will be attending the local community college. On a nice day, it's just a fifteen-minute walk across town.

THE SLEEPOVER
BREAKFAST

I never liked sleepovers when I was a kid—my father can tell you countless stories of midnight rescues from friends' houses, even though I'd insist that *this time I can do it.* The problem with sleepovers, I found out pretty quickly, was that they were all about *not* sleeping. My energetic pals would stage contests, like who could stay up the latest, or who could eat a tablespoon of toothpaste and be the first to whistle. Or *Who wants to play truth or dare?* This last one was the worst because it usually involved talking about boys, another pastime my fifth-grade self had no interest in. All I wanted was to be home, in my rainbow comforter–covered bed, the hum of my parents' TV in the next room lulling me to sleep. I always felt bad picking up the phone and dialing home— I could hear the rattling ring of the phone next to my dad's pillow, and see his initial look of panic, before, likely, figuring out exactly what little voice was on the other end of the line.

"Hi Dad. Can you pick me up?"

If there was any annoyance about getting out of bed and driving across town in his pajamas, he never let on.

"On the way," he'd say.

When Phoebe was five or six, she decided she was ready for her first sleepover at my sister's house. We had been there all evening for a big family dinner and, caught up in the cousin energy (see Cousinland, page 28), Phoebe and my niece Alison begged for her to stay the night. *Please please please?*

I was a little wary, given my own experiences when I was her age, but I didn't say anything. I never liked being the kid who hated sleepovers, and sleeping at her cousin's seemed like a safe introduction to the sport. "Of course," I said. "We'll pick you up in the morning."

An hour later, Andy and I were reading in bed across the county when the phone rang.

It was my mom, who was still at my sister's house helping with the clean-up. "Someone wants to talk to you." Off to the side she said, *"Phoebe, Mommy's on the phone."*

I heard a little rustle and some heavy breathing.

"Phoebe? Sweetie?" She wasn't talking. "Pheeb? Are you there?"

In between some heaves, she spoke three words, which took an amazing amount of energy for her to get out, and which I will remember for the rest of my life.

"I . . . want . . . you."

I thought of my father, not just because of my response ("On the way," natch), but because the guilt over all those late-night rescue APBs had lifted. I didn't feel inconvenienced at all by the prospect of driving back to my sister's to retrieve Phoebe. In fact, a small part of me even kind of enjoyed being able to play the white horse role for my kindergartner. Especially when I could be the one to field the call, and then dispatch Andy to do the actual driving.

Phoebe got over it eventually, but for a long while after that experience, sleepovers took place at our house. Which was just as well, because it gave us a chance to go all out for breakfast. What better excuse than a pajama-clad little kid to forgo our usual boring Cheerios or yogurt for some real morning hedonism? My niece Alison is a chocolate fiend, so when she was the guest, inevitably I'd make a batch of chocolate chip pancakes. But on any given sleepover, there might also be popovers, muffins, and Abby's favorite, apple-cinnamon fritters, which would give any shaky guest some delicious motivation to make it through the night.

Three Sleepover Breakfasts

Though we generally reserve our super-deluxe morning moves for sleepovers or birthdays (see page 196), there should be nothing stopping you from making these recipes on Saturdays, Sundays, and any other days deemed special in your house. Also, it should be noted that making pancakes from a mix does not disqualify you, as long as you remember the chocolate chips.

SLEEPOVER CHOCOLATE CHIP PANCAKES

This is a nice everyday recipe for pancakes, whether you have a little guest sleeping over or not. Feel free to have fun with the add-ins. No kid will ever complain about M&M's.

MAKES 6 TO 8 (MEDIUM) PANCAKES

1 cup all-purpose flour

2 tablespoons sugar

1 tablespoon baking powder

1 teaspoon kosher salt

1 large egg

1 cup milk

1 tablespoon melted butter or vegetable oil

¼ cup chocolate chips or chunks (or M&M's)

2 to 3 tablespoons vegetable oil, for the pan

sliced strawberries (optional), butter, and

    pure maple syrup, for serving

• In a medium bowl, whisk together the flour, sugar, baking powder, and salt. In a small bowl, whisk together the egg, milk, and melted butter. Slowly whisk the wet ingredients into the flour mixture. Fold in the chocolate chips. Heat a cast-iron griddle or skillet to medium. Add a tablespoon of vegetable oil and tip the pan to make sure the entire surface of the pan is coated.

• Spoon ¼-cup portions of pancake batter onto the griddle, separating chocolate chips that might end up too close to each other.

• Cook until small air bubbles appear on the surface of the pancakes, about 3 minutes, then flip to the other side and cook for another 3 minutes, until golden and crispy.

• Serve with strawberries (if desired), a pat of butter, and pure maple syrup.

POPOVERS WITH HOMEMADE STRAWBERRY JAM

You might want to test one of these by breaking it open. The inside should be airy and slightly cruller-like. P.S.: No need to limit them to the breakfast table. One of the girls' favorite dinners is a popover stuffed with chopped salad.

MAKES 12 POPOVERS

> 1 tablespoon butter (for greasing the pan)
>   plus 1 tablespoon butter, melted
> 1 cup all-purpose flour
> ½ teaspoon salt
> 3 eggs, at room temperature
> 1 cup buttermilk
> homemade strawberry jam (recipe follows)

• Preheat the oven to 425°F. Grease a 12-cup muffin tin with butter.

• In a large bowl, whisk together the flour and salt. In a small bowl, lightly beat together the eggs, buttermilk, and melted butter. Using an electric mixer, blend the wet ingredients into the dry to form a batter; you want it to be as lump-free as possible. Pour the batter into the greased muffin tin, filling each cup about halfway.

• Bake for 25 minutes, until puffed and golden brown, without opening the oven door. Remove and allow to cool. Serve warm, with jam.

STRAWBERRY JAM

It goes without saying that this recipe is best in the spring, when the strawberries are small and vibrant red through and through. In addition to complementing popovers so beautifully, it also tastes amazing on toasted pound cake, waffles, or pancakes, or drizzled over vanilla ice cream for strawberry sundaes.

MAKES ¾ CUP

> 1½ cups strawberries, sliced and de-stemmed
> ⅓ cup sugar
> juice from 1 small lemon

POPOVERS WITH JAM
Make these for a
sleepover guest
and you've won her
over for life.

- Add the strawberries, sugar, and lemon juice to a small saucepan. Let the mixture cook on low heat for 15 to 20 minutes until everything is syrupy. Cool, then whirl in the bowl of a food processor for about 3 seconds until it's smooth and spreadable. Spread on fresh popovers and save the leftovers in a jam jar for up to a week.

APPLE-CINNAMON FRITTERS

These are based on the same pancake mix you see on page 149, but they earn fritter status due to the high apple-to-batter ratio.

MAKES 12 TO 14 FRITTERS

1 tablespoon unsalted butter

2 cups peeled and finely chopped apples
   (I've used just about every kind, but Granny Smith
   and Fuji are probably my favorites)

¾ teaspoon ground cinnamon

1 cup all-purpose flour

1 tablespoon baking powder

2 tablespoons sugar

1 teaspoon kosher salt

1 egg

1 cup milk

vegetable oil, for the pan

powdered sugar, for serving

- Heat a cast-iron skillet to medium low. Melt the butter in the pan and add the apples and cinnamon, stirring every now and then until they are soft-ish, 6 to 8 minutes (or until someone walks in the kitchen and asks, "Are you making apple pie?"). Using a slotted spoon, remove the apples to a small bowl.
- While the apples are cooking, whisk together the flour, baking powder, sugar, and salt in a medium bowl. In a small bowl, whisk together the egg and milk, then slowly whisk this into the flour mixture.
- Using the same skillet you used for the apples, increase the heat to medium and add a tablespoon of vegetable oil, tipping to make sure the entire surface of the pan is coated.

- Using a tablespoon measure, spoon 3 small clusters of apples into the skillet, about 2 inches apart, flattening each of them a bit so that most of the apples are touching the surface of the pan. Drizzle ⅛ cup of the batter in and around each cluster so the batter holds the apples together. (They will be misshapen, that's okay! Charming, even!) Cook until small air bubbles appear on the surface of the fritters and the edges look golden, about 3 minutes, then flip gingerly to the other side and cook for another 2 minutes, until golden and crispy. Serve right away showered with powdered sugar.

VACATION RITUALS

Summer vacation is, of course, fertile ground for family rituals, and though I have yet to find the hard science to back up this theory, I'm positive that parents get way more bang for their memory-making buck when the weather is warmer, the air is brinier, and there's always the promise of an ice-cream cone in the not-too-distant future. For some people, summer rituals act as annual checkpoints with old friends or extended family: renting a place on the lake with the college roommate who lives on the opposite coast; returning to the same hotel at the same beach every year with your siblings, nieces, and nephews. Once, when I asked readers of *Dinner: A Love Story* about their summer traditions, I noticed that the rituals they looked forward to the most were either food-related or just simple shifts in the daily routine: Eating a lobster roll or an ice cream every day. Never turning on the oven. Collecting shells. Drinking an ice-cold Coke after a day at the beach. Eating s'mores by a campfire. Picking blueberries. Playing mini-golf, but only at the course that's next to the soft-serve ice-cream truck. Our vacation rituals, as you'll see in the next few pages, tend to be a combination of both.

Vacation Ritual 1: Cook at Home

Back in the day—that is, before we had kids—Andy and I took our vacation dinners very seriously. We'd start reserving tables within minutes of booking our flights. We'd procure our Zagat guide and begin plotting our sightseeing itinerary around the places that served the most authentic migas/coffee/minestrone/cassoulet/lobster rolls/etc. From a cultural perspective, this may not have been the best way to approach a new city, but from a food perspective? God, it was fun. Once, in the late nineties, after booking a trip to San Francisco, we set an alarm for the exact minute the French Laundry started taking reservations for the one night we'd be traveling through Napa—and after a Muzak-filled hour on the line, we landed a two-top for seven thirty and high-fived like two bros who had scored tickets to the champagne room at the Super Bowl.

We are still fixated on food when we travel, but once we had kids, our energy shifted more toward *cooking* it, especially for dinner. Why? Because we found it far less stressful to cook in a rental kitchen than sweat through fancy dinners in restaurants with Michelin stars—and nowhere to stash the Snap-N-Go. Because we came to dread that particular brand of disappointment one feels from dropping too much money on those epic meals, only to have someone complain the food is "too squishy." And because eating out prevents us from experiencing the thing we love best about travel: finding great markets and specialty shops and discovering ingredients we can't get at home.

So many moments on our Vacation Memory Highlight Reel center on all of us sitting down in some new and distant place, eating a meal we've made, using ingredients we've found, from a recipe we've grabbed in the Local Cuisine section of a bookstore. Cooking where we are with what we find connects us to a place in a different way, like performing in a show instead of watching it.

In Alaska, this meant making gravlax and scraping roe from the skein of a salmon that was delivered to us by a guy in a boat; in New Mexico, it was sitting on the patio in the morning, hummingbirds circling, and dumping Hatch chiles and cotija cheese on our scrambled eggs. On Block Island, it's steaming the lobsters we buy at the dock where the ferry comes in and tossing them with cucumbers, tomatoes, and whatever else we find in front-yard farm stands around the island. (Heed this travel rule: Never drive by a farmer's market without stopping.) It's not that we never go to restaurants on vacation. Lunch is *always* fair game, and we try to do at least one big dinner out. But while we're there, we make sure to ask the waiter where he buys his fish so we can go there first thing the next morning.

Note #1

Upon reading about this ritual, some readers might reasonably retort, "Uh, I thought this was *vacation.*" It's true that when you're responsible for producing three meals a day all year long, it can be a drag to keep that up on vacation, and it can be even more drag-like if there are young children in the equation. For you guys, I understand if this ritual is lower on your list of priorities than, say, having someone *else* make you a gin and tonic, no matter how much more it costs in a restaurant.

Note #2

If you follow our cook-at-home advice, remember: Always assume the worst about the vacation rental's utensil drawer. It's officially a ritual to bring our own knives whenever possible: one four- or five-inch paring knife, and one six- or seven-inch chef's knife. I create little sheaths for the blades out of cardboard and throw them in the suitcases. (Not in the carry-ons, obviously!)

GRILLED FISH SANDWICHES WITH SALSA FRESCA

Chances are, if you're on a beach vacation, you're near a great fish market.
Seek it out, then make these sandwiches to start your trip off right.

MAKES 4 SANDWICHES

2 tablespoons soy sauce

2 teaspoons dark sesame oil

freshly ground pepper

1½ pounds tuna or swordfish steaks
   (or whatever firm local fish you can find), sliced in half horizontally if thick

juice from ½ lime

spicy mayo (see next page)

salsa fresca (see below)

1 long, skinny baguette (enough for four sandwiches)

• Make a charcoal fire or preheat a gas grill to medium-high.

• In a small bowl, whisk together the soy sauce, sesame oil, and pepper. Place the fish on a large dinner plate and pour the marinade on top. Marinate for about 15 minutes, flipping halfway through. Five minutes before you grill, squeeze the lime juice over the fish, flipping the fish to fully coat it. Grill over medium-hot coals for 1 to 2 minutes a side. (Fish cooks fast when it's this thin, and if it's tuna we like it on the rare side.)

• While the fish marinates, make the spicy mayo and salsa fresca. (Recipes follow.)

• Slice the baguette into 4 sandwich-size pieces, then halve each lengthwise. Spread mayo on each half, then top each half with fish and salsa fresca and the other baguette half. Serve open-face if you like your sandwiches on the less bready side.

SALSA FRESCA

If your tomatoes aren't quite as flavorful as you'd like, whisk a little tomato paste
into the red wine vinegar before tossing with the tomatoes.

MAKES ENOUGH FOR 4 SANDWICHES

• In our house, salsa is one of those recipes that change every time, but the general idea is this: Chop up 1 or 2 of the freshest tomatoes you can find—heirlooms are best, but any good summer tomatoes will do. For every cup of chopped tomatoes, add 2 tablespoons chopped fresh cilantro, 1 tablespoon finely diced red onion, ¼ cup red wine vinegar, ¼ cup good-quality olive oil, a dash of hot sauce, salt, and pepper. That's your baseline salsa fresca, but even that is flexible depending on how juicy the tomatoes are (and how juicy you like your salsa). Once you have your base, you can add whatever you'd like: corn, chopped yellow bell peppers, chopped peaches, pineapple. Serve on top of fish sandwiches. Use any leftovers for tomorrow's tortilla chips.

SPICY MAYO

Make a double batch, because once this is in the fridge, you'll want to spread it on or mix it into everything.

MAKES ENOUGH FOR 4 SANDWICHES

• You don't need a lot of spicy mayo for these sandwiches; you will have enough by stirring together 3 tablespoons mayo with 1 teaspoon Sriracha sauce. Use extra on burgers or turkey sandwiches, or with french fries.

Vacation Ritual 2: Break Some Rules

You know how everyone says that sleepaway camp is good for kids because it gives them a chance to reinvent themselves outside of their everyday lives? To be someone else for a little while, try on a new costume, and not have to worry about being accepted? I would say that's a pretty good summary of our family's vacation philosophy. The way I see it, vacation exists to bust us out of our newspaper-club-on-Monday-piano-on-Thursday routines, to jump in the pool instead of the shower, to order the local grouper instead of the plain old salmon, to live out of a suitcase instead of drawers. Actually, I take that back. Girls, if you are reading this, that last example does not apply to you. You still need to put your clothes away.

Another major display of maverick vacation behavior? The Supermarket Shop. As much as we love stumbling into obscure markets and trolling roadside farm stands when we are traveling, food shopping isn't all about the local perch and the Georgia

GRILLED TUNA WITH SALSA FRESCA
You know it's summer
vacation in our family
when there's fresh
fish on the menu,
good tomatoes at
the market, and a
bottle of Coke to
wash it all down
(page 158).

peach. We're just as excited by, say, a Food Lion or a Piggly Wiggly, two southern grocery store chains considered downright exotic to a Northerner. (They also stock the holy grail of gifts to bring back to New Yorkers: Duke's mayonnaise.) Unlike at home, where breakfast starts with fruit, and milk is mandatory at dinner, anything is fair game. Go wild, we tell them. Two-liter bottles of Coke? Sure. Cinnamon Toast Crunch? Yum. Pop-Tarts? Wouldn't be vacation without 'em! It's on these shopping trips that I realize how much psychic energy I expend saying no to things all year long, and being able to let go of that for a week might be more relaxing for me than an hour at a hotel spa. Our days are not twenty-four-hour bacchanalias, but we *need* (not want, *need*) to have an icy Coke with our grilled cheese after a day on the beach to feel like vacation has officially started.

POST-BEACH GRILLED CHEDDAR AND APPLE SANDWICH WITH A SIDE OF COKE

It goes without saying that your everyday grilled cheese on white bread with American cheese would be just fine, too. But here's our grown-up version, which is even better when made in a waffle iron or panini press.

MAKES 1 SANDWICH

> 2 pieces hearty white bread
> 2 tablespoons butter, softened
> smear of grainy mustard
> 2 slices sharp cheddar cheese (or to taste)
> 2 to 3 slices of peeled Granny Smith or Fuji apple

• Heat a cast-iron skillet or grill pan to medium. Spread one side of each piece of bread with butter. On the other side of one slice, spread mustard, then one slice of the cheese, apples, then another slice of cheese. Top with the second buttered slice. Fry on both sides until the cheese is melted and the bread is toasted and golden. Serve with Coke or your favorite "vacation-only" soda.

"COOKING FOR OURSELVES WHILE TRAVELING, USING WHAT WE FIND, CONNECTS US TO A PLACE, LIKE PERFORMING IN A SHOW INSTEAD OF WATCHING IT."

COLD BREWED COFFEE
This. On a Patio. After a workout. Before a swim. Can vacation please last forever?

Vacation Ritual 3: Iced Coffee Every Morning

There is something else you're likely to see wedged between the jars of Duke's and the cans of Cokes in our summer vacation refrigerator: a large pitcher of iced coffee. Home-brewed by Andy, always. As soon as the last dinner dish is cleared on the first night of vacation, my husband is scooping his favorite blends into the Chemex for a pour-over, or, if we're lucky, into his cold-brew apparatus, which sounds fancier than it actually is: a basic French press. He is as fetishistic about this ritual as any Brooklyn barista is about latte art. The brew does its thing overnight, and in the morning, our coffee awaits, ready to be served with ice and a snaky swirl of whole milk. If I were a business type, I'd say the Return On Investment of this ritual is on the impossibly high end of the spectrum: Knowing it's there for me when I wake up, or, the best, right after a morning run, upgrades the day in a way that is completely out of proportion to the work involved in making it happen. Especially since I don't *do any of the work.*

COLD-BREWED ICE COFFEE

We've been known to travel with our own coffee, but it's way more fun to seek out some local beans.

MAKES 8 TO 10 CUPS

• Place 6 ounces (about 2 cups) of coarsely ground coffee into a 48-ounce French press, fill with cold water (almost 6 cups), stir until the grounds are coated, and let sit on the counter for 12 to 24 hours. (The longer it sits, the more concentrated it is, and the more concentrated it is, the better.) When you are ready for your coffee, plunge down the press. You now have cold-brew concentrate, which can be diluted with water or milk to taste. (We generally prefer one part concentrate to one part water or milk.) Add ice, then stash the rest in a pitcher in the refrigerator for later.

Vacation Ritual 4: Quiet Time Every Day. Make It Sacred.

One of our more memorable family trips was a week on Block Island during the summer of 2008. In a caption on the first page of the iPhoto album devoted to the trip, I wrote, "It was a vacation for the books." The weather had been picture-perfect—not humid but hot enough to swim in the ocean. The house where we stayed had a distant view of Great Salt Pond and a driveway lined with blackberry bushes. We went on hikes with 360-degree views of the Atlantic, discovered the girls' penchant for boogie boarding, and spent a good part of the late morning tracking down the best lobster rolls for lunch. We packed a *lot* into our days, but somehow, what I remember the most fondly was the time spent doing nothing. This occurred from one thirty to three thirty every day and marked the start of our long-standing vacation ritual of post-lunch Quiet Time. Capital Q, capital T.

The girls were six and almost five that summer, and we had officially entered the phase that everyone promised was the best part of having kids so close in age. "It'll be tough for a couple years," they'd say like grizzled war vets, "but once they start playing together, you'll never need a babysitter." Unlike most from-the-trenches parenting advice we had received thus far, this was advice that actually seemed to ring true. And best of all: It was ringing true on vacation! Almost as an afterthought, I had packed a little travel dollhouse, plus a few animal and princessy figurines, for the trip, and by some miracle, the girls would retreat into this imaginary world for roughly two straight hours after lunch *every single day.* It's hard to overstate how satisfying this development was. It meant we had two straight hours to ourselves, to take a nap, to read a newspaper. For the first time since becoming parents, starting and finishing a novel while on a weeklong vacation was in our sights. We christened this period Quiet Time, just like their kindergarten teachers did, and called it that over and over, in hopes that the girls would recognize it as official and sacred, just like in school. It worked. Seven years later, they know exactly what to expect after lunch on vacation, and even though we don't crave the downtime as much as we did when we were new parents, and even though they're often out on their own riding bikes, no supervision necessary, it's nice to have a little block of time to finish that novel—or at least pretend to finish the novel, but nap on the hammock instead.

Vacation Rule 33:
Never change out of
your bathing suit.

MIRACLE MASHED POTATOES

Twelve years into this whole parenting thing, I know a few things for sure: The baby will need your attention at the exact moment the garlic in the pan goes from golden to blackened, bribery is a necessary evil, and—perhaps most relevant for the phase I'm in right now—mashed potatoes are crucial for surviving the middle-school years. I'm not talking about the kids' survival here. I'm talking about my own.

In the spring of 1983, I was probably the happiest twelve-year-old who ever lived. I had the starring role of Adelaide in my elementary school's production of *Guys and Dolls*; I was on the travel soccer team; I never lacked for lunchroom companions. I had my own CB windbreaker, which wasn't a hand-me-down from my sister (a first), and I even had a requited crush (another first) on a kid named Mike, who was cool enough to pull off a shell necklace.

By the fall it was all gone. My cozy class of one hundred kids matriculated to the much larger middle school, where my lunchroom companions found new lunchroom companions, who were interested in makeup (I was not), snapped each other's bras at gym (I was years away from wearing one), and made fun of me when I asked them to "play." ("We say 'hang out' now, Jenny.")

Even when I said it the right way, though, no one wanted to play or hang out. Maybe it was because I wore a really uncomfortable retainer that made me talk funny. I tried to look on the bright side, telling myself, *At least I don't have braces.* But that only worked until Mike ditched me in favor of his next crush, who had top and bottom braces, as well as the much coveted red CB down jacket, the one with the quilted back.

God, middle school sucked.

Somehow I clawed my way back, and along the way found my best friend, Jeni, with whom I've remained close, but thirty years later, like most people I know, I can still tap into the acute pain of being unceremoniously dumped and lonely and confused.

For years I thought my fall from grace would make me a great mother to girls, that I'd be more attuned to their socio-emotional temperature and more equipped to protect them from whatever middle-school situation reared its ugly head. That is to

168

say, I wasn't afraid to do a little micromanaging if it meant, somehow, that I could spare them the pain of being excluded down the road by any bra-snapping, blue-mascara'd monsters.

This worked out fine when they were little. I called other moms and arranged play-dates with kids who appeared to have soulmate potential. I picked up the phone and raised a tiny bit of hell when the summer-camp director put one in a group without the friend we had requested. More than once, I'm not proud to admit, I made place cards for my daughters' parties to ensure that they were sitting next to the kids who made them happiest. God forbid my children's birthdays end up not being The Day of All Days.

But then I entered middle school—I mean, my kids entered middle school—and it became clear that the issues we were dealing with were not ones I could control. At the dinner table and during carpools, I'd hear stories about girls excluding other girls from parties and excursions for reasons that no amount of questioning on my end could get to the bottom of.

All I could do was listen and play out the imaginary conversation I'd have with the Queen Bee's mother. In the worst-case scenario, she'd take offense; in the best-case scenario, she'd talk to her daughter and say . . . what exactly? That my daughter told on her and got her in trouble?

I don't know a lot, but I do know that a meddling mother is among the lowest forms of life on a seventh-grader's food chain. Sure, I can talk to school administrators about getting the girls matched up with the right teachers, and I can look for a new soccer program if the old one isn't working out. But negotiating the politics of middle-school girls? If ever there was a situation where a mother was utterly powerless, this was it. There was no phone call I could place to fix the problem.

Except to my own mom. I could call her, and during one particularly dicey drama, I did. She told me what I already knew: I'd have to sit this one out, as well as the next one and the one after that and the one after that, too. It was time to let the kids figure this stuff out on their own. But in a vehement tone that I imagine she reserves for her most unruly clients (she's a real estate attorney), Mom gave me one piece of advice that I think about all the time: "You just make sure that when those girls walk in that door every day," she said, "they never doubt that home is the most comforting place for them to be. That is what you can do."

This made a lot of sense to me. Comfort was something I could get a handle on. And as a food writer and blogger, I knew better than anyone that comfort was, in fact, something I could cook. I started to feel a new swell of appreciation for the family dinner table, a place that allowed for a safe, happy break from whatever else was going on—in both the kids' and the parents' lives. I also started thinking more carefully about what I served at those dinners and which dishes shouted "I Love You!" the loudest.

I kept coming around to mashed potatoes.

Once, after a particularly medieval braces-tightening session, I asked my twelve-year-old what she was in the mood to eat for dinner. Her beleaguered response: "Advil." Then: "I don't care what you make, as long as there are mashed potatoes on that plate." A few weeks later, when she and her sister were slogging their way through state tests, the request came again. And these days, whenever there is a rough day in the lunchroom or the classroom, an ortho appointment, a crushing loss in a double-overtime shoot-out, or anything that falls under the category of "something Mom can't make a phone call to fix," I find myself making mashed potatoes.

Will it exorcise my own middle-school demons? Will it solve every one of my daughters' adolescent anxieties from now until college? Of course not. But I'll tell you one thing: However small it is, it sure feels good to do something.

THE ELIXIR

Comfort can come in many forms, but I think both my daughters would agree that the best form is one involving a few russet potatoes that have been whipped with milk and butter (Classic Mashed Potatoes, page 175).

"HOWEVER SMALL IT IS TO COOK HER FAVORITE DISH, IT SURE FEELS GOOD TO DO SOMETHING."

CLASSIC MASHED POTATOES

When I'm trying to figure out how many mashed potatoes to make, whether I'm preparing a school-night dinner for my family of four or a Thanksgiving dinner for a table of twelve, I go by a simple formula: Count on one regular-size baking potato for each diner, which will yield just enough for a generous dinner portion, plus leftovers. (Leftovers, Phoebe will tell you, are crucial.) Also: We are big fans of the mix-ins and usually end up adding horseradish, caramelized onions, or freshly grated Parm; see variations below.

SERVES 4

4 baking potatoes, peeled and chopped into thirds or quarters
1 tablespoon kosher salt, plus more for serving
4 tablespoons butter, plus more for serving
¾ to 1 cup whole milk, cream, or half-and-half
freshly ground pepper

• In a large pot, cover the potatoes with water, add 1 tablespoon salt, and bring to a boil. Reduce the heat to a simmer and cook until a knife can slip through the biggest one with no resistance. It usually takes about 15 minutes. Drain and return the empty pot to the stove.
• Add the butter and about ½ cup of the milk to the pot, and heat until the milk is warm and the butter has melted. Heat the remaining milk in the microwave for about 30 seconds.
• Add the potatoes back to the pot and, using a hand mixer, whip until smooth, slowly adding more warm milk until you reach the desired consistency.
• Season with salt and pepper to taste. Serve each portion with another pat of butter so it creates the necessary little pool of melted fat on top.

Variations
• For Horseradish Mashed Potatoes: Mix in 1 tablespoon prepared horseradish.
• For Parm Mashed Potatoes: Mix in ½ cup freshly grated Parmigiano-Reggiano.
• For Caramelized Onion Mashed Potatoes: Heat 1 small onion (sliced) in olive oil over low heat for 30 minutes until the onions get sweet and caramelly. Stir the onions into the mashed potatoes.

APRÈS SKI

The "après ski" ritual conjures a certain kind of image: for some, a group of ruddy-faced J. Crew models wearing Uggs and sipping pale ale around a rough-hewn coffee table; for Andy, a Manhattan on the rocks soothing burning muscles in front of a roaring fire; for Phoebe, reading a comic book under a blanket in her pajamas. For me, it means one thing: skiing is over, and I am alive.

It's not that I don't like skiing. When the stars align—rental gear fits right, slopes aren't icy, trails marked green actually *are* green, I have feeling in all twenty digits—I totally get the exhilaration thing. But the problem is, I learned in my thirties, the decade I had kids, the decade when my mantra became, "Why have fun when I can be safe instead?" I grew up playing tennis, where the worst thing that could happen was stubbing my toe on the way to the Igloo cooler that contained the ice-cold water bottles. I can't tell you how many times I've pulled off to the side of a ski trail pretending to take a break or wait for the kids, when I'm really just pausing to let the fear pass, or giving myself a pep talk before a particularly steep downgrade, or redirecting my thoughts away from the mental catalog of ski injury stories I've accrued over the years and tap into as soon as I pick up a little speed. When I really think about it, given how much of a gigantic wimp I am, it's a miracle anyone got me to try this sport. And that I keep trying it. More than one time I've made a panicky declaration to myself mid-run: *Just make it down this slope without crashing, or through that narrow pass without fainting, and then you never have to get on skis again. What are you trying to prove with this whole skiing thing, anyway? Next time, just sit by the lodge's fire in your slippers or babysit a big hunk of meat as it braises in something stewy back at the house. Do we have a deal?*

Whenever I float this plan by the girls, of course, they are incredulous. *How is sitting by a fire or cooking more fun than skiing?* they ask. And though the answer to that question can fill—and has filled—three books, I know they are right. One of the main reasons I locked my boots into skis in the first place was so the girls wouldn't end up like me, someone whose first instinct when trying something new was to begin itemizing everything that could go wrong, someone who categorized walking under scaffolding as a "high-risk" activity. In the best possible world, they'd see their mother confronting her fears head-on and, God willing, triumphing over them. For now, they only see their mother do things like kick off her too-tight boot and fall sideways wailing into the snow after the first run of the day because her foot is asleep. True story.

It takes a little of the pressure off that when we ski, we usually do it with friends, and it just so happens that almost all of these friends have been skiing double black diamond trails for most of their lives. (One of these friends, Sarah, is a trauma surgeon in Salt Lake City, married to an orthopedist, and is obviously my very first choice for a ski partner.) I'm so grateful my kids can look to them as role models of grace and confidence. I am also grateful that when we return home to the rental, there is usually a bottle of bourbon, a pair of slippers, and something on the dinner menu that will satisfy the particular brand of voraciousness that results from a day of breathing in all that mountain air, sometimes by way of hyperventilating. The dinners almost always fall into the comfort-food category—think meatballs and pizzas—so they work for any wintry day, whether skiing is part of that day or not.

CIDER-BRAISED PORK MEATBALLS WITH CREAMY POLENTA

It's practically law that the word "creamy" or "braise" appear in an après-ski recipe.
To cut some of the richness, we often eat it with a bright Kale Salad with Pomegranates
(page 110).

THE RECIPE MAKES 16 TO 18 MEATBALLS AND SERVES 4

1¼ pounds ground pork

¾ cup plain breadcrumbs

2 eggs

1 tablespoon chopped fresh sage leaves

½ teaspoon grated lemon zest

2 teaspoons kosher salt, plus more to taste

¼ teaspoon freshly ground pepper, plus more to taste

3 tablespoons good-quality olive oil

1 large shallot, sliced

1 tablespoon tomato paste

1 tablespoon sugar

1 cup chicken stock

1 cup hard cider

½ cup apple cider vinegar

1 tablespoon butter

• Using your hands, in a bowl mix together the pork, breadcrumbs, eggs, sage, lemon zest, salt, and pepper, then form into golf-ball-size meatballs.

• Set a medium saucepan or Dutch oven over medium-high heat and add the olive oil. Brown the meatballs on all sides (in batches if necessary), about 3 minutes, and remove to a plate. They do not have to be cooked through.

• Turn down heat to medium and sauté the shallot for about 1 minute. Add the tomato paste and sugar and cook for another minute. Whisk in the chicken stock, cider, vinegar, and butter and bring to a boil. Turn the heat to low and add the meatballs back to the pot. Cover and simmer for 15 to 20 minutes, until cooked through.

• Remove the meatballs from the pot and turn up the heat for about 5 minutes, until the braising liquid has thickened slightly. Serve the meatballs with sauce spooned on top.

CIDER BRAISED PORK MEATBALLS
Do not forget to drizzle a little of that sweet-and-sour sauce on top of the meatballs and polenta. So so good.

CREAMY POLENTA

Polenta is always comforting on a winter plate, but I find it's even more so when it's made with homemade stock (page 52).

SERVES 4

4 cups chicken or vegetable stock

1 cup medium or fine cornmeal

1 teaspoon kosher salt

2 tablespoons butter

• Bring the stock to a boil in a heavy saucepan over high heat. Pour the cornmeal into the pot slowly, whisking as you go. The mixture will thicken after 2 or 3 minutes. Reduce the heat and let the mixture bubble on the stovetop for another 30 minutes, stirring every 5 minutes and adding water if it becomes too thick for your liking. Before serving, remove the polenta from the heat and stir in the butter.

BROCCOLINI-CHICKPEA PIZZA

This calls for a sprinkling of salami, but feel free to omit it if you'd like to go vegetarian. Also, broccoli rabe makes an excellent substitution for the broccolini, if you think the kids can handle its bitterness.

THIS RECIPE MAKES 1 PIZZA THAT SERVES 4; MAKE 2 PIZZAS IF YOUR SKIERS ARE PARTICULARLY RAVENOUS.

4 tablespoons good-quality olive oil, plus more for brushing

1 16-ounce ball store-bought pizza dough, preferably sitting out at
    room temperature for about 15 minutes to warm up a bit and rise

1 8-ounce ball fresh mozzarella cheese, thinly sliced

1 large bunch of broccolini (about 8 ounces), roughly chopped
    (including stems and leaves)

1 cup cooked chickpeas (canned are fine, just make sure they are drained,
    rinsed, and thoroughly dried)

¼ cup finely chopped Genoa salami or cooked,
   crumbled bacon (about 2 ounces)

1 teaspoon grated lemon zest

½ teaspoon garlic powder

kosher salt and freshly ground pepper

⅓ cup freshly grated Parmigiano-Reggiano

• Preheat the oven to 475°F. Using your fingers or a pastry brush, grease a 17 x 12-inch rimmed baking sheet with 1 tablespoon of the olive oil. Drop the pizza dough into the center of the baking sheet and, using your fingers, press out and flatten the dough so it spreads as close as possible to all four corners. (This takes time, but you want it to be thin so it cooks evenly and quickly.) Cover the dough with mozzarella slices, leaving a ½-inch border around the perimeter.

• In a large bowl, toss the broccolini, chickpeas, salami, lemon zest, and garlic powder. Season with salt and pepper to taste and drizzle in the remaining 3 tablespoons olive oil, then give it all another toss. Using your hands, add the broccoli-chickpea mixture on top of the mozzarella in an even layer. Shower with the grated Parm and brush the exposed edge of the crust with a little oil. Bake for 15 minutes, until the crust looks golden and the broccolini looks crispy and dark brown, but not black-burnt. (You can always cover the toppings with foil if the broccolini looks ready before the crust is.) Remove the pizza to a cutting board to cool. Slice into eight rectangular pieces and serve.

BROCCOLINI-CHICKPEA PIZZA

If you have the kind of kid
who wouldn't think twice
about barreling down a double-
black-diamond trail, but hides
under the table at the sight
of broccolini, don't force
it. Just make a separate
tomato-sauce-and-marinara pie
for him, and focus on your
après-ski Modelo.

PART III

BIRTHDAYS

Abby's Birthdaypalooza

Andy's Birthday Breakfasts / Jenny's Mud Cake

Phoebe's Ice Cream Cake

Pick a Country, Any Country

A Sane Parent's Guide to Throwing an
At-Home Birthday Party

ABBY'S BIRTHDAYPALOOZA

One summer, on vacation in South Carolina, I was pretending to read my (very slow) book club book, but really drifting off into a poolside nap, when nine-year-old Abby started tapping my shoulder.

"Mom?"

"I'm not awake."

"Mom? Do you have any paper?"

"Ask Dad."

I drifted off again into daydream-land, focusing on the distant cry of seagulls.

Tap. Tap. Tap.

"Dad doesn't have any paper. Can I rip out a page of your book to write on?"

Nap over.

"What? Why? What's so important that you have to write down this second? Why don't you go swimming or get yourself a Good Humor bar?"

"I have to plan my birthday."

I sat up on my elbows. I had to shield my eyes from the sun to look at her. Did I hear her right? Or was I still half sleeping?

"Your *birthday*? Your birthday is in three months. You don't need to plan your birthday right now. And you certainly don't need to rip out a page of my novel to plan your birthday right now."

"I thought you hated that book," she said.

She had a point.

"Please, please, please, Mom. I'll do *anything*."

I should've known by that point in my little litigator's nine-year-old life that when these words are uttered in the middle of a conversation, she's not letting go until she wins.

"Fine," I said, and tore out the back page, which was mostly blank. "But now you have to let me finish my nap. Deal?"

"Deal."

When I woke up, she handed me her birthday plan. It was titled "Abby's Tenth Birthday":

When the birthday box comes out of the cabinet, it usually means good things are about to happen.

- *Breakfast: homemade waffles with whipped cream and berries*
- *In-Class Celebration: doughnut cake (topped with one pink-frosted, sprinkled doughnut for the birthday girl)*
- *Birthday Party: around-the-world theme*
- *Celebrating with Cousins and Grandparents: dinner at home— pappardelle with pork ragu—followed by gift opening.*
- *Soccer Team Celebration: homemade chocolate chip cookies (with M&M's) after a game*
- *Actual Birthday: dinner at the Japanese restaurant that has the excellent appetizers*

It's not her fault, really. For the most part, our family likes to get things done in as nonfussy, no-nonsense ways as possible. (In the case of our "garden" and my front hall closet, this can, in fact, mean doing nothing at all.) But when it comes to birthdays, we are the opposite. We go kind of nuts. Though we never tick off *all* the boxes on Abby's master birthday checklist, it's not uncommon for multiple celebrations to take place across multiple days and to have many discussions about presents, party themes . . . and food. Lots of food. In our house, we don't celebrate birthdays as much as we stage birthdaypaloozas.

This is because, the way I figure things, a) we don't have that many years to go crazy for our daughters' birthdays, and b) rituals related to birthdays, in my experience, have more warm-and-fuzzy memory potential than most. When I think about my own childhood memories, the ones that exist in high relief are almost always birthday related: candle-blowing, duck-duck-goose playing, and the party in the early eighties when every single one of my friends gave me a stuffed Smurf. (And yet no Smurfette, which flummoxed me.)

In short, the theory driving our madness, which you are welcome to steal, is this: *If you can figure out a way to make your kids feel off-the-charts special on their birthdays, then you can pretty much let yourself off the hook on all parenting duties for the rest of the year.*

We have a few birthday rituals that carry over from celebrant to celebrant. For instance, all birthday mornings start with a properly tablecloth-ed four-top, and something diner-worthy like waffles or popovers (see page 152) on the menu. The birthday girl gets to pick a restaurant for dinner out (see page 211). And, if it's a kid we're talking about, the celebrant is guaranteed a rockin' at-home party (page 214). (That is, until they turn twelve or thirteen, at which point, they reject all notions of "games" and "parties," invite a handful of friends to Smashburger, and call it a day.) But for the most part, each member of the family gets to dictate how to celebrate on his or her own terms. Birthday pie instead of cake? Ice cream cake in the middle of winter? A sausage-egg-and-cheese biscuit for breakfast? A recipe that beams you back to your childhood? Your birthday wish is our command.

Though we are all bananas for birthdays, I would like to go on record and say that there is no kid on this planet who gets more excited about her big day than Abby. In addition to the topic being part of the regular family conversation all year long, she will go into a deep state of mourning the second it's over, inevitably announcing, "I can't believe I have to wait three hundred sixty-four days for the next one."

This is partly because she is her father's daughter (a true enthusiast) and her mother's daughter (a natural-born celebrationist), but my secret theory is that having a birthday gives her an excuse to do something she likes to do more than almost anything: organize.

Abby loves a list. We find them all over the house written in all different colors of ink: "Stuff Abby Likes" (Robert Downey, Jr., Ronaldo, Yummi Desserts, Tokidoki, sushi erasers, or whatever miniature Japanese collector's item she's into that week); "What I Want for My Bedroom" (wallpaper, swing, Robert Downey Jr. poster); "Favorite Pixar Movies" (*Inside Out, Up, The Incredibles, Finding Nemo*); "Songs I Love on *Glee*" ("Don't Stop Believin'," "Take a Bow," and, much to Andy's dismay, "Don't Rain on My Parade"). We find checklists and to-do lists, with a box beside each task that needs to be x'd out. Sometimes the list is assembled out loud in the form of rankings. "List your favorite places to vacation from best to worst," she'll put forth on a road trip from the backseat. Or "What are your top five favorite Taylor Swift songs?" For Abby, it seems there's no issue too insignificant to work through with good old-fashioned bullet points.

Like her mother, she also gets an inordinate amount of pleasure from drawing up a schedule. Once, when Andy and I were traveling for a few days, leaving the girls in the care of a few tag-teaming babysitters, I handed them a stapled single-spaced

189

packet at the breakfast table. It was an hour-by-hour schedule of when they had to be where, who was driving who to what, and cell numbers for everyone involved, from the high school senior who was picking them up at school to the soccer coach they can always count on to answer her cellphone. Phoebe, justifiably, took one look at the thing, squinted in a way that indicated her mother was insane, and went back to her bagel. Abby pored over the schedule, studying it line by line, before looking at me and saying, "Thank you, Mom. This is the best thing ever."

Thanks to our resident organizer, we have very little to do in terms of planning her birthday. Beyond figuring out what celebratory foods she'd like, she comes up with the invitation list for her party, designs the invitation and emails it to her friends, writes down theme ideas and party activities, and assembles all the goodie bags.

The astute reader might pick up a glaring omission, something that doesn't appear on any of her lists, and something most celebrants could never do *without* on their big day: a birthday cake. Abby claims it's because she's "not a cake girl" (her words), but I secretly think it's because she places a premium on the unpredictable—and the idea of two monogrammed pies lit up with candles is, to a tween, just about the most radical move you could make at a party. I gotta hand it to her, it's also pretty delicious.

BROWN BUTTER APPLE PIE

Since Abby's birthday is in October, it's only natural that her pick of pie is apple.
The truth is, though, it's her favorite pie any day of the year. And one of mine, too.
This recipe is a slight twist on the classic: The brown butter adds a little more
dimension and makes the house smell amazing.

SERVES 8 (I USUALLY MAKE 2 FOR A BIRTHDAY PARTY)

5 cups tart baking apples (such as Granny Smith,
   Mutsu, Honeycrisp), peeled and sliced

⅓ cup sugar

1 tablespoon fresh lemon juice

2 teaspoons ground cinnamon

¼ teaspoon freshly grated nutmeg

¼ teaspoon kosher salt

2 store-bought or homemade 9-inch pie crusts (for top and bottom)

4 tablespoons (½ stick) unsalted butter

1 egg, whisked

vanilla or cinnamon ice cream, for serving

- Preheat the oven to 425°F. In a large bowl, toss the apples with the sugar, lemon juice, cinnamon, nutmeg, and salt.
- Line a 9-inch pie dish with one of the crusts, pressing firmly around all sides and smoothing out any cracks.
- Add the butter to a medium saucepan set over medium-low heat. Do not leave your stovetop perch. Watch as the butter melts, then foams, then begins to brown, swirling occasionally as you go. The whole process should take about 4 minutes, but it's really an eyeball (and an aromatic) thing: As soon as the butter starts to turn brown and smell nutty, remove the pan from the heat so the butter doesn't burn. Toss the brown butter with the apples, then add the entire mixture to the pie dish. Top with the second crust, cinching the perimeter of the dough with a fork or your fingers to seal. (For more creative perimeter options, see page 121.)
- Using a sharp knife, cut 5 or 6 air slits into the top of the crust and brush the crust with the egg wash.
- Bake at 425°F for 15 minutes. Then reduce the heat to 350°F and bake for 30 more minutes or until the crust is golden brown and the filling is bubbly. Serve studded with birthday candles and top slices with vanilla or cinnamon ice cream.

DOUGHNUT CAKE

When I debuted this doughnut cake at school I was embarrassed by how slapdash it was. (Though not embarrassed enough to scrap it and bake a cake from scratch.) But the kids went bonkers when I removed the foil, and pretty soon I started getting emails from parents: Anna wants some doughnut cake for her birthday and told me to ask you? My friend Sue told me that your daughter had some crazy cake in class? Erin told me to ask you about the Munchkin cake. Do you know what she's talking about? If so, can you pass along instructions?

SERVES A CLASS OF ABOUT 25 KIDS

• Here they are. Make sure you are paying close attention because it's kinda complicated: Cover a concave platter with tissue paper. Stack 3 doughnuts in the middle and shove the candles in the top one. (The top one should be festive with sprinkles; if you are feeling ambitious you can pipe a "happy birthday" message on it as well.) Dump 75 assorted Munchkins around the stack. Serve.

BIRTHDAY RITUALS 101

Note: While birthday celebrations can veer toward the absurd in our house, it's here that I'd like you to recognize that each one of the dozen or so rituals that make up a birthdaypalooza is not terribly complicated, and could stand alone as its own special birthday ritual. I'd also like to note that, even though cribbing celebratory ideas from me in this chapter is encouraged, a birthday is another good place to take stock of the little traditions you already have in place. Some examples: How about that time when your son turned double digits and you spontaneously treated him to a double scoop at the local ice cream shop? Or snuck a happy birthday note into his spelling workbook? Or the time you discreetly asked the waiter to place a candle in his hamburger when you went out for dinner on his sixth birthday? These might've been one-time gestures that you've long forgotten, but I'd be willing to bet they are preserved in happy memory amber somewhere in your child's brain. Ask him about his most favorite birthday memories, take careful notes, and then milk them for all they are worth for as many years as you possibly can.

DRIVE-THRU CAKE
Pile up some Munchkins, pipe your message on a strawberry-glazed, and call it birthday cake.

ANDY'S BIRTHDAY BREAKFASTS

I like my husband a lot. He throws a killer spiral; he makes a mean Manhattan; he is deft with nicknaming (thanks to him, no one in our house goes by their given name); he's not afraid to belt along with Taylor Swift, should the situation call for it. (It's amazing how often the situation calls for it.) He is also, as I've established, gifted in the pickling department.

But I'll tell you when I *don't* like my husband at all: in the morning. Before we are all properly caffeinated, the man is a monster. Let me give you some examples:

- On a weekday morning, he frequently tries to start conversations with me within seconds of the alarm going off. ("Good morning! How'd you sleep?")
- He frequently ignores my mumbled response ("not awake yet") to this affront and continues trying to talk to me.
- On alternating weekday mornings, he gets up an hour earlier than the rest of our house and runs four to five miles outside, even in single-digit winter weather, even when the sky is black as ink.
- He often walks into the house after these runs, headphones still on, singing. Singing!
- While I call on every ounce of maternal instinct in order to grunt a "good morning" to my daughters, Andy greets their entrances at the breakfast table as a booster squad might greet its football team at the pep rally. WHAT'S UP, ROZELLE? HOW'S IT GOING, DOODLER? (See: Nicknamer.)

Ugh, morning people! Are they not the *worst*?

I have never been a morning person, in case that needs clarification. Every now and then, on a summer day, when I manage to get myself up with the sun to walk our dog, Iris, or go for a run, I can see the appeal, and on those occasions I feel a wave of superiority over all the lazy-heads still in bed. More often than not, however, I am the lazy-head.

But there are three days a year when I always match Andy's Morning Energy Bunny: on each of my family members' birthdays. Considering there are only about fourteen hours in a day to celebrate the honoree, I figure we might as well start at the breakfast table. If the big day falls on a school morning, this usually means I'm up early tucking chocolate chips into waffle divots or sticking candles into a stack of silver-dollar pancakes. But God help us if the birthday falls on a weekend. Then the celebration automatically balloons into a bona fide sit-down affair with offerings like Belgian waffles, French toast with almond-extract-spiked freshly whipped cream, or— Andy's favorite—sausage-egg-and-cheese biscuits. The first time I made one of these for his birthday breakfast, I didn't mean to make it entirely from scratch (including the sausages) but . . . well, did I tell you how we feel about birthdays? The best thing about the sandwich, besides how buttery and delicious it is? The sausage patties are easy enough for Phoebe to prepare—and she has, many times—which means if I want to (and usually I want to) I can deputize her to get breakfast going and then press my snooze button one more time.

HOMEMADE SAUSAGE, EGG, AND CHEESE ON HOMEMADE BISCUITS

Regarding the cheese: only American will do.

MAKES 6 SANDWICHES

Biscuits

4 cups all-purpose flour, plus more for rolling the dough

2 tablespoons sugar

1 tablespoon baking powder

2 teaspoons baking soda

1 tablespoon kosher salt

¾ cup (1½ sticks) cold unsalted butter, cut into small pieces

1½ cups buttermilk

- Preheat the oven to 425°F. Line a rimmed baking sheet with parchment.
- In a large bowl, whisk the flour, sugar, baking powder, baking soda, and salt until combined. Add the butter and toss to coat. Using your fingers, quickly and firmly rub the butter into the dough to create some pieces that are flat and others that are chunks the size of peas. Stir in the buttermilk with a fork until the dough just comes together.
- Turn out dough onto a lightly floured surface and roll to 1 inch thick. Using a biscuit cutter or a straight-sided drinking glass, cut 10 to 12 biscuits. (Even though you'll only need 6. You'll be glad you have extras.) Place on the baking sheet. Bake for 17 to 19 minutes, until golden brown. Cool on a rack.

Sausage Patties

1 pound ground turkey

1 teaspoon kosher salt

1 teaspoon ground cumin

½ teaspoon onion powder

½ teaspoon paprika

½ teaspoon freshly ground pepper

1 small clove garlic, very finely minced

4 teaspoons pure maple syrup

1 tablespoon olive oil

- Combine all of the ingredients (except oil) and form into 6 flat patties. Place a large skillet over medium-high heat until hot. Add the olive oil, then cook the patties until browned, 2 to 3 minutes. Repeat on the flip side. Set aside.

Eggs

- Add 1 tablespoon butter or olive oil to a large ovenproof skillet set over medium heat. Whisk together 4 eggs with a little salt and black pepper and pour into the heated pan like a very large pancake. Heat until the underside is cooked, about 1 minute. Place the pan under the broiler and cook the other side for an additional minute. Turn the egg pancake onto a clean surface and, using a knife, divide into six pieces.

Biscuit Sandwich

- Split 6 biscuits in half horizontally. On the bottom half, place 1 sausage patty and 1 egg piece (you might have to fold or trim slightly) on a biscuit and drape a slice of American cheese on top. Place on a cookie sheet and heat under the broiler for 1 minute, or until the cheese melts. Top with the other biscuit half and serve, with or without a candle.

JENNY'S MUD CAKE

A few years ago Andy made me the best birthday dinner: a big bowl of salty, buttery egg noodles, served with a side of zucchini wedges sautéed in olive oil and garlic and finished with salt and pepper.

If you're sitting there scratching your head, wondering how on earth a bowl of buttered egg noodles qualifies as birthday-worthy, let me assure you it was about a hundred times more celebratory than, say, a grilled porterhouse or a steamed Maine lobster. Why? Easy. Because I didn't grow up eating grilled porterhouses or steamed Maine lobsters. No matter how good either one of those tastes to me now, neither could ever beam me back to my mustard-yellow linoleum childhood kitchen the way a bowl of egg noodles and zucchini can.

When I was in high school, egg noodles were my go-to after-school snack, and the zucchini was a side dish on just about every dinner plate in our household in the 1980s. I complained about this a lot growing up, until I had my own family to feed and was shocked to discover that no one in my brood liked zucchini—or anything in any way related to the squash family, for that matter.

"It's mushy," said Abby.

"It's watery," said Phoebe.

"It's completely tasteless," said Andy. "It's like reading a boring book."

Well, sure, the humble zucchini is not going to have much luck in a match-up with an heirloom tomato, a crunchy slaw, or a peak-season ear of sweet corn. But no one was tasting the zucchini with the sauce that mine was tossed with—*a hefty dollop of Nostalgia.* As I'm sure you know, that stuff can be magical. (Have you ever tried a drop on top of Triscuits with American cheese?)

My point is, sometimes all you need to make a birthday feel special is a little sensory throwback, and that night I got it. Dinner was executed to perfection and was delicious, even though the rest of the family dined on take-out pizza that night.

Dessert, though: That was another story. I didn't have to convince anyone to partake in Rosa's Mud Cake, which no Nostalgia Night would be complete without.

I've had many culinary heroes in my lifetime, but Rosa was my first. She was the mother of my childhood best friend, Jeni, and was a rare bird in the 1980s: a woman who took pride in ambitious, home-cooked food. While shoulder-padded, shortcut-obsessed moms were clearing the supermarket shelves of Chef Boyardee and embracing their microwaves, she was driving to Arthur Avenue's famous Italian markets in the Bronx to procure fresh bread and pastas, assembling shepherd's pie from scratch, and tossing lentil salad with homemade dressings that called for exotic ingredients like tarragon vinegar. For the longest time, I viewed that lentil recipe, and all her recipes, as official legislation handed down from a high court, never swapping ingredients, even though tarragon vinegar was expensive for a recent college grad, and just about any other vinegar would've worked fine. Rosa's well-worn wooden recipe box was a treasure chest, overstuffed with yellowed recipe clippings from *The New York Times* and handwritten index cards that I still sometimes fantasize about stealing off with in the middle of the night.

On one of those cards was something called Mud Cake. It was a classic dump-it cake—all the ingredients, including a cup of strong black coffee, mixed artlessly in one large bowl, my kind of recipe—and the result was a rich chocolate cake that was somehow still light as air. Rosa made it for Jeni's birthday every year, and I loved it so much that I adopted the tradition as soon as I had kids. I made her give me the recipe and started baking it for seemingly every occasion that presented itself, sometimes even with frosting. You'll see it provides the layers for Phoebe's Mint Chocolate Ice Cream Cake with Ganache (page 208) or takes the form of two dozen cupcakes to be carted into the classroom or a bake sale (page 203). On my chocolate-loving father's birthday a few years ago, I dusted one with powdered sugar and studded the top with a few berries. On Valentine's Day, I bake it in two pans, one round and one square, and turn it into a heart cake (see page 24.) For my nieces, nephews, and neighbors, I tend to go classic, layering two rounds, then slathering with chocolate frosting. On my birthday, though, I like it plain with a dollop of you know what. It doesn't need anything else to taste exactly right.

MUD CAKE

It's not a birthday until my favorite chocolate cake makes an appearance. P.S.: A Dum Dum lollipop perimeter definitely makes it party-worthy.

ROSA'S MUD CAKE

Rosa's recipe calls for a cup of brewed coffee, which will help give the cake its dark "muddy" color, but the final product won't taste like mocha. Just really outstanding chocolate. Also, warning: The cake can be extremely delicate, so make sure you are not stingy with the butter when greasing the pan, which will help remove it without any breakage.

MAKES ONE 9-BY-13-INCH SHEET CAKE, TWO 9-INCH LAYERS, OR 25 TO 30 CUPCAKES
(Cupcake instructions below.)

butter, for greasing the pan

2 cups sugar

1¼ cups flour, plus more for dusting the pan

¾ cups unsweetened cocoa powder

2 teaspoons baking soda

1 teaspoon baking powder

2 large eggs

1 cup room-temperature strong black coffee
   (brewed, not grounds)

1 cup buttermilk

½ cup canola or vegetable oil

1 teaspoon pure vanilla extract

⅔ cup semisweet chocolate chips (optional)

• Preheat the oven to 350°F. Grease a 9 by 13-inch sheet pan or two 9-inch round cake pans with butter, and lightly flour, shaking off any excess. (See note on the next page for cupcake instructions.)

• In a medium bowl, whisk together the sugar, flour, cocoa powder, baking soda, and baking powder. Add the eggs, coffee, buttermilk, oil, vanilla, and chocolate chips, if using. Stir until incorporated, then pour into the prepared pan. Bake for 30 to 33 minutes or until a toothpick inserted in the middle comes out clean. Transfer to a wire rack and let cool in the pan for 20 to 30 minutes. Run a serrated knife along the edges until they pull away from the sides. Place a cooling rack on top of the cake and slowly, carefully invert the cake onto the rack to finish cooling.

• When the cake is completely cooled, you have many options: You can top it with chocolate frosting (recipe follows); you can set the cake on a wire rack on top of a rimmed cookie sheet and pour ganache glaze on top (see page 210); or, you can simply top it with freshly whipped cream (see page 59) or vanilla or cinnamon ice cream.

• *Cupcakes:* Since the cake is relatively delicate, I strongly recommend using cupcake papers instead of baking the batter directly into greased cupcake tins. Fill to two-thirds capacity and bake at 350°F for 18 to 20 minutes, until a toothpick inserted in the center of one comes out clean. Top with chocolate frosting, below.

Chocolate Frosting

MAKES 1¼ CUPS

½ cup (1 stick) unsalted butter, at room temperature

1½ cups powdered sugar

2 ounces unsweetened chocolate, melted and cooled

1 tablespoon whole milk

½ teaspoon pure vanilla extract

• In the bowl of a stand mixer fitted with the paddle attachment, beat together the butter and powdered sugar on medium speed until light and fluffy, 2 to 3 minutes. Reduce the speed to low and beat in the chocolate, milk, and vanilla until the mixture reaches spreadable consistency, 1 to 2 minutes.

Phoebe's lair contains multitudes.

PHOEBE'S
ICE CREAM CAKE

My eldest refuses to read *Harry Potter*. Actually, "refuses" is not entirely accurate. We read the first one together when Phoebe was seven or eight, and she got through half of the second book on her own before deciding that the series just wasn't doing it for her.

It made me crazy. "But you *love* a good fantasy series," I insisted. "And every person on earth loves *Harry Potter*." Plus, I had bought the entire eight-volume set for *one buck* at a garage sale, and it killed me to see a bargain like that go to waste. "Maybe you should give it another shot?"

"No thanks," she'd reply.

Though it sounds like a polite response on paper, a "no thanks" from Phoebe is, to quote my husband, "a hammer wrapped in velvet." It's the equivalent of her saying, "This conversation is over. And it would be wise to never bring up the topic again because I'm never going to change my mind."

When she applies this I-won't-budge philosophy to other things—like, for instance, giving pasta another shot—it's not my most favorite character trait. But her stubbornness seems to be a two-sides-of-the-same-coin issue, the other side translating to one of my most favorite character traits ever: She's a radical loyalist. The girl knows what she likes. And once she decides she likes something, she *locks in.* When she was six, she picked up a graphic novel about Zeus, by George O'Connor, and she hasn't stopped obsessing over the Greek gods (or graphic novels) since. From the moment she got wind of the fact that she was named after Holden Caulfield's sister in *The Catcher in the Rye,* she began lobbying her parents to bring home a copy, and when we finally did, she read it in two days, then carted it with her everywhere like a security blanket, reading it over and over again. My sister bought her a multivolume set of *The Adventures of Tintin* when she was in first grade and she's read them so many millions of times that it was only natural for Tintin, Snowy, Captain Haddock, and Professor Calculus to accompany her to sleepaway camp. (In her words, "It was nice to have a good friend around.")

It goes beyond books. When I ask her what she wants for dinner, 100 percent of

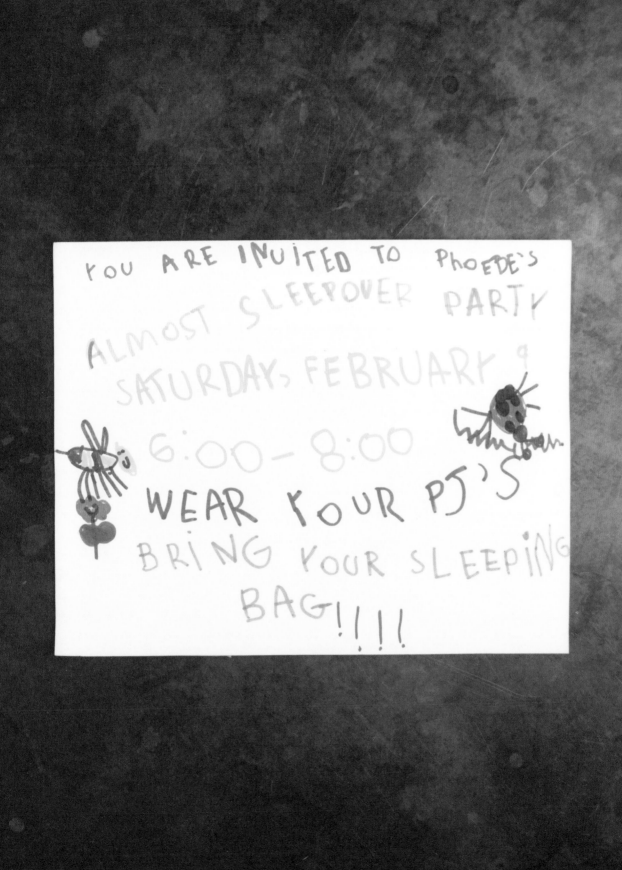

the time her answer will be salmon salad. (Unless she's gotten her braces tightened, in which case 100 percent of the time the answer is mashed potatoes; see page 175.) When we return to a vacation spot, she begs to visit the same ice cream parlor, go on the same hike, swim at the same beach.

And once, when my mom made Phoebe a mint chocolate ice cream cake for her fifth or sixth birthday, she sat down, eyed it, took a bite, locked in. Right there, she decided that that was going to be her birthday cake for all her parties for all eternity. No matter that her birthday is in February, the coldest month of our New York winter, and ice cream cake is something most kids generally crave on a hot summer day.

It's not stubbornness. It's loyalty. It's not a lack of adventure. It's the comfort of ritual.

PHOEBE'S MINT CHOCOLATE ICE CREAM CAKE WITH GANACHE

My friend Sara Schneider, a world-class baker, once gave me a version of this recipe in three or four text messages, so don't be intimidated by all the steps here. It looks complicated but is pretty much a straight assembly job. This one starts with Rosa's Mud Cake (page 202), of course, which makes exactly enough batter to fill a 2½ by 9-inch springform pan, producing a cake that will then be horizontally sliced in two. (You can also make two thinner layers in two separate 9-inch pans, then return them to a springform pan for the layering.)

SERVES 12 TO 14

Step 1: Make the Cake

    butter, for greasing the pan

    1¼ cups all-purpose flour, plus more for
        dusting the pan

    2 cups sugar

    ¾ cup unsweetened cocoa powder

    2 teaspoons baking soda

    1 teaspoon baking powder

    2 large eggs

1 cup room-temperature strong black coffee

   (brewed, not grounds)

1 cup buttermilk

½ cup canola or vegetable oil

1 teaspoon pure vanilla extract

• Preheat the oven to 350°F.

• Butter and flour a 9-inch springform pan and set aside. In a medium bowl, whisk together the sugar, flour, cocoa powder, baking soda, and baking powder.

• Add the eggs, coffee, buttermilk, oil, and vanilla. Stir until everything is incorporated, then pour into the prepared pan. Lightly tap the pan on a hard surface to release any air bubbles. Bake for 30 to 33 minutes or until a toothpick inserted in the middle comes out clean.

Step 2: Allow Cake to Cool Completely

• Once the cake has cooled, remove it from the pan and slice it in half horizontally. Place the two halves on separate plates and freeze (covered) for an hour. (This isn't 100 percent necessary, but I find it makes the airy, fragile cakes easier to handle and less likely to fall apart when I am transferring them from place to place.) Wash the springform pan and set it aside.

Step 3: Thaw the Ice Cream and Crush the Crunchies

72 ounces (1½ rectangular 48-ounce cartons) mint chocolate chip ice cream

   (You can also use two separate flavors of ice cream,

   in which case 36 ounces of flavor one and 36 ounces of flavor

   two in two separate bowls.)

1 dozen Oreos or chocolate wafers

• Scoop the ice cream into a large bowl and let it soften. Stir the ice cream with a wooden spoon sporadically as it thaws until it's the consistency of really thick soup. You do not want it to be liquidy.

• While the ice cream thaws, place the Oreos or chocolate wafers in a large zip-top plastic bag, seal the bag, and crush the cookies with a rolling pin.

Step 4: Assemble the Ice Cream Cake

• Tighten the springform pan and place it on a cooling rack that has been placed on top of a cookie sheet. Set the first layer of chocolate cake into the springform pan. Hopefully it is just about hugging the sides of the pan. Spread half of the ice cream in a thick layer on top of the cake. Flatten as much as possible. Using your hands, distribute a thick layer of cookie crumbs on top of the ice cream. Add the second layer of ice cream, spreading so the top is flat. Add the second layer of cake. This is your last layer. Cover with foil and place the entire cake, cooling rack, and cookie sheet assembly in the freezer. Freeze for a minimum of 4 hours, or preferably overnight.

Step 5: Make the Ganache

COATS 1 CAKE

> 1 cup heavy whipping cream
> 6 ounces semisweet chocolate chips

• In a small saucepan, heat the cream over medium-low heat until tiny bubbles are forming around the edge, 3 to 4 minutes. Meanwhile, add the chocolate chips to a medium heat-proof bowl. Pour the warm cream over the chocolate chips and let sit for about 2 minutes without stirring. Whisk together and let cool for about 10 minutes (very important).

Step 6: Glaze the Cake

• Remove the cake from the freezer and set on the counter. Carefully remove the cake from the pan, keeping it on top of the rack and cookie sheet. Once the ganache has cooled to room temperature (Did I mention? Very important!), slowly pour the glaze in the very center of the top layer of cake, allowing it to drip down the sides. It's fine if it looks a little uneven and even a little messy. At this point, you may sprinkle more mix-ins on top, or pipe a happy birthday message on top, or just behold the cake in its pure, simple, chocolate-glazed glory. Using two large spatulas and as much emotional support as you can dredge up, transfer the cake to a large round serving platter.

Step 7: Serve the Cake

• Using a hot knife, slice the cake into wedges. Serve with whipped cream.

PICK A COUNTRY, ANY COUNTRY

When the girls were little, we started a birthday tradition in our house: If it was your birthday, you got to go to any restaurant you wanted. There was only one rule: The restaurant you picked had to be specific to a certain country. For instance, on her sixth birthday, Phoebe chose Sweden. It's not as random as it sounds: Abby's best friend at the time was from Stockholm, and our kids also happened to be in the midst of a powerful Muppets obsession. (Remember the Swedish Chef?) Then, Abby, all of age six, chose Japan. Then, Phoebe picked . . . Morocco. (We gave her "Middle Eastern"; she never knew the difference.) Some of these adventures (Sweden, with its creamy meatballs . . . jammy lingonberries . . . whipped potatoes) were more successful than others (Brazil, with its amazing barbecue, but not-so-child-friendly dive-bar vibe), but the meal was only half the point. The point was that this was one of those rare nights the kids got to orchestrate themselves. It was a night that involved pulling out world maps and our book of flags and thinking about where on earth they wanted to go, what they wanted to show *us*. It involved tasting something new, even if it was only a falafel platter. And it involved dressing up and going out, getting on a train, and riding all thirty-two minutes to Grand Central Terminal in a window seat, watching Yonkers roll by. Which, to them, back then, was about as exciting as riding a pink unicorn through an enchanted forest.

211

Part Fifteen
of Our Fifteen-Part
Birthdaypalooza:
Andy serves the cake.

A SANE PARENT'S GUIDE TO THROWING AN AT-HOME BIRTHDAY PARTY

I am well aware that the birthday party, specifically *the at-home birthday party,* is a term that sends a shudder down many a parent's spine. True, the at-home birthday party has the power to make time move at a quarter speed while you're in the middle of hosting one; and true, it can involve Herculean levels of endurance and patience; and true, it's bordering on absurd to throw a party at your house given all the good options these days for outsourcing. But I find that if I can survive the at-home birthday party unscathed, I can live off the resulting high for weeks.

Don't turn the page! Trust me on this one.

I remember swearing off the at-home birthday party when Phoebe turned two. I'll never forget the sight of Andy surrounded by empty pizza boxes and a dozen toddlers waving paper plates (screaming *"me me me me"*) while he attempted to summon his inner Buddha and slice through a pink-frosted sheet cake with a piece of dental floss. (*Real Simple* promised it worked better than a knife. It did not. Curse you, *Real Simple*!) At some point in the middle of all this, my husband turned to me, with genuine despair in his eyes, and discreetly mouthed the words, *"This is a death march."*

Since that party, however, we've picked up many strategies that help us get through the event with as little nerve damage as possible, while simultaneously optimizing the happy childhood memory potential. The key, naturally, is all in the organizing. You have to have a game plan. And you most certainly have to have a schedule. (I learned this lesson the hard way: ten four-year-olds, one hour remaining, zero plan.) There's psychological prep work to do as well as logistical: You have to steel yourself to either a) be cleaning the entire time or b) embrace the spiraling mess that ensues when a dozen kids are tearing through the living room. Perhaps hardest, though, is really turning yourself *on* (i.e., being fully engaged, present) for the duration of the party. In short, it's important to know that if you're anything like me, the whole thing will be anxiety-inducing, but after it's over—after you've put your exhausted, euphoric birthday honoree to bed, after you've seared the image of her blowing out the candles on your brain forevermore, after you've reminded yourself, again, not to take any of this for granted—you might find yourself in a state of euphoria yourself. (Related: childbirth.)

After the dental floss episode, we did two kid parties a year for about seven years straight and got the schedule down to a science. My little secret is that even though the theme changed every year, the general party plan was, with a few exceptions, exactly the same. They were all two hours (any longer than that and my brain liquefies) and follow the same basic template.

Basic Party Template
- *Arts and Crafts Project (20 minutes)*
- *Game 1 (20 minutes)*
- *Game 2 (20 minutes)*
- *Food and Cake (20–30 minutes)*
- *Pass the Parcel (20 minutes) or Gift Opening*
- *Time Killer until Pickup (whatever time is leftover)*

Once you have this basic template down, it's easy to slot in the activities based on the theme. Let's take Activity 1: Arts and Crafts Project, for instance. One year, for Phoebe's Almost Sleepover Party, the project was a make-your-own pillowcase using a kit I found at an online party shop. For Abby's ninth, a Cooking Party, we filled the project slot with chef hat decorating. (Hello, photo op!) For Phoebe's ninth, a Secret Agent Party, the project was Make Your Own I.D. Badge. As soon as the party-goers walked in the door they were handed a spy packet with their code name ("Pork Chop") inside in the tiniest font our MacBook was capable of printing. Once they used the magnifying glass (which—bonus—doubled as a party favor) to discover what their code name was, they wrote it on I.D. badges (procured at Staples) and

"IN OUR HOUSE,
WE DON'T CELEBRATE
BIRTHDAYS AS
MUCH AS WE STAGE
BIRTHDAYPALOOZAS."

decorated them with stickers and their own fingerprints (messy, but worth it). One of us was around to fit it into a lanyard, which they wore for the duration of the party. See, easy! First twenty minutes: Done.

In other words, the trick is to think about the party in terms of six or seven of these twenty-minute blocks, instead of one big amoebic blob of sugary-juice-induced chaos that no amount of parental determination will be able to surmount. This helps get your head in the right place. (Of course, if you are lucky enough to have a kid with a warm-weather birthday—and you can set them loose outside—the chaos is much easier to embrace.) It also helps to have someone else do all the think work for you, which is exactly what I've done in the following pages. Don't thank me yet; you still have to host the actual party. The games and art projects mentioned are all fleshed out more on pages 220–21, including Pass the Parcel, which is practically mandatory at our parties, but which you should feel free to interchange with simple, old-school gift opening if you think it's a little too much.

One last thing to remember: The schedule is a loose guide to make sure you stay on track, but you shouldn't cut short a good game of Ninja just because it's running over its allotted time. Going through the schedule too fast? That is something you want to avoid. Unless you're prepared to play Freeze Dance for a *looong* time.

MASTER PARTY CHART

THEME	ART PROJECT	GAME 1	GAME 2
COOKING PARTY	Decorate Chef's Hats with Names using markers and stickers	This Is Jeopardy! (see page 220) played with food categories: Local Restaurants, School Cafeteria, Birthday Girl Favorites, Candy, and Ice Cream	Cookie or Cupcake Decorating Contest (teams of three or four). Have the cookie dough and an array of mix-ins already made. Kids get to choose combos.
ALMOST SLEEPOVER PARTY	Decorate a Pillowcase	Purple Socks (see page 221)	Jelly Bean Counting Contest or Candy Hunt (see page 220)
PUPPY PARTY	Dog Ear Headbands (cut out floppy ears from felt and help the guests staple to headbands) and puppy face painting.	Simon Says (mix in commands like "bark like a dog," "play dead," or "roll over")	Dog-themed Celebrity (see page 221; mix in names like Beethoven, the host's dog, Snoopy, Benji, Clifford, Goofy, and Toto)
SOCCER PARTY	Decorate a Water Bottle	Soccer Bowling: Line up targets in your backyard and have the guests try to knock them down by kicking a soccer ball.	Soccer scrimmages if your backyard allows
SECRET AGENT PARTY	Decorate I.D. badges with secret code names and attach to lanyards	Scavenger Hunt around the house. (Split party into two teams.)	Frog Detective (see page 221)
JAPAN PARTY	Make your own Ninja headbands	Ninja!	Celebrity (page 221), the Japanese edition (Think: Totoro, Hello Kitty, Pokémon, the proprietor of your kid's favorite Japanese restaurant)

ALL GAMES ARE DESCRIBED IN THE GLOSSARY ON PAGE 220.

FOOD (or just make subs, page 223–25)	CAKE (or just make mud cake, page 202)	PARTY FAVORS (or gifts for Pass the Parcel, page 220)
Make-Your-Own Pizzas	Huddle all the contest cookies or cupcakes together, stick some candles in there, and start singing!	Cooking-themed stickers, cookie cutters, small chocolates, wooden spoons, photocopy of the birthday girl or boy's favorite recipe
Pigs in a Blanket	"Sheet" Cake decorated like a bed, with halved marshmallows for pillows.	Small stuffed animals, glow-in-the-dark ceiling stars, chocolate mint squares, fairy stickers
Hot Dogs; snacks and chips served in doggie bowls	Sheet cake (or any cake) topped with puppy figurines. Puppy-face cupcakes.	Dog bone–shaped candies, dog stickers, puppy figurines, paw-print rubber stamp or pencils, paw-print temporary tattoos
Stadium food—hot dogs, pizza, popcorn	Soccer-field sheet cake frosted green with white piping (much easier than a World Cup ball covered with a layer of draped and shaped fondant—people are really out of their minds)	Soccer ball key chains, hair wraps for girls, shoelace wraps for cleats, soccer tattoos and stickers, eye black, neon soccer socks, neon cleat laces, referee whistle, soccer ball chocolates, FIFA cards
Scent-sniffing (hot) dogs; pitchers of fruit smoothies labeled "Truth Serum"	Any kind of cake, but "Happy Birthday" written in code (backward? scrambled?) across the top	Spy glasses, fake mustaches, small magnifying glasses, Top Secret rubber stamps
California rolls, shrimp tempura, vegetable tempura, shu-mai dumplings	Forget the cake—it's candy sushi time! Form Rice Krispies Treats into rectangular sushi-size pieces, then top with Swedish fish, gummy worms, jelly beans.	So many options here—manga comics, those little Japanese erasers, chopsticks, bento boxes, Hello Kitty or Pokémon stickers

THE GAMES GLOSSARY

Pass the Parcel

If we had a signature party game in our house, this would be it. We buy the same number of presents as guests (one main present, like a small stuffed animal or a box of Japanese erasers, and then lots of tiny presents, like gum, a pair of vampire teeth, or stickers), then wrap each one in a single layer of gift wrap, with the big present being the "core" of the parcel. The kids pass this multilayered parcel around in a circle to music, and when the music stops, whoever is holding it gets to peel off a layer. Whichever parent is on music duty coordinates the music-stopping so everyone gets to open one. Stick to gifts that are small, flat, or compact. It will make your life much easier and the earth will thank you for not using a ton of gift wrap and tissue paper.

Jelly Bean Counting Contest

I love this because it gives the kids a purpose the minute they walk in the door. As soon as the guests arrive, direct them to a Mason jar filled with jelly beans. (Or M&M's or marbles, or candy corns or sweethearts, depending on your theme.) Place a piece of paper next to the jar with a list of all the guests' names, then have each guest write (beside his or her own name) how many jelly beans they think are in the jar. In addition to being a real head-scratcher for kids, this exercise is hilarious for grown-ups. One year, I remember the range in guesses spanned from twenty-four to one million.

Candy Hunt

While kids watch a quick movie (defined in our house by a seven-minute Pixar Short), "hide" candy all over the first floor. Depending on how young they are, you don't have to hide very thoroughly—a "scatter" might be more their speed. When the movie is over, give each kid a bag and tell them to go hunting. Be sure to save a few candies to bulk up the bag of the kid who inevitably ends up with one piece of Laffy Taffy and starts crying. (Does anyone actually like Laffy Taffy?)

This Is Jeopardy!

You know the drill here: Create six categories that the kids are likely to get excited about such as: Animals, Your Town, School Cafeteria Food, Sports, Maroon 5, and of course "The Birthday Girl/Boy." (I think my favorite moment in birthday history is Abby screaming, "I'll take Abby for five hundred!") On a poster board, draw a grid of boxes—six across, six down. You want your boxes to be the size of small Post-It notes. Write categories in the top row, then in each box of the grid write a Jeopardy question that relates to the category, keeping in mind that the harder ones should be worth more points and closer to the bottom. Cover each question with a Post-It note marked with the point value it's worth. The Post-Its across the top row should all say 100, the second row should all be 200, and so on. Divide the guests into two groups. When it's time to play, the first group picks a category and point value (such as "Music for 300!"), then you remove the Post-It to reveal the question. ("What famous singer shares a last name with the fourth planet from the sun?"*) If they get the question right, hand them the Post-It with the point value. If they don't get the question right, the other team gets a shot. Whichever team has the most points at the end of the game wins.
*Bruno Mars

Purple Socks

I grew up playing this game, and somehow I seem to be the only person who has ever heard of it. Cut about a hundred sock shapes out of purple construction paper (they don't have to be perfect, and it goes a lot faster when you fold over and layer your paper). Make a list of about twenty things the kids might show up with. For instance, for an Almost Sleepover Party, you might list "sleeping bags that are pink," or "sleeping bag that has a soccer ball on it," or "stuffed animal," or "pajamas with a princess on it," or "anything that sparkles." The last item should always be purple socks. The leader says, "Raise your hand if you have . . . ," and reads each item from the list, for example, "Raise your hand if you have a stuffed animal." The leader then gives a purple paper sock to every kid who has brought a stuffed animal. Kids get double points for wearing actual purple socks. At the end, whoever has the most cutouts wins.

Celebrity

We've been known to play this at Thanksgiving and big family get-togethers in addition to just birthday parties. (That way, all the grown-ups can try to outdo one another with obscure names. Jane Pauley? Kirk Cameron?)

For birthday parties, though, it works like this: Give each kid five small pieces of paper and have them write one celebrity on each. (Explain to them that a "celebrity" can also be a teacher, a pet, a coach, and not necessarily someone who appears regularly in *Us Weekly*.) Collect all the slips of paper in a hat or a bowl, weeding out what will likely be multiple entries of Taylor Swift or LeBron James or whoever happens to be president of the United States. Divide the guests into two groups and explain the rules. We favor the three-round version of Celebrity: *Round 1:* Decide which group will go first and have that group elect one person to be the first name-picker. The name-picker selects a slip of paper from the bowl, then tries to describe the celebrity to her team without identifying that celebrity by name. (For instance: If she selects the name "Katniss Everdeen," the name-picker might say, "She's the hero in *Hunger Games*! Jennifer Lawrence plays her in the movie!" If she selects "Mrs. Metrano," she might say "Phoebe's third-grade teacher!") Once the team gets it right, the name-picker sets the slip of paper aside, then selects another celebrity from the bowl and on and on. They get one point for

every name they guess right in the course of one minute. (The other team should be timing.) The next group does the same thing, and the teams go back and forth, rotating name-pickers, until the bowl is empty. Round 2: Same thing, same names in the pot, but during this round, the name-picker only has three words to describe the celebrity on the paper. For instance, "Hunger Games Hero" or "Third-Grade Teacher." Round 3: Same thing, same names in pot, but no words at all, so essentially it's charades. For instance, acting like you are shooting a bow-and-arrow might be a wise approach to Katness Everdeen. I love this game because it requires no special gear, just paper and pens.

Frog Detective

Everyone sits in a circle. One girl or boy—the frog detective—leaves the room, then a parent appoints a leader among those left behind. The leader starts a pattern (clapping hands, tapping shoulders, etc.) and everyone follows when he or she changes the pattern. The Frog Detective comes back into the room and is charged with figuring out who is changing the pattern. Once she guesses the leader, it's the leader's turn to play detective.

FOOT-LONG PARTY SUBS
One classic Italian, one vegetarian, piled high. (Note: They also come in handy on Super Bowl Sunday.)

The Sick-of-Pizza Party Food Option: Foot-Long Subs

These can be made up to a day ahead of time—but to avoid soggy bread, don't drizzle the dressing on the baguette until right before the party starts. Note: While it's exciting and dramatic to stuff these subs nice and high, keep in mind the mouth sizes of the party guests, which I'm guessing are on the small side. (To combat this, feel free to pull some of the bread out of the baguette—so the crusts look sort of like canoes—before you start assembling.) Plan on about five sandwiches per twelve-inch baguette. (Anything left over goes right into the lunch box.)

CLASSIC ITALIAN SUB

This is what you will need for one twelve-inch sub to feed five small people. Double or triple as needed depending on the size of the party. I like to halve all the meat and cheese rounds so it's easier to slightly overlap as you assemble.

SERVES 5 KIDS

1 12-inch baguette, the best quality you can find

3 ounces roast turkey

3 ounces salami or soppressata

3 ounces bologna (we like turkey bologna)

3 ounces provolone cheese

1 large tomato, the best you can find,
    sliced horizontally and thin

8 to 10 lettuce leaves from a head of Bibb,
    Boston, romaine, or oak leaf

¼ small red onion, very thinly sliced

¼ cup red wine vinegar

⅓ cup good-quality olive oil

½ teaspoon dried oregano

• Slice the baguette in half lengthwise and on one half, start layering each of the meats in rows (overlapping slightly), then the cheese, then the tomato. Distribute the lettuce and onion evenly on top.

- When ready to serve, whisk together the vinegar, olive oil, and oregano until emulsified, and then drizzle down the top half of the baguette.
- Close the sandwich with the top baguette half, then stick in 5 toothpicks, one every 2 to 2½ inches along the top. Place on a cutting board and slice into 5 separate sandwiches.

VEGETARIAN SUB

I once brought this veggie sub to a family picnic as an option for a few adults I knew wouldn't necessarily want to eat a stack of cured Italian pork for lunch. (I had also brought along the Classic Italian Sub on page 223.) The adults were out of luck, though, because almost all the kids opted for the veg version over the meat. Below is what you will need for one twelve-inch sub to feed five people. Double or triple as needed depending on the size of your party. You can use the classic Italian red wine vinegar and oregano dressing for this since you probably already have that on hand—but also keep in mind that the Basic Vinaigrette on page 118 works well, too.

SERVES 5 KIDS

1 12-inch baguette, the best quality you can find

1 avocado, halved and sliced into thin half-moons

3 ounces Swiss or provolone cheese

24 thin slices of hothouse cucumbers
   (the narrow kind you don't have to peel or seed
   that usually comes wrapped in plastic),
   from about 1 small cucumber

1 large tomato, the best you can find, sliced (very thin)
   horizontally and then in half

8 to 10 lettuce leaves from a head of Bibb, Boston,
   romaine, or oak leaf

¼ small red onion, very thinly sliced

¼ cup red wine vinegar

⅓ cup good-quality olive oil

½ teaspoon dried oregano

1 tablespoon mayonnaise

- Slice the baguette in half lengthwise and on the bottom half, start by layering the avocado then the cheese, slightly overlapping as you go. Lay down the cucumbers in two adjacent rows, overlapping slightly, on top of the cheese. Distribute the tomato halves, overlapping as well, then the lettuce and onion.
- When ready to serve, whisk together the vinegar, olive oil, and oregano until emulsified, then drizzle on the top baguette half. Spread the mayo on top of the vinaigrette.
- Close the sandwich with the top baguette half, then stick in 5 toothpicks, one every 2 to 2½ inches along the top. Place on a cutting board and slice into 5 separate sandwiches.

Sun 2/22   Sweet + Spicy Shrimp + Scallops
Mon 2/23   Pork + Kale Stir-whatever [Asian?]
Tue 2/24   Mercurio? Baked Ziti + Meatballs
Wed 2/25
Thu 2/26
Fri 2/27   Herring's Dinner
Sat 2/28   Lasagna   (Phoebe out)
Sun 2/29 3/1 Lawlers   Meatloaf + Potatoes
Mon 3/2   Pork + Kale w/Tomatoes /Bugialli   blackbeans + cotija
Tue 3/3   Roast Chicken + Salad
Wed 3/4   Pomegranate-Soy Pork Tacos with Guac + Pom seeds
Thu 3/5   Turkey meatloaf
Friday 3/6 PHOEBE's PARTY (a little late) Frank Pepe's

Friday 3/7 Navia - Peter - Bonnie - Jonathan
Sat 3/7
Sun 3/8   Thai Red Lentil Soup w/ Snap Peas
Mon 3/9   Ravioli + Marsala Burgers [soccer]
Tue 3/10   Miso-Butter Tofu
Wed 3/11   Salad Sandwiches
Thu 3/12   SOUP-OFF Springhurst
Fri 3/13   Chicken Piri Piri
Sat 3/14   Fried Flounder
Sun 3/15   Pan-Fried thighs with leeks
Mon 3/16   BBQ chicken sandwiches
Tue 3/17
Wed 3/18
Thu 3/19   Pork Tacos

PART IV

FAMILY DINNERS

Did I Ever Tell You . . . ? / Sunday Dinners
Eating in Front of the TV
After-Dinner Rituals / On Signature Dinners

DID I EVER TELL YOU . . . ?

A few years ago, I discovered an eight-word phrase that added a whole new energy to family dinner. And, it's not "Finish your vegetables or else there's no dessert."

The phrase? It's more like a question, and it goes like this:

Did I ever tell you about the time . . . ?

As in: "Did I ever tell you about the time the suitcases flew off the roof of Papa's car on the New Jersey Turnpike?"

As in: "Did I ever tell you about the time I came home at four o'clock in the morning and got in *huuuuge* trouble?"

As in: "Did I ever tell you about the time Uncle Mike tried to cook a turkey with a lightbulb?"

As in: "Did I ever tell you about the time Uncle Tony drove the Ford Pinto through the garage door?"

As in: "Did I ever tell you about the time Aunt Lynn shook the bottle of salad dressing at the dinner table . . . without realizing that the bottle's top was off?"

As in: "Did I ever tell you the story about the time Daddy's high school girlfriend asked him to throw a fastball to her as hard as he could—which she ended up catching with her forehead?"

As in: "Did I ever tell you about the time my high school boyfriend, a six-one, two-hundred-pound tight end, came over for dinner and Nana served him a single hamburger that fit in the palm of his hand?"

As in: "Did I ever tell you about the time we accidentally shut my childhood cat in the refrigerator all day?"

As in: "Did we ever tell you about the time Daddy cooked soup for your grandparents and Nana called it . . . *interesting*?"

That soup story was the first time I discovered the eight-word trick. It wasn't a premeditated question. I hadn't been saving it up all day to trigger dinnertime conversation. We were eating soup that night, so the story just happened to come out. As soon as it did, though, as soon as I uttered those magic words—*Did I ever tell you about the time*—I noticed the focus adjust in their eyeballs like the lens on a camera. I had their undivided attention, something that hadn't happened in hours, maybe days.

I used to turn
on the fairy
lights only
when we had a
special guest
or if there was
something to
celebrate. Now,
they're pretty
much illuminated
24/7.

Did I ever tell you about the time . . .

Storytelling. It's as good a hook as any I know. As good a strategy for instigating meaningful conversation as I can think of.

I started blogging about family dinner in 2010, when my daughters were six and eight years old. At that point in our lives, "how to have meaningful conversation" fell somewhere around number thirty-five on the family dinner checklist. Ranked much higher were the logistical concerns: *How* to get home in time to cook? *When* to shop? *Who* will cook? *How,* dear Lord, HOW will we convince the kids to like Ottolenghi's Black Pepper Tofu? If I could get those questions answered, and sit down to a meal I felt good about serving the kids, soul intact, I was grateful for whatever conversation transpired at the table—meaningful or not. How was your day? Who'd you sit with at lunch? Who does your best friend have a crush on *now*? Not to sound like a self-help book you'd find at the airport, but that day-to-day stuff isn't the small stuff. It's everything.

These days, there are still dinner logistics to negotiate, of course, but they tend to be more manageable ones. For instance, two to three nights a week I find myself alone in the house at seven o'clock waiting for my kids to come home from their late-afternoon activities. After so many years of the reverse, of *them* waiting for *me* to return from work, after so many years of having a ticking stopwatch be the soundtrack to my working-parent life, this scenario is still hard to get my head around.

(Also hard to get my head around: They still won't go near tofu.)

Family dinner will always be a place to recharge and reassure, and, ahem, reject, but as the kids have gotten older, I've found I appreciate the ritual for a different kind of perk: It appears to be the most natural place to tell stories. I'm not talking Garrison Keillor on *A Prairie Home Companion* here. (Though if you are capable of that, go for it!) I mean bringing up the simplest moments in family history, like the ones I mentioned earlier—A fastball that went awry? A mishap with a cat? A bad choice for dinner? None of these on their own would ever be categorized as "epic," or even that fascinating, but it hardly matters. If your kids are like mine, they love hearing stories about where they came from and who we are as a family. Particularly when those stories include a glimpse of their parents behaving in a way that is far from perfect. Beyond just having their attention, beyond giving us something to talk about besides the meatballs, all these stories help us build up the family narrative, the never-ending, multilayered yarn they've been hearing their whole lives.

Is the dinner table the only place this can happen? Of course not. But in our world, it certainly appears to be the most logical, considering it's the only guaranteed undivided family time we have all day.

Great, I'm sure you're thinking. *Now, in addition to nailing down a repertoire of healthy, wholesome, local, seasonal, organic, and quick weeknight recipes, I also have to show up to the table with an entertaining tale to tell?*

No. Obviously. But I'll bet you can find some creative inspiration from the food that's right in front of you.

That soup story, for instance. A few weeks ago, when I decided to experiment with a red lentil soup for dinner, the girls were incredulous. *Soup for dinner? Soup's not a dinner, soup's an appetizer!* It reminded us of the time Andy invited my parents over for dinner to his first Brooklyn apartment in 1994. It might have been the first time he ever "officially" entertained. (Which, when you really think about it, is pretty gutsy for a twenty-three-year-old.) What did he decide to serve? Chicken and barley soup, one of his childhood favorites. I think it was the first time in my parents' lives they ever had soup as a main course. After the meal was over and I asked my mom what she thought, she famously declared the meal "interesting." Thanks to years of stories just like this one—the *interesting* sweater unwrapped on Christmas morning, the *interesting* chairs we selected for our living room, the *interesting* idea to use raw cranberries instead of cooked on Thanksgiving—we now recognize that this word is really code for, "Yeah, I appreciate the effort and all, but I'm not buying it."

Is this story meaningful to anyone outside of my family? No. But it doesn't have to be. The only audience that counts is the one sitting around my dinner table. And the same applies to yours.

CURRIED RED LENTIL SOUP WITH GREENS

There's still one stubborn holdout at our table who, like her grandmother, doesn't love the idea of soup and only soup for dinner. But this one's so good and so easy that I make it all the time anyway. It's an especially great soup for the end of the week, when you don't feel like a high-maintenance dinner and you're trying to get rid of the almost-wilted greens and vegetables in the refrigerator. Our favorite leafy green here is Tuscan kale, but you can use spinach or chard, too.

SERVES 4 TO 6

2 tablespoons neutral oil (such as sunflower
　　or grapeseed, but olive oil is okay in a pinch)

½ medium onion, finely minced (about 1 cup)

1 clove garlic, minced

1 tablespoon peeled and minced fresh ginger
　　(from about a ½-inch piece)

kosher salt and freshly ground pepper

¼ teaspoon Thai curry paste

2 teaspoons curry powder

2 cups (14 ounces) red lentils

4 cups vegetable stock

1 tablespoon white miso (optional)

⅓ cup light coconut milk

handful of shredded dark leafy greens

suggested toppings: plain yogurt, squeeze of fresh lime juice,
　　chopped fresh cilantro, drizzle of Sriracha sauce

• In a medium pot over medium heat, heat the oil. Add the onion, garlic, and ginger, season with salt and pepper, and cook until soft. Using a wooden spoon, smush in the Thai curry paste and curry powder until blended. Add the lentils and stir until they are all glistening with oil. Add the vegetable stock and bring to a boil. Lower the heat to a simmer and cook for 15 to 20 minutes, until the lentils are tender and start breaking apart. (You might have to add up to 1¼ cups water as the soup simmers; the lentils should always be slightly submerged.) Whisk the miso, if using, with a little water and add to the soup, then, using an immersion blender, whirl the soup until it's smooth and blended. Turn off the heat. Drizzle in the coconut milk and stir in the greens. Serve with desired toppings.

Curried Red Lentil Soup:
So easy, all the instructions
fit on a single Post-It note.

BROTH

— CILANTRO
— YOGURT
— SRIRACHA
— GREENS
Saute ginger, garlic,
onion. Smush in
curry paste, salt &
pepper. Add lentils.
— Veg broth, simmer.
— whir w/
immersion blender.

SUNDAY DINNERS

Back in the olden days, before we had kids, when we slept until our bodies, and not the baby monitor, told us to wake up, when our biggest decision was whether to check the luggage or go with carry-on, my coworker Meryl asked Andy and me out to dinner.

"Sure! That sounds like fun—when were you thinking?"

We had one of those familiar back-and-forths, cross-referencing our leather-bound Filofaxes (told you: olden days), checking with our spouses off to the side of the receiver, resisting the urge to joke "How 'bout never?" *Ha ha ha.* "Does never work for you?" Now that I am so used to kids' sports hijacking our weekends, it's hard to remember what we were all so busy with, but nonetheless, we couldn't come up with a date that worked. We started flipping pages in our calendars, looking a few weeks out.

"How about three weeks from now? Sunday the twenty-first?" Meryl said.

I gasped privately. *Did she say Sunday the twenty-first?*

Sunday the twenty-first was totally free. Of course it was . . . it was a *Sunday*! Who makes plans on a Sunday for dinner with anyone but family?

"Can't that day," I finally told her. "I have plans."

When I hung up on her, I turned to Andy and said, "She wanted to make plans on a *Sunday*."

As far back as I can remember, it's been a given that we end the weekend with family at our own table, whether that table has been in our Brooklyn apartment, in our first house in the suburbs, or in my parents' or sister's house across the county. Only under special circumstances—Super Bowls, Oscar Nights, invitations we can't weasel our way out of—do we stray from this policy. I realize I'm not alone here. No matter what Sunday dinner looks like in your house, whether it involves a proper roast on a Wedgwood platter, some dogs on the backyard grill, or the ambient roar of an NFL crowd on TV pulsing in the background, I'm guessing the philosophy behind it is most likely the same: *Rest, recalibrate, reconnect. We've got a long week ahead of us.*

When people ask me for advice on how to make family dinner happen more regularly, I always tell them to start with Sunday dinner. For a lot of families, it's the only guaranteed day when there's a little more time—maybe even a whole glorious afternoon—to focus on *making* a meal, and not just consuming it. It's the one day a week when people who hate to cook might understand the idea that putting together a big meal can actually be therapeutic. The one day when you might have the patience to build a lasagna with your toddler. Or the one day when spying something like *gochujang* in a recipe doesn't read like an affront to your very existence. In fact, on Sunday, that kind of moment, instead of stoking your ire at the whole dinner-making enterprise in general, might even inspire you to make a pit stop at that Korean market you always pass on the way to the baseball game.

My family manages to sit down together most weeknights, but that doesn't make Sunday dinner any less sacred in our house. We cook differently on Sundays. In colder weather, we might start the main dish early in the day, braising a pork shoulder or short ribs for a few luxurious hours that we'd be hard-pressed to find during the week, letting the caramelizing vegetables and simmering meat perform their most important duty, i.e., infusing the house with a smell that telegraphs warmth, happiness, and home.

On warmer nights, our big Sunday meals center around the grill and whatever bounty we've brought home from our farmer's market the day before: Persnickety, high-maintenance fava beans, which on any other day of the week would require a small army of prep cooks to shell and blanch and peel if we wanted to eat dinner before midnight; maybe some celeriac? Or purple peppers or rhubarb or garlic scapes or a whole yellow-spotted mackerel that the fish guy said had been swimming a few hours earlier? How on earth does one turn all these things into dinner? Good thing we have a few hours to do nothing else but figure it out.

WINTER SUNDAY DINNER

Shredded Pork Lettuce Wraps with Pomegranates

Cilantro-Lime Rice

SHREDDED PORK LETTUCE WRAPS WITH POMEGRANATES

I love this meal, especially toward the end of winter when I've had my fill of starchy, cheesy, rich comfort food. It's somehow both indulgent and bright tasting, and, unlike most braised meat dishes, it won't leave you rolling away from the table, swearing off food until the spring crocuses rear their hopeful little heads. Make sure you freeze any leftover meat. Your weeknight self will thank you.

SERVES 4

3 tablespoons good-quality olive oil

1 boneless pork loin (2½ to 3 pounds), patted dry and salted and peppered

1 small onion, chopped (about 1 cup)

1 tablespoon minced peeled fresh ginger (from about a ½-inch piece)

1 clove garlic, minced

kosher salt and freshly ground pepper

½ cup low-sodium soy sauce

1½ cups pomegranate juice

¾ cup water

1 tablespoon Sriracha sauce

10 to 12 sturdy, concave Bibb lettuce leaves

suggested toppings: pomegranate seeds, sliced avocado,
    chopped apples, diced jicama

• Preheat the oven to 325°F. In a large Dutch oven set over medium-high heat, add the olive oil. Brown the pork loin on all sides so you get a nice golden crust, about 5 minutes

One crucial qualification for a
winter Sunday dinner recipe: It
must make the house smell obscenely
delicious. The shredded pork
in these lettuce cups takes care
of that handily.

per side. (Warning: It's going to splatter. Wear an apron.) Remove to a plate. Decrease the heat to medium low. Add the onion, ginger, garlic, and salt and pepper, then cook until the onion is soft, about 3 minutes.

• Return the pork to the pot. Add the soy sauce, pomegranate juice, water, and Sriracha, whisking to combine. (You want the liquid to come a third of the way up the loin.) Bring to a boil, then transfer to the oven with the lid slightly ajar. Cook for 3 hours, flipping once at the 1-hour mark and again at the 2-hour mark. It's ready when the meat falls apart easily if pulled with a fork. Shred the pork in the pot and toss in what remains of the braising liquid, which should be thick and saucy. (If the liquid is not saucy, remove the pork before shredding, place the pot on a burner, and turn the heat to high. Boil down until the sauce reaches the desired consistency.)

• "Stuff" each lettuce leaf with a little pork, and place on plates or a platter. Serve with toppings on the side and have diners customize their own wraps.

CILANTRO-LIME RICE

If your children are wary of the lettuce wrapping part of this meal, you can just as easily turn the recipe into a Rice Bowl with Shredded Pork, topping with the pomegranate seeds and avocado. Either way, you want a bowl of this rice accompanying your main.

SERVES 4

1½ cups white or brown rice
1 tablespoon butter
1 teaspoon kosher salt
⅓ cup chopped fresh cilantro leaves
juice from 1 lime

• Prepare the rice according to the package directions. While the rice is still warm, toss it with the butter, salt, cilantro, and lime juice.

```
┌ ─ ─ ─ ─ ─ ─ ─ ─ ─ ─ ─ ─ ─ ─ ─ ─ ─ ─ ─ ─ ─ ─ ─ ─ ┐
```

SPRING SUNDAY DINNER

Harissa Roasted Chicken / Baked Polenta with Feta

Greenest Green Salad

```
└ ─ ─ ─ ─ ─ ─ ─ ─ ─ ─ ─ ─ ─ ─ ─ ─ ─ ─ ─ ─ ─ ─ ─ ─ ┘
```

HARISSA ROASTED CHICKEN

Nothing says Sunday quite like a roasted chicken. This version calls for harissa, a chile paste used in Middle Eastern cooking, which adds a nice kick if you're in the mood to switch things up a bit. It can be found in Middle Eastern markets or the international aisles of better supermarkets.

SERVES 4

4 tablespoons (½ stick) butter

1 whole roasting chicken (3 to 4 pounds),
   giblets removed from inside, patted completely dry
   inside and out with paper towels

1 small onion, halved

½ lemon

3 to 4 cloves garlic, halved

kosher salt and freshly ground pepper

3 tablespoons harissa

• Preheat the oven to 425°F.

• Melt the butter over low heat in a small saucepan. Turn off the heat. Place the chicken on a rack inside a roasting pan and stuff the cavity with the onion halves, lemon, and garlic. Tie the chicken's legs together with kitchen twine, then brush the chicken all over with about a tablespoon of the melted butter. (Do not discard the butter that remains in the saucepan; you should have about 3 tablespoons left.) Sprinkle salt and pepper all over the chicken.

• Roast the chicken for 45 minutes. Meanwhile, add the harissa to the melted butter.

241

Turn the heat to medium low and stir until combined. Remove from the heat and let rest on the stovetop.

• After 45 minutes, generously brush the chicken with the harissa glaze. Roast for another 20 minutes. Glaze again. Roast for another 10 minutes or until the chicken is cooked through and the legs wiggle easily. (The general rule for making sure a chicken is done is to roast for 18 to 20 minutes per pound.) Slice and serve.

BAKED POLENTA WITH FETA

This side dish isn't just for Sunday dinners—we make it ALL. THE. TIME. When we entertain, too.

SERVES 4 TO 6

2 tablespoons unsalted butter
5 cups good-quality chicken stock
   (homemade if you can swing it)
1¼ cups finely ground cornmeal
kosher salt (the amount depends on the saltiness of your stock)
drizzle of half-and-half or heavy whipping cream
handful of crumbled feta cheese
good-quality olive oil, for drizzling
sea salt and freshly ground pepper, for sprinkling

• Grease a 9-inch pie plate with 1 tablespoon of the butter, reserving what remains. Bring the stock to a boil in a medium saucepan, then lower the heat to a simmer. Gradually add the cornmeal, whisking constantly to prevent clumping. Add salt to taste. Continue to whisk for another 10 to 12 minutes, until the polenta thickens and pulls away from the sides of the pan. Remove from the heat, stir in the remaining butter (including what was left over from greasing the pie plate), and stir in the cream. Pour into the pie plate and allow to cool slightly. Chill covered for at least an hour.

• Preheat the oven to 425°F. While the oven heats, remove the polenta from the refrigerator and sprinkle the feta on top. Bake for 20 minutes, until the cheese is slightly golden. Serve drizzled with olive oil and sprinkled with salt and pepper.

"I'M GUESSING THE
PHILOSOPHY BEHIND
MOST FAMILIES'
SUNDAY DINNERS
ARE THE SAME:
REST, RECALIBRATE,
RECONNECT.
WE'VE GOT A LONG
WEEK AHEAD OF US."

Nothing shouts
"Spring is here!"
quite like our
Greenest Green Salad.
If you have access
to good avocados,
throw in one of those
(sliced) as well.

GREENEST GREEN SALAD

The goal with this salad is to make it as monochromatically green as possible.
The way I see it, if you're going to do it, do it.

SERVES 4

Dressing

2 teaspoons Dijon mustard

¼ cup red wine vinegar

¼ teaspoon honey

squeeze of fresh lemon juice

kosher salt and freshly ground pepper

½ cup good-quality olive oil

Salad

1 bunch of asparagus (about 1 pound)

¾ cup green peas (fresh or thawed frozen)

1 head of Bibb lettuce, washed and leaves torn

½ cup chopped fresh cilantro leaves

¼ cup chopped fresh mint leaves

¼ cup chopped fresh dill

freshly grated Parmigiano-Reggiano

• Make the dressing: In a small jar or measuring cup, shake or whisk together the mustard, vinegar, honey, lemon juice, and salt and pepper. Add the olive oil and shake or whisk again until emulsified.

• Prepare the salad: In a deep-sided skillet, bring salted water to a gentle boil. Add the asparagus and peas and cook for 3 to 4 minutes (depending on the thickness of the spears), then plunge the vegetables into a bowl of ice water to stop the cooking and preserve the bright green color. Drain and allow to dry completely.

• Add the peas and asparagus to a large bowl along with the lettuce, cilantro, mint, and dill. Toss with the dressing. Scatter on a serving platter and top with freshly grated Parm.

GRILLED SOY-GLAZED PORK CHOPS

Sweet and spicy, smoky and tender, I beg Andy to make these for us all summer long.

SERVES 4

4 bone-in pork chops, about 4 pounds total

kosher salt and freshly ground pepper

¼ cup soy sauce

1 tablespoon rice wine vinegar

1 tablespoon fresh lime juice (from about ½ lime)

1 teaspoon light brown sugar, packed

¼ teaspoon Sriracha sauce (optional)

• Make a fire in a charcoal grill or preheat a gas grill to medium.

• Sprinkle the chops with salt and pepper. Bring them to room temperature. In a small bowl or measuring cup, mix together the soy sauce, vinegar, lime juice, brown sugar, and Sriracha, if using. Grill the chops over medium-hot coals, turning frequently, until cooked through, 10 to 12 minutes total. Right before you are about to remove the chops, brush them with the soy glaze and flip 4 or 5 more times until they look glazed and lacquered.

When grilled soy-glazed pork chops are on Sunday's menu, you might even forget—at least momentarily—that the work week starts tomorrow.

GRILLED HALLOUMI AND ASPARAGUS WITH PESTO

Halloumi is a firm Greek sheep-goat blend that is available at most cheese shops and specialty markets, and it holds the distinguished honor of being a cheese you can actually grill right on the grates. (And in the off-season, you can pan-fry it.) This dish works as either a side or a vegetarian main, especially if you toss in a cup of quinoa or farro. P.S.: When your kids ask you what's for dinner, tell them "grilled cheese."

SERVES 4

Pesto

1 large bunch of basil, stems removed, rinsed
    (about 2 packed cups)
⅓ cup good-quality olive oil, plus more for serving
¼ cup pine nuts
3 tablespoons freshly grated Parmigiano-Reggiano
1 tablespoon fresh lemon juice
kosher salt and freshly ground pepper

Asparagus and Halloumi

1 bunch of asparagus, trimmed
½ red onion, sliced in ¼-inch wedges, root end intact
½ lemon, sliced in rounds
¼ cup good-quality olive oil
kosher salt and freshly ground pepper
1 8-ounce block halloumi cheese,
    sliced horizontally and brushed with olive oil

• Make the pesto: Bring a small saucepan of water to a boil, then reduce to a simmer. Blanch the basil for 30 seconds, then immediately plunge in an ice bath (this helps it stay greener longer). Pat basil dry with paper towels. Do not discard the warm water.

• Whirl together the basil and the remaining ingredients in a blender. Slowly drizzle a little of the hot water into the pesto until it reaches a saucy, but not liquidy, consistency. Remove to a small bowl and set aside.

• Make a fire in a charcoal grill or preheat a gas grill to medium.

• In a medium bowl, toss the asparagus, red onion, and lemon with the olive oil and salt and pepper. If you have a grill basket—and you should, these things are lifesavers, especially in the asparagus department—add the vegetables and lemon to the basket and grill over medium-hot coals until everything is softened and charred, 5 to 7 minutes, though the onions might take a bit longer. (If you don't have a grill basket, you can use skewers.) Meanwhile, if there's room, add the halloumi slices to the grill and cook until slightly softened and grill marks appear, about 4 minutes a side. (If there isn't room, just grill the cheese after the vegetables come off.) Add to a large platter along with the vegetables, drizzle with the pesto, and serve.

SLICED TOMATOES WITH SEA SALT AND CHIVES

Every year I try to come up with some new way to take advantage of in-season, heavy, full-bodied heirloom tomatoes, and every year I end up in the same place: a platter of multicolored beauties, drizzled with good olive oil, and sprinkled with sea salt and fresh-snipped chives. It's like Dorothy said: "If I ever go looking for my heart's desire again, I won't look any further than my own backyard."

PEACH BERRY COBBLER

This recipe is a real stand-by in our house and, in fact, hails from Andy's mom, who's been baking it for decades. You can go straight-up peach or any direction the market is telling you to, but we tend to favor a peach-blackberry or peach-blueberry blend. (In that case, I use about nine medium peaches with one cup of berries.) The key is to almost fill the baking dish with whichever fruit you choose.

SERVES 6 TO 8

7 to 8 cups peeled, sliced fresh peaches or nectarines,
   blackberries, blueberries, or raspberries, enough to mostly fill
   a 9 by 13-inch baking dish
2 tablespoons fresh lemon juice (from about ½ lemon)
1 cup all-purpose flour, whisked
1 cup sugar
1 teaspoon kosher salt
¾ teaspoon ground cinnamon
1 egg, lightly beaten
5 tablespoons butter, melted
vanilla ice cream or whipped cream (see page 59), for serving

- Preheat the oven to 375°F.
- Place the peaches and berries in a 9 by 13-inch baking dish. Sprinkle with the lemon juice and toss. In a medium mixing bowl, whisk together the dry ingredients. Add the egg, tossing with a fork until the mixture is crumbly, using your hands if you want. (It should not be mushy.) Sprinkle the flour-egg mixture over the fruit until it's mostly covered (with little pieces of fruit poking out here and there), then drizzle as evenly as possible with the melted butter.
- Bake for 40 to 45 minutes, until the fruit is bubbly and the crust is golden.
- Serve the cobbler warm with ice cream or whipped cream (see page 59) if desired.

FALL SUNDAY DINNER

Grandma Jody's Lasagna
"Leaf"

When we do Sunday dinners at my parents' house, my father will make sure we know "not to expect anything fancy." I'm pretty sure he thinks that saying this out loud will somehow prevent my mother from sending him all over town to procure various specialty items for her specialty-loving grandkids. It never works. In the end the sideboard in their dining room will be lined up with all the girls' favorite foods: crispy chicken Milanese or lasagna with a simply dressed green salad (my mom has always called this "leaf"). Like a true Italian, she'll end the meal with a platter of fresh fruit.

GRANDMA JODY'S LASAGNA

My mom has never messed around with the traditional béchamel when making lasagna. Her recipe is a strict assembly job, making it a perfect dinner for kids to help out with, something neither the kids nor the grown-ups in our house seem to ever find time for on a weeknight.

SERVES 8

4 cups homemade marinara sauce (recipe follows)
    or good-quality store-bought marinara
      (we love Rao's, Cucina Antica, or Ooma Tesoro's)
2 tablespoons good-quality olive oil
1 clove garlic, halved
¼ cup finely chopped onion

1 cup frozen spinach, thawed
   (or one 9-ounce bag or bunch spinach, trimmed,
   rinsed, and cooked) and squeezed dry

pinch of freshly grated nutmeg (⅛ teaspoon)

kosher salt and freshly ground pepper

2 links (about 8 ounces) good-quality sweet Italian sausage
   (or to taste, or eliminate to make this vegetarian), skins removed

1¼ cups fresh ricotta cheese

1 egg, lightly beaten

¾ cup freshly grated Parmigiano-Reggiano

2 cups grated fresh mozzarella cheese
   (from an 8-ounce ball mozzarella)

1 pound no-cook lasagna noodles

- Preheat the oven to 350°F.
- If you are making your own marinara, do that first. If you're not, place the jar on the counter. It is the first ingredient in your Lasagna Assembly Line. (No need to heat it up.)
- Add the olive oil to a skillet set over medium heat. Cook the garlic halves cut side down to infuse the oil, about 2 minutes. Remove. Add the onions and cook until wilted, about 2 minutes. Add the spinach, the nutmeg, and salt and pepper to taste, and cook until the spinach is warmed through (or wilted if you're using fresh). Transfer to a bowl and set on your assembly line. To the same skillet, over medium-high heat, add the sausage, breaking it up into crumbles with a fork, and cook until brown, about 5 minutes. Remove from the skillet to a bowl. Add the bowl to your assembly line.
- In a medium bowl, stir together the ricotta, egg, ½ cup of the Parm, and all but about ¼ cup of the mozzarella. Season generously with salt and pepper. Add the bowl to your assembly line.
- Now, time for the fun part. Scoop about ½ cup of the marinara into the bottom of a 9 by 13-inch baking dish and "paint" the bottom completely with the back of a spoon. Place lasagna noodles on top, trimming the noodles if you have to in order to cover the sauce completely. Add another layer of sauce on top, then top with sausage crumbles and dollops of both the cheese mixture and the spinach mixture, flattening them a bit with your spoon. Repeat with the remaining noodles and toppings, finishing with only a thin layer of sauce, the remaining mozzarella, and the remaining Parm.
- Cover the dish with foil and bake for 40 minutes, until everything looks bubbly. Remove the foil and bake for another 10 minutes.
- Allow to cool slightly, which will make it easier to cut.

GRANDMA JODY'S MARINARA

Freeze any leftover sauce in flattened zip-top plastic bags.

MAKES 4 CUPS

¼ cup good-quality olive oil

4 heaping tablespoons finely chopped onion (about ½ small onion)

1 clove garlic, minced (2 cloves if you are a garlic lover)

kosher salt and freshly ground pepper

1 tablespoon dried oregano

quick shake of red pepper flakes

2 teaspoons sugar

2 tablespoons tomato paste

¼ cup water

1 28-ounce can tomato puree

2 basil leaves, torn (optional)

• Set a medium saucepan over medium heat. Add the olive oil and onions and cook until the onions have softened, about 3 minutes. Add the garlic, salt and pepper, oregano, and red pepper flakes and cook for another minute, watching closely so the garlic doesn't burn. Add the sugar and smush in the tomato paste, along with the water, until all the onions are coated in tomato. Stir in the tomato puree and basil, if using, and bring to a boil. Reduce the heat and simmer covered, lid slightly ajar, for 20 to 25 minutes.

"LEAF"

Yes, this hardly belongs in a book that's shelved in the Culinary Arts section of the Library of Congress. But the truth is, when I am eating something as substantial and cheesy as lasagna, all I want next to it is something that epitomizes simplicity and freshness. And that's exactly what my mom's "leaf" delivers. As always when making something with so few ingredients, it's important that those few ingredients be of the best quality you can get your hands on, including the olive oil.

SERVES 4 TO 6

2 heads of Bibb lettuce, washed and torn into bite-size pieces

1 shallot, minced

squeeze of fresh lemon juice

drizzle of good-quality olive oil

kosher salt and freshly ground pepper

• Add the lettuce to a salad bowl and top with the shallots, lemon juice, olive oil, and salt and pepper to taste.

2 cans crab meat (Geisha $1.2?)
3 cups milk
6 eggs   beat
1 3/4 tea. salt)
1-2 tea. dry mustard

Place 1/2 of bread in buttered casserole.
Add 1/2 crab. Sprinkle 1/2 cheese. Repeat.
Pour liquid over top and add mustard. Sprinkle
with paprika.
Make day before   and refrigerate over
night.
Bake 350° for 50 to 60 minutes.

Scalloped Oysters

Mix together 1 1/2 cups water cracker crumbs and 1/2 cup melted butter. Put a thin layer of the mixture in the bottom of a well-buttered shallow baking dish and cover it with a layer of shucked oysters. Season the oysters with salt and pepper and dot with 1 tablespoon sweet butter. Add another layer of the crumb mixture and oysters and repeat the seasonings. Finish the dish with a layer of crumbs. Pour enough oyster juice into the sides to moisten the crumbs well and dot thickly with sweet butter. Bake the oysters in a hot oven (400° F.) for about 15 minutes, or until   (Continued on page 66)

LIFE **Great Dinners**

...owned and tender, turning and bast-
... them frequently with the soy mari-
...le so they won't dry out.

Salade Niçoise

...is is so easy it's almost hard to be-
... that it's going to be any good.
... for boiling up a few eggs, beans
... potatoes all the work has been
... by the people who put the ingre-
... to their cans and jars. I have
... plenty of arguments about

Take a moment

RHUBARB PIE

2 cups unpeeled, diced rhubarb stalks
2 cups sliced strawberries
3½ tablespoons cornstarch
1¼ to 2 cups sugar, depending on tartness of fruit
1 teaspoon orange rind
1 tablespoon butter.
1. Brush pie crust with lightly beaten egg white.
2. Combine all of remaining ingredients and let stand for 15 minutes.
3. Place filling in unbaked pie crust. Cover with top crust. Trim crust so there is a one-quarter-inch overhang.

Wet edges of lower crust and seal crusts together by pinching dough.
4. Bake pie at 450 degrees for 15 to 20 minutes. After first 10 minutes, remove pie and cut vents in top crust.
5. Reduce temperature to 350 degrees and continue baking pie for another 30 minutes, until golden brown and fruit is bubbling.
6. Cool and serve, while still warm, if desired.
Yield: 8 servings.

Bean

... beans
... water
... cup salt
... onions - chopped
... peppers "
... cloves garlic   crushed
1/2 teas cumin
1/2 " oregano
1 tables salt
Rice
Ravioura
Sherry
stock
... cups sliced onions
" leeks
chop tomatoes
... garlic
... cup alc= oil
... water
... sprigs parsley
... leaf
... teas tyme
Basil
... pepper
... 1 teaspoon sal
4 th Fishheads - bones

1 cup sugar

STUFFED
24 Mush.
6 Butter
1/2 veal
1/2 pork
1 cup crumbs
1 can anchovies chopped
1/2 salt - teas
pepper
1 egg
1/4 chop celery

375
15 to 20 min.

Brandy Alex.
Pie

---

2 T plus 1 T gelatin
over 1 cup cold water —
add 1½ c. boiling water
2 cups tomato juice
1 cup ketchup c chopped
celery - 1/2 cup minced
onion - 1/2 c thump
1 green pepper - 1/4 c
lemon juice 1 t

NEW YORK TIMES MAGAZINE, JULY 2, 1967

EATING IN FRONT OF THE TV

Are you wondering if that is a misprint? The whole eating-in-front-of-the-TV idea? Isn't that, like, Public Enemy Number One for a family-dinner nut like me? Well, yes. Sort of. But mostly no. I love many things about well-worn family traditions, but here's something I love the most: When you establish rituals and routines and spend night after night faithfully sticking to the script, in my book, when the situation calls for it you earn the right to completely break with tradition and revel in it. This is a common theme in our house—in fact, an alternate title for this book might have been "What's the Point of Rules If You're Not Allowed to Break Them?" The point is, yes, rituals like eating together every night are psychologically grounding and offer important family bonding opportunities and blah blah blah. But busting out of the routine, eating dinner in front of the TV, napkin in lap, so that we can observe the year's first major holiday (Super Bowl Sunday) or watch Lindsey Vonn take the gold or Phillip Phillips be crowned on *American Idol* or two presidential candidates battle over the state of healthcare reform? Now, that's just plain fun. (Well, most of it is, anyway.)

When I was growing up, my mother would no sooner serve dinner in front of the TV than let us have Pop Rocks with Coke for breakfast. She'd come home from work, do a Superman-quick change of clothes, turn the dial on the black-and-white kitchen TV to Channel 4, and bake some chicken. But as soon as the dinner bell rang (yes, she rang an actual dinner bell, which even in the 1980s struck my brother, sister, and me as ironic and hilarious), Tom Brokaw would be shut off and my family of five would all squeeze around the mustard-colored linoleum table to eat.

It wasn't until after college, when I was first dating Andy, that I could picture dinner at home looking any other way.

I was living on the Upper East Side, and he was on Hoyt Street in Brooklyn. I am not lying when I say that every night that I found myself in his apartment between the months of April and October, he would cook us dinner—pasta, usually, or those spicy rice and beans that came in the little foil pouch—flip on local Channel 11 WPIX, collapse on the couch, and say, "I can't believe I get to watch the Yankees *every single night they play.*"

It never occurred to me that this was something to get excited about, or—maybe I shouldn't admit this—that Yankee games weren't already broadcast on every station across the country. Growing up in the New York area with my brother, Phil, who idolized Ron Guidry and Mickey Rivers, and with a father whose childhood apartment was on 165th Street, in the shadow of Yankee Stadium, the Yanks were *always* on. It was as predictable a scenario in our house as that chicken on the dinner table. Andy, who was raised by displaced Yankee fans in Virginia, was not as lucky.

Though it's true that while Andy was watching his Yanks every night, I secretly would have preferred watching Must-See TV (Rachel and Ross were my Derek Jeter and Bernie Williams), I still got way into the ritual of eating dinner in front of a game. It wasn't *too* much of a hard sell for me: Baseball had always been synonymous with longer days and warmer, softer-lit nights, and watching my hometown team while eating a bowl of penne and marinara felt less like a catatonic TV dinner than it did a true American's rite of spring.

So from April to October, three or four nights a week, I found myself looking forward to parking myself in front of the TV for dinner. Even when I wasn't at Andy's, and the game was important enough (playoffs, World Series, any match-up against the Mets or Boston), we'd watch it together over the phone—him in his Carroll Gardens living room, me in my East Eighty-Seventh Street roach-infested studio. I was in that studio, sitting on the ten-year-old corduroy couch inherited from my parents, eating an experimental risotto, when the Yankees beat the Braves in the 1996 World Series, winning four games in a row after losing the first two of the series.

I know it's not breaking news to say that it can be really fun to witness something huge and exciting, to feel like you're part of something that the whole city, the whole country, or the whole world is into—whether it's the World Series or the World Cup or the presidential debate or the Super Bowl or the Olympics. But when we had kids six years and three (!) Yankee championships later, it somehow became very important to us to impart this universal experience to the kids. Especially since, thanks to DVR and On Demand, and a little thing called the Internet, the world they

"WHEN YOU SPEND NIGHT AFTER NIGHT STICKING TO A ROUTINE, YOU EARN THE RIGHT TO COMPLETELY BREAK TRADITION AND REVEL IN IT."

were born into offers so few big events that can be enjoyed in real time in that kind of Big World Communal Way.

When I was a kid, *Charlotte's Web* was on TV once a summer, and the night it aired, the streets were empty: We were all at home parked in front of the TV eating our Chef Boyardee dinners. And for weeks after that, every elementary-school-age kid I knew was walking around with the same songs in their heads. When I watched Borg sink to his knees after beating McEnroe in the 1980 Wimbledon finals, I was watching with all the neighborhood kids. When I watched Christian Laettner nail the game-winning shot at the buzzer to win the 1992 NCAAs, I was with about two hundred college classmates in the basement of an old frat house. When I watched Mookie Wilson's easy grounder go through Bill Buckner's legs in the 1986 World Series, I was with my brother, who was *incredulous* (and sort of confused: As a Yankee fan, it was hard to figure out who he wanted to lose more, the Mets or the Red Sox). When I watched the series finales of *The Cosby Show, Cheers,* and *Seinfeld,* it felt like I was watching with the entire Western Hemisphere, and we were all somehow connected for those brief thirty minutes. I'm pretty sure I wouldn't feel that way had I watched any of these things on Hulu on my iPad, during my commute home, a few weeks after the fact.

So when big world events come along, I have no problem whatsoever eating in front of the TV, no problem whatsoever with staring at the screen instead of at each other. In fact, I look forward to it. The trick, of course, is to decide what televised event is important enough to merit this kind of status. That hilarious episode when Patrick babysits SpongeBob's pet snail Gary? No. *The SpongeBob Christmas Special*? Maybe! A DVR'd EPL game of Tottenham vs. Manchester United: No. Live World Cup or Olympics or other major sporting event that happens once every four years? Yes. *American Idol* auditioning rounds: No. *American Idol* finale: *Hell,* yeah!

The other trick is to pick the right kind of dinner. One-bowl recipes that require only a single utensil—chicken and rice, stir-fries, thick soups (there I go with the soup again)—are always going to be a good idea. But as far as I'm concerned, the one that says Big Exciting Event the loudest in our house is our Big World Event Dinner Nachos. The stewed chicken makes it a meal, and the mandate to eat with your fingers makes it memorable.

Big World Event Super Nachos work when you're watching the Super Bowl, obviously, but they are also an excellent choice for presidential debates, the World Cup finals, or anything involving a red carpet.

BIG WORLD EVENT SUPER NACHO PLATE

You can easily make this vegetarian by skipping the chicken. Just add the chili powder and chipotle adobo to the refried beans as they warm.

SERVES 4

For the chicken

2 to 3 split chicken breasts (about 1 pound)

2 to 3 tablespoons good-quality olive oil

2 cloves garlic, halved

1 medium onion, chopped

1 14-ounce can diced tomatoes, with juices

½ cup apple cider vinegar

¼ cup water

3 tablespoons chili powder

1 chipotle in adobo (not the sauce, just the dripping single pepper;
  you can freeze the rest)

For the nachos

1 14-ounce can refried beans (I like pinto, but if you prefer black, go for it)

1 18-ounce bag tortilla chips (look for thick and sturdy ones)

2 cups grated sharp cheddar cheese

½ cup chopped red onion

¼ cup pickled Fresno or jalapeño chile rounds

Toppings

¾ cup sour cream

Quick Guacamole (page 280)

Salsa Fresca (page 158) or store-bought salsa

½ cup crumbled queso fresco

thinly sliced butter radishes, from about 2 radishes (optional)

pickled Fresno or jalapeño chiles, seeds removed (optional)

½ cup chopped fresh cilantro leaves

Make the chicken:

• In a Dutch oven or heavy-bottomed pot over medium-high heat, brown the chicken in the olive oil on all sides, 4 to 5 minutes a side. Remove, then add the garlic and onions and cook until soft, about 2 minutes. Return the chicken to the pot, then add everything else so the chicken is just barely immersed in liquid, and stir. Bring to a boil, then lower the heat to a simmer. Cover, leaving the lid slightly ajar, and cook for about 30 minutes, until the chicken is cooked through. Remove the chicken, shred with two forks (discard the bones), and place back in the braising liquid.

Make the nachos:

• Preheat the oven to 325°F. In small saucepan, heat the refried beans until smooth and somewhat thinned out. Cover a large rimmed baking sheet with foil. Distribute the tortilla chips on the foil. Evenly distribute dollops of refried beans and pulled chicken on top of the chips. (If you'd like part of the nacho plate to remain vegetarian, limit chicken to only one side of the baking sheet.) Evenly distribute the cheese on top of the chicken and beans, being sure to cover as many chips as possible. Top with the red onions, then top with the pickled jalapeño rounds, keeping some sections free of chiles if your kids don't like the heat. Bake for 20 minutes, until the cheese is bubbly and golden.

• While the nachos bake, get the toppings ready. Remove the nachos from the oven and let cool slightly, then top as desired with fixings, keeping in mind not everyone will want every topping. Place the nacho platter on a trivet or wooden cutting board in the TV room. Give everyone small dinner plates and have each viewer assemble his or her own nacho plate as desired.

WORLD CUP BREAKFAST FRY-UP

Of all the unhealthy things we ate when we visited England a few years ago—to name a few:
rock cake, apple tart, banoffee pie, Cadbury bars, clotted cream, chocolate éclairs, scones, currant scones,
cheese scones, lamb shoulder, beef roasts, fish and chips, Victoria sponge cake, summer pudding,
maple pecan ice cream—none was more bald in its unhealthiness, or more satisfying, than the fry-up. It's one
unapologetic, greasy, bursting plate of deliciousness. We'd like to live long enough to see our kids
reach their teenage years, so we're not making a habit of this, but man (blimey?): The Brits know from
breakfast, and it seems especially appropriate to serve this in front of a World Cup match.
There's no real art to the fry-up, as far as I can tell, but here's how Andy describes his technique:

• Preheat the oven to 350°F. Halve 6 tomatoes, slice 1 yellow onion, de-stem a dozen cremini mushrooms, and toss it all into a roasting pan. Drizzle very lightly with olive oil, salt, and freshly ground pepper. Place a cooling rack—the kind you use for cookies—on top of the roasting pan, and place one large coil of sweet sausage (or breakfast sausage if you have it), so that the drippings fall into the pan below as it cooks. Bake for 20 minutes, until the sausage is mostly cooked through. Remove the pan from the oven, put the sausage down below with the vegetables, place the strips of bacon on top of the cooling rack, and return to the oven. Bake for another 20 to 25 minutes, allowing the bacon drippings (Like we said: Best not to think about this too hard) to fall into the pan as it cooks. Remove from the oven. In separate pans, warm some baked beans and fry a bunch of eggs, sunny-side up. Put everything—except for the beans—on a platter and top with the eggs. Serve with beans and toast. Buttered toast. Of course.

AFTER-DINNER RITUALS

When the girls were little and we were still waking up in a slight state of panic every day—about how exactly we were going to get *through* the day—family dinner crystallized as one of our more cherished rituals, mainly because both Andy and I were working full-time, and it was guaranteed check-in time with the kids. Back then, I was obsessed with how much time I was spending (and not spending) with the girls, as though someone somewhere was keeping score. I'd sit on the train counting the hours I had spent with Abby and Phoebe (predawn wake-ups, evenings, weekends, phone calls home from the office) versus the hours I spent with my coworkers (weekdays, nine to five). Every time, I somehow made the two columns come out even.

It was fuzzy math to say the least, but the way I convinced myself that all was well was by weighting the hours of quality time more heavily. Family dinner, which represented roughly 50 percent of our evening time home with the girls, was an excellent example of quality time, even though it was often spent cajoling a supposedly fish-loving kid to eat fish, lasted roughly ten minutes, and frequently required retrieving the Hoover from the basement to suck up whatever the dog didn't. These things didn't bother me, though, because there were way more ticks in the plus column than the minus column where family dinner was concerned, and no matter how logistically challenging the meal, it was too important to me to ever consider surrendering to takeout. Instead, I began obsessively assembling a massive archive of under-thirty-minute meals, lest I spend a single extra second doing something that would register in the not-with-the-kids column. Even while I was in the middle of this, I realized my internal scorekeeping was irrational, if not slightly insane. But I know that for every person reading this essay who is questioning my mental health, there is someone else nodding his or her head in recognition.

When our energies weren't directed toward family dinner, they were directed to "winding-down" activities that we hoped might make the transition to bedtime a little saner for everybody, including the parents. Sometimes we'd tell the girls it was "movie night" and we'd screen a Pixar Short, those legendary five- or six-minute mini-movies that preceded *Finding Nemo* and *The Incredibles* in the theater or were included as bonus content in the DVD versions. On movie night, we'd head up to the small home office, shut the door, turn off the lights, and let the girls watch *Boundin'*, or *Lifted*, or *For the Birds*, or *Jack-Jack Attack*—an outtake from *The Incredibles*, and the one they asked for over and over again. Other times after dinner, we'd force ourselves to play board games, an activity that became decidedly less torturous as soon as they graduated from Candy Land and Life to Pictionary and Clue, games that required the use of actual brain cells.

The best post-dinner ritual of all, though, was what came to be known as the "Hallway Shows." On show nights, the girls would usher us to one end of the small upstairs hall and tell us to sit while they disappeared into their bedrooms to nail down what to perform. When I was feeling ambitious, I'd lay down a strand of Christmas lights around the perimeter of the hall to create a stage.

The earliest shows were inspired by our collective obsession with *Annie*, the musical. Phoebe, about four, would sing "Tomorrow," allowing Abby, then two or three, to play Sandy the dog, if she was lucky. During the ballet years, they graced us with Sugar-Plum-Fairy dancing, then moved on to *Backyardigans* jingles and Black-Eyed Peas routines. In that small hallway, over the course of a decade, we watched Abby air-guitar to Wilco, the Drive-By Truckers, and the Clash. We witnessed Phoebe becoming Wendy to Abby's Peter Pan, and Michael Jackson in "Thriller," and perform a G-rated interpretation of Beyoncé's "Single Ladies" video. They've rehearsed harmonies for their school chorus concerts and done their best imitations of various *American Idol* contenders. Both of them have at some point had a moment—I'm sure of it—where they've convinced themselves they will grow up to be Taylor Swift. It was the best kind of quality time, and I can't recommend this ritual enough to any work-weary parent out there, not least of all because it allows you to *sit down* while partaking.

Another boon to quality-time seekers? Daylight savings. On the spring day we turn our clocks forward an hour, I always get a note or a call from my mother with the same basic theme: "Happy times are here again!" My mom and I are both warm-weather fanatics who view the vernal equinox not only as the great signifier that spring is finally here, but as the day the Scheduling Gods grant us an *extra hour in our day.* One we can use to hang out in the backyard, or grill in the backyard, or kick the soccer ball, or take a walk *after* dinner. Somehow, the bedtime deadlines that we are so Draconian about in the winter lose a little of their urgency when the sun is just starting to slip down over the horizon. So the girls go to bed at 9:15 instead of 8:30? What's the difference? So we eat a little later? Who cares? Not me. What's the rush? Bonus: I get an extra hour in the plus column.

Quick Weeknight Dinners

Most of the weeknight meals I discovered during this period are in my first book, *Dinner: A Love Story.* These next few recipes weren't in the repertoire back then, but that is only because I hadn't discovered them yet. If I had, they'd be VIPs in the rotation, as they are now. All of them serve four.

ORECCHIETTE WITH SWEET SAUSAGE BOLOGNESE

This is a quick dinner, made even quicker if you've thought to cook and freeze it ahead of time. Freeze in flattened BPA-free zip-top bags so it thaws faster under running water. (Ever try to thaw a football-size block of sauce at seven o'clock on a weeknight? Not fun.)

SERVES 4

½ small onion, finely chopped

1 clove garlic, minced

2 tablespoons good-quality olive oil

¾ to 1 pound good sweet Italian pork sausage, casings removed

⅓ cup red wine

kosher salt and freshly ground pepper

1 28-ounce can whole tomatoes with their juices

1 pound orecchiette

1 tablespoon butter

¼ cup freshly grated Parmigiano-Reggiano, plus more for serving

fresh basil or oregano, for serving

• In a large saucepan set over medium-low heat, add the onion and garlic to the olive oil and cook until soft, about 3 minutes. Add the sausage and turn the heat to medium high, breaking up the meat with a fork or wooden spoon. When the pink of the meat is almost gone (about 8 minutes), add the wine and raise the heat, cooking until the meat has absorbed most of the wine. Season with salt and pepper.

• Add the tomatoes and use kitchen scissors to roughly chop them. (You could also just hand-smush the tomatoes before they go in the pot. But then you get your hands all messy.) Bring to a boil, then turn down the heat to low and simmer uncovered for 45 minutes to an hour.

• (If not serving right away, allow to cool, and freeze in a BPA-free zip-top plastic bag.)

• While the sauce is simmering down, bring a large pot of salted water to a boil and cook the orecchiette according to the package directions. Drain the orecchiette, then return it to the pot with the butter and toss. Add the sauce and cheese and toss until the sauce is clinging to every piece of pasta. Serve in bowls topped with more cheese and fresh herbs.

SALMON AND POTATOES WITH YOGURT SAUCE

I love this dinner because everything bakes on one baking sheet. Translation:
less dish-washing, more hallway hanging.

SERVES 4

1 bunch of lacinato kale, center ribs and stems removed,
    torn into 2-inch pieces, or flat-leaf spinach, thick stems removed

6 red potatoes, unpeeled, very thinly sliced

2 medium shallots, thinly sliced

4 6-ounce salmon fillets

kosher salt and freshly ground pepper

1 lemon, seeded and sliced into very thin horizontal rounds

2 tablespoons good-quality olive oil

Yogurt Sauce

½ cup plain yogurt (whole or low-fat)

2 tablespoons chopped fresh dill

1 tablespoon Dijon mustard

1 tablespoon prepared horseradish

kosher salt and freshly ground pepper

- Preheat the oven to 400°F.
- Lay 4 large rectangular pieces of parchment paper on a work surface. Place a few kale leaves on each sheet and top with potatoes, shallots, then salmon; season with salt and pepper. Top the fish with lemon slices; drizzle with the oil. Fold the parchment over the fish, crimp the edges tightly to form a sealed packet, and fold the side overhang underneath the packet. Place the packets on a large rimmed baking sheet. Bake for 20 minutes. While the salmon is baking, in a small bowl whisk together the yogurt, dill, mustard, and horseradish. Season with salt and pepper. Carefully open the salmon packets (the steam will be hot) and top with the sauce.

Quick, healthy, delicious,
minimal cleanup . . .
Salmon with Potatoes and
Yogurt Sauce: Will you
marry me?

CRISPY CHICKPEAS WITH YOGURT SAUCE AND NAAN

This makes a lot of appearances in the weeknight dinner rotation because it's flavorful and healthy—but mostly because 90 percent of the ingredients have long shelf lives so it's always there for me.

SERVES 4

5 tablespoons vegetable oil

2 14-ounce cans chickpeas (garbanzo beans), drained, rinsed, and dried completely

2 tablespoons finely minced onion

¼ teaspoon cayenne

½ teaspoon garlic powder

¾ teaspoon smoked paprika

kosher salt and freshly ground pepper

¾ cup plain yogurt (whole, nonfat, low-fat, any kind)

¼ teaspoon garam masala

small squeeze of fresh lime juice (about 1 teaspoon)

1½ teaspoons good-quality olive oil

½ teaspoon Sriracha sauce, plus more for serving

4 individual whole wheat naan breads

tamarind chutney, for serving (optional)

handful of chopped fresh mint or cilantro leaves, or both

• Add the vegetable oil to a cast-iron skillet set over medium-high heat. When the pan is hot but not smoking, add the chickpeas (in batches, if necessary, or use a large skillet—you want a single layer of chickpeas on the pan's surface). Fry for about 15 minutes, tossing every 5 minutes, adding the onion during the last 5 minutes. Remove with a slotted spoon to a paper-towel-lined bowl. Once all chickpeas are fried and drained, remove paper towel, then add the cayenne, garlic powder, and paprika along with salt and pepper to taste. Toss.

• While the chickpeas fry, in a small bowl whisk together the yogurt with the garam masala, lime juice, olive oil, and Sriracha. Season with salt and pepper.

• Toast the naan and serve with chickpeas, yogurt, chutney, Sriracha, and fresh herbs.

Crispy Chickpeas with
Naan: our go-to my-mind-
is-completely-blank
pantry dinner.

ON SIGNATURE DINNERS

When I was growing up, my mom made the best meatballs. And roasted chicken. And lasagna with the local market's sweet Italian sausages (see page 252). These days, when I take my family for dinner at my parents' house, I beg her to make one of these dishes for me. (See Sunday Dinner, page 236.) How could I not? They were the tent-poles of my culinary upbringing—the family dinner rotation—and I must've had each of them once a week for eighteen years. If there were other things worth eating out there, I didn't care to know about them.

For a while there, the dinner situation with my kids was the polar opposite of this. My kids never had any idea what was going to be on the menu. They knew what *wouldn't* be on the menu (tofu, eggs, and other well-established Enemies of the State), but otherwise it was anyone's guess. This is because they are members of a small club: kids whose mother's career depends on mixing things up at the table. Just like any job, it's important to keep up to speed on the latest industry trends, which, in my case, means exploring einkorn berries if ancient grains are suddenly getting a lot of ink, or reading up on bone broth if that seems to be what's trending on social media.

Being the children of a food writer is not without its privileges. During one stretch back in 2011, when I was in pursuit of a perfect galette, Abby came home from school to a warm, freshly made open-face apple pie five days in a row. At least once a week, the UPS man shows up with treats from various food vendors hoping I'll write about them on my blog or elsewhere. Sometimes, when my workday consists of testing paella or something any normal working parent would consider a complete dinner deal-breaker, someone at the table will say, "I can't believe we get to eat this on a random Tuesday night."

But the lab rat thing can get old, too. During the launch of my blog, when I was posting five days a week and photographing food in real time, dinner was often an exercise in patience for the pre-tweens at the table. As if they weren't already starving enough when they sat down to eat, they'd have to wait for the clouds to diffuse the sun just enough to create optimum photographic conditions to shoot what was set before them. They'd have to hear their parents earnestly discuss things like acidity in their freaking salad dressing. And God forbid they loved something as much as I loved my mom's meatballs; they might never see it again. I remember Phoebe, then eight years old, begging for a reprise of a lemony chicken dish I served one autumn night. The Lemon Chicken! Of course! I promised her. But first we have to retest the fish cakes for the cookbook, and after that I have to turn in my copy for a magazine story, so I need to double-check that the marinade is getting the right flavor on the grilled flank steak. And remember how we were going to taste-test all those jarred pasta sauces? Sorry, sweetie, maybe next week?

Things have calmed down a bit since then. The truth is, I have hundreds of recipes in my rotation, most of which are immortalized on my blog or in my books by now, but in the past few years, I've made a point to pay more careful attention to the answer when I ask my kids "What do you want for dinner?" Because what I'm really asking is: "What foods will someday have the power to transport you back to your childhood?" (Or maybe "What foods will someday be powerful enough to make you literally transport yourself back to your mother's dinner table, no matter how far away you live from her?") The answers, not surprisingly, have nothing to do with what's trending on Instagram. They couldn't care less about ancient grains or bone broth. Their list can be reduced to what all kids want: pizza, roasted chicken, tacos, or burrito bowls. Especially burrito bowls. So long as Mom and Dad are making them, they can't get enough.

Note: See my first book, *Dinner: A Love Story,*
for two other signature recipes:
Chicken Milanese and Hawaiian Pizza.

BURRITO BOWLS

Here's the thing about burrito bowls: If you go all out and make every component from scratch, it will be delicious, but it will be a real pain in the neck. That's why here, you'll see shortcut versions of everything except the chicken. On a weeknight, pick or choose what you want to spend time on and don't look back. To serve: Present the fixings on the table or counter, serve everyone rice, then let them top as they please. I like this meal to be more veg-heavy, so I usually only cook 4 small boneless chicken thighs. You can add another if you think your family will want more.

SERVES 4

By this point in my parenting life, I know exactly which meals will be greeted with zero resistance at the dinner table (#1: Burrito Bowls, page 277), but I still have no idea how to execute the girls' secret sister handshake.

Chicken

1 tablespoon vegetable oil

1¼ pounds chicken thighs (about 4 chicken thighs),
     pounded to even thickness (you can also use
     chicken breasts cut into 1-inch pieces)

1 teaspoon chili powder

2 teaspoons dried oregano

kosher salt and freshly ground pepper

squeeze of fresh lime juice

• Heat the vegetable oil in a skillet set over medium-high heat. Sprinkle one side of the chicken thighs with half of the chili powder and half of the oregano, and season with salt and pepper. Add the chicken, spiced side down, to the hot oil. Let the chicken brown, sprinkling the remainder of the chili powder and oregano on the raw side of the chicken and seasoning with salt and pepper. After about 5 minutes, flip and brown on the other side. When cooked through, about 5 minutes more, remove to a cutting board and cut into strips. Squeeze a little lime juice on top.

Beans

• In a small saucepan, heat 1 tablespoon vegetable oil. Add 2 tablespoons diced onion and cook until slightly softened, about 2 minutes. Add ¼ teaspoon ground cumin, salt, and pepper and stir for another minute. Stir in a 14-ounce can of black beans (rinsed and drained) and a bay leaf, and simmer until the beans are heated through, about 5 minutes. Discard the bay leaf before serving.

• *Shortcut:* Heat a 14-ounce can of rinsed and drained black beans in a small saucepan until warmed through, about 5 minutes.

Rice

• Prepare white or brown rice according to the package directions—enough to yield 2½ cups of cooked rice. (This is based on a little more than ½ cup cooked rice per diner; you know your family better than I do, so make more if you think you'll need it.) When the rice is finished, toss in 1 tablespoon finely chopped fresh cilantro leaves, the juice of ½ large lime, and a generous sprinkling of kosher salt. (Skip the cilantro if you think the kids will balk.)

• *Shortcut:* Prepare white or brown rice according to the package directions—enough to yield 2½ cups of cooked rice.

Salsa

- Finely chop 2 cups grape tomatoes (or any tomato if it's summer) with 1 tablespoon chopped red onion, 2 tablespoons chopped fresh cilantro leaves, 1 tablespoon red wine vinegar, salt, pepper, and ½ minced jalapeño chile (seeds and most of the pith removed) or a dash of hot sauce.
- *Shortcut:* Use your favorite store-bought salsa.

Quick Guacamole

- Using a fork, mash 1 avocado with a pinch of ground cumin, salt to taste, and a heavy squeeze of fresh lime juice.
- *Shortcut:* Slice an avocado and fan out on a plate.

Other components

4 to 5 cups shredded romaine lettuce

3 ounces sharp cheddar cheese, sliced or grated (about ¾ cup)

handful of fresh cilantro leaves, chopped

4 ounces sour cream (about ⅓ cup)

lime wedges

GRILLED SPICY SHRIMP TACOS WITH AVOCADO BUTTER AND SUMMER CABBAGE

These tacos are best eaten outside, preferably in a place where you have access to fresh shrimp and fresh napa cabbage. The epiphany for me here was spreading avocado on the tortilla before the shrimp, instead of dolloping it all on at the end. That way, you get some in every bite.

SERVES 4

Slaw

1 shallot, minced

¼ cup red wine vinegar

½ head of Savoy cabbage, shredded

good-quality olive oil

handful of fresh cilantro leaves, chopped

Avocado Butter

1 to 2 really ripe avocados, pitted and peeled

juice from ½ lime

kosher salt

Shrimp

about 2 pounds shrimp (small, sweet preferred), shelled

generous drizzle of olive oil

1 teaspoon Sriracha sauce

kosher salt and freshly ground pepper

juice from ½ small lime

Tortillas

8 tortillas

• Make a fire in a charcoal grill or preheat a gas grill to medium high. Meanwhile, as the grill heats, prepare the toppings.

• For the slaw: In a small bowl, soak the shallot in the vinegar for 15 minutes. In a large bowl, toss the cabbage with the olive oil, shallot-vinegar mixture, and cilantro.

• For the avocado butter: Mash the avocado in a small bowl with lime juice and salt to taste. Set aside.

• For the shrimp: About 20 minutes before you want to start grilling, place the shrimp in a medium bowl and toss with the olive oil, Sriracha, and salt and pepper to taste. About 3 minutes before you grill, toss in the lime juice. If you are using large shrimp, thread them onto skewers; if you are using small shrimp, place in a grilling basket. Cook for 1 to 2 minutes a side, tossing as you go if they are in a grill basket. If using skewers, turn once halfway through cooking. Remove from the grill and heat the tortillas, about 30 seconds a side, watching so they don't burn. Remove and cover with foil so they stay warm.

• Spread avocado butter on each tortilla, then add shrimp and slaw.

"THE CRUCIAL QUESTION: WHICH DINNERS WILL SOMEDAY HAVE THE POWER TO TRANSPORT OUR KIDS BACK TO THEIR CHILDHOODS?"

ONE-PAN LEMON CHICKEN WITH ASPARAGUS AND CHIVES

Tomorrow, Phoebe, tomorrow. I promise.

SERVES 4

kosher salt

1 bunch of asparagus, trimmed of woody stems

3 tablespoons good-quality olive oil, plus more to taste

5 chicken breasts (about 1½ pounds), pounded to ½-inch thickness
   and cut in half

⅓ cup all-purpose flour, salted and peppered, for dredging

¾ cup chicken stock

3 tablespoons fresh lemon juice

2 teaspoons Dijon mustard

chopped fresh chives

• Add about 1 inch water and a pinch of salt to a large, deep-sided skillet, and bring to a boil. Add the asparagus spears and cook for 2 minutes. Using tongs, remove the asparagus from the water and immediately plunge into an ice-water bath to stop the cooking and preserve the bright green color. Remove from the ice bath, pat dry, and chop into 1-inch pieces. Drain the water from the skillet and set it back on the stovetop over medium-high heat. Add the oil.

• Dredge each chicken breast in the seasoned flour and add four or five of them to the skillet at once, being careful not to crowd the pan. (The pan should be hot enough so that the chicken sizzles upon contact.) Cook each breast for 3 to 4 minutes a side, until firm to the touch but not rock-hard. Remove the cooked chicken breasts to a plate and continue with the remaining dredged chicken, adding oil as necessary, until they are all cooked.

• Turn heat to medium high and add stock, lemon juice, and mustard, stirring to combine and scraping up any brown bits that might have collected on the surface of the pan. Season with salt and pepper. Heat until the stock simmers and thickens slightly. Add the chicken and asparagus, heat through, then serve in a rimmed platter, topped with the sauce and showered with chives.

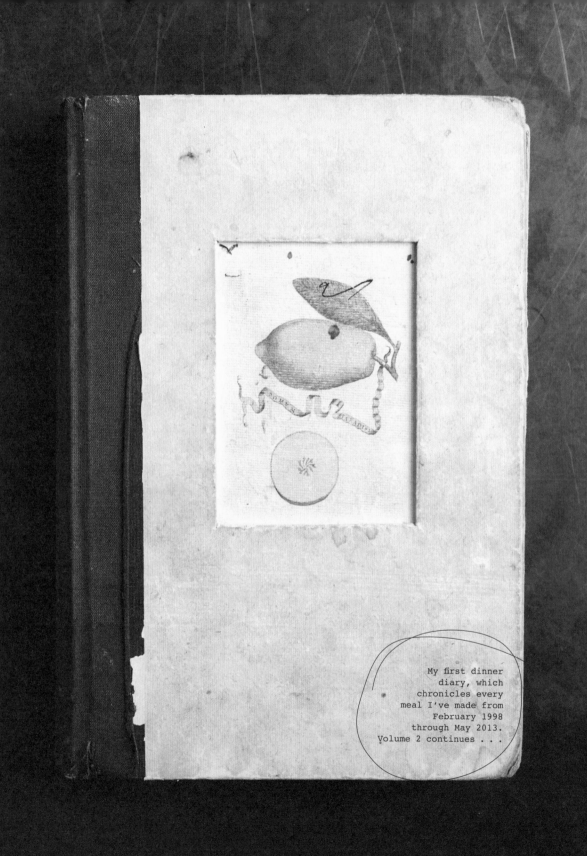

My first dinner
diary, which
chronicles every
meal I've made from
February 1998
through May 2013.
Volume 2 continues . . .

IN CONCLUSION

I'd like to conclude by reminding you, once again, that the family rituals you have just finished reading about are *our family rituals.* I'd be thrilled if they sparked ideas for traditions to kick-start in your own life—or if they give you ideas for things to cook for dinner tonight—but what I really hope they've done is illustrate how some of my most cherished rituals involve hardly any fanfare, multicourse menus, or (hallelujah!) multicourse dishwashing. Again, I am positive you have family rituals already in place and happening before your eyes without even realizing it—it's just that nobody has pointed them out to you yet.

I'll tell you one last story.

On hot summer nights when I was little, my mom would come home from work and take me to our local pool so she could do laps—or just cool off after a soupy New York July day before making dinner. I'd try to keep up, or, more often, take a few dives off the diving board. Our evening swim usually took place around seven o'clock, just as the pool was emptying and just as the sun was that diffused orangey-gold color, its reflection dancing on the surface of the water. At least, that's how it always seemed to me, admittedly a world-class over-romanticizer. It was one of my most favorite rituals of summer, and I found myself rooting for the mercury to rise to suffocating heights, which pretty much guaranteed a night swim. To this day, I find myself making excuses to go to the pool with the girls not in the middle of the day, when the sun is at the highest, hottest point in the sky, but in the early evening, pre-dinner. I think of my mom every time I do this, even though—here's where it gets interesting—she has very little memory of our sunset pool visits being a regular thing.

Have I taken a small memory and turned it into something more? Or was she simply not registering how much more meaningful those swims were for me, and therefore not holding on to it in the same way that she might've held on to, say, my solo in the sixth-grade production of *Hello, Dolly!*?

I thought about this the other night, not as I was doing a few laps at sundown, but after carrying up a huge load of just-dried, not-yet-folded laundry from the basement. Bear with me here.

You know how some people get all Zen with their laundry—ironing sheets, tucking in the sleeves of T-shirts Gap-style to make nice, neat stacks? I am not one of those people. I am a legendary laundry-hater. After a quarter-century of washing my own clothes, I still don't know what requires a warm versus cold wash, gentle versus regular. The dingy whites my daughters sport about town offer incontrovertible evidence to my impatience: Why do two separate loads of whites and colors over the course of three hours when you can do one in half the time? Perhaps most annoying to my family is that I'm not shy about my resentment of the fact that it somehow *all falls on me*. And in order to make a big show of my resentment—and to lay on the guilt as thickly as possible—I dump the big mess of clean clothes on my bed, then sit down where everyone can see me folding and hear me whining.

But apparently all of my complaining has had the opposite effect on Abby, who, one night, spied the laundry basket of unfolded clothes and said to me, "Don't start folding until I can come upstairs with you." I hadn't realized it, but all along, she had been sitting with me while I matched black sock to navy sock (close enough) and earmarked each corner of the bed for a family member's piles. And though Abby fell short of actually *helping* me, she kept me company, experimenting with some new hairstyles in the mirror as she talked (*If I get my hair cut to here, do you think I could still wear a high pony?*); filling me in on school news (*There's another new kid in school who moved from Brooklyn*); working through the kind of hypotheticals that weigh on an eleven-year-old's mind (*If you could be rich or famous, but not both, which would you be?*). On some level, I realized, this had become something she looked forward to. My folding and whining, her hanging out: It had become a ritual.

In other words, remember this: Sometimes the sweetest—if most unlikely—rituals happen by accident. So don't put too much pressure on yourself if you're not actively creating them. It's pretty likely your kids are already seeking them out on their own without you even knowing about it.

RITUALS AND HOLIDAYS
ORGANIZED BY CALENDAR

— January —

Super Bowl Sunday,
page 264

— February —

Après Ski, page 176

Valentine's Day, page 15

— March —

Spring Sunday Dinner, page 241

Easter, page 9

— April —

Farmer's Market Walk, page 98

— May —

Mother's Day, page 15

— June —

Father's Day, page 15

World Cup Finals, page 266

Summer Sunday Dinner, page 246

— July —

Fourth of July, page 28

— August —

Summer Vacation, page 156

— September —

Fall Sunday Dinner, page 252

The Jewish Holidays, page 2

— October —

Pickling, page 135

Halloween, page 37

— November —

Thanksgiving, page 43

— December —

Winter Sunday Dinner, page 238

The Holidays (Christmas, Hanukkah,
Interfaith Parties), pages 68 to 88

Christmas, page 86

New Year's Eve, page 89

— Year-Round Rituals —

The One-on-One Date, page 122

Fruit First Thing, page 133

Lunch with Dad, page 143

Sleepover Breakfasts, page 146

Birthdays, pages 185 to 213

Birthday Parties, page 214

Family Dinners, pages 227 to 283

ACKNOWLEDGMENTS

If you really want to know How to Celebrate Everything, the easiest thing to do is surround yourself with people who have big hearts, big talents, and, of course, big recipe collections. It just so happens this was also the secret to writing the book you just finished, so I'd be remiss if I didn't raise a glass to the following people:

To Team Ballantine: Gina Centrello, Kara Welsh, Pamela Cannon, Robbin Schiff, Mark Maguire, Evan Camfield, Sharon Propson, Nina Shield, Betsy Wilson, Janet McDonald, Richard Callison, Maggie Oberrender, Libby McGuire, and especially my editor, Jennifer Tung, whose grace and friendship I'm grateful for every day.

To my agent, Elyse Cheney, for being so badass in the best possible way.

To Victoria Granof, the LeBron James of food stylists: Yes, you help make the meatballs look real pretty, but mostly you just make me laugh.

To Chelsea Cavanaugh, for your amazing photographic talents. Thanks to your calm, confident presence, five days of shooting nearly a hundred recipes felt like a vacation in Hawaii.

To Olivia Anderson, Jess Damuck, and Amy Tischler, for your A-game recipe prepping and testing; and to digital technician Ted Cavanaugh for being so organized— and for being so nice to Iris.

To my *Dinner: A Love Story* partner, Applegate, who supplied all the natural and organic meats and cheese for the foot-longers on page 223. (Make them now!)

To my designer, Kristina DiMatteo: I trust you so implicitly, it's hard to overstate how lucky I feel to have you in my corner. Thank you for (yet again) bringing my vision to life so beautifully.

To my *Bon Appétit* editors, Meryl Rothstein and Adam Rapoport, who cook for us, inspire us, and extend our deadlines when we need it most.

To my Eleventh-Hour Squad: Tom Prince, Rory Evans, and Yolanda Edwards, who I can always count on for crucial (sometimes brutal) last-minute feedback.

To my photo shoot helpers, Madeline Lawlor and Lily Jebejian. If you two ever get tired of playing midfield, perhaps you might consider a career in hand modeling?

To my nephews and nieces: Nathan, Sophia, Aidan, Luca, Alison, Amanda, Owen. Now that you have my book, you guys are in charge of Thanksgiving.

A big reason why the recipes in this book are so special to me is because almost all of them have been shared or swapped with family and friends, both old and new. Big huge thanks to: Lynn Zerbib, Nick Zerbib, Phil Rosenstrach, Tony Ward, Patricia Sullivan, Selma Sherman, Ronnie Fein, Patty Rockmore, Sicily Rockmore, Rosa "Mud Cake" Goldman, Jeni Goldman, Ben Silbert, Anne Scharer, Todd Lawlor, Evan Lawlor, Joel Lovell, Kate Porterfield, David Sedaris, Jim Nelson, John-Mario Sevilla, Lia Ronnen, Naria Halliwell, Peter Levine, Sara Schneider, Liz Vales, Tom Vales, Andrea Montalbano, Susan Dominus, Alanna Stang, Lori Slater, Jon Slater, Carly Slater, Helene Godin, Seth Godin, Ed Nammour, Joanna Goddard, Pilar Guzman, Bonnie Stelzer, and Jonathan Abady.

To Andy, Phoebe, and Abby. With you guys around, every day is a party.

INDEX

Page numbers in **bold** are the location of the recipe.

Abby's Homemade
Gnocchi with Basil and
Cheese, 126, 127, **129–30**

alcohol
Classic Negroni, **xxix**

appetizers
Caviar on Potato
Chips, 90, **92**
Phoebe's Fried
Pineapple, **92**
Truffle Popcorn, **92**
Warm Artichoke Dip, **92**

apples
Apple-Cinnamon Fritters,
154–55
Brown Butter Apple Pie, **193**
Sausage and Apple
Stuffing, **53**

Apricot-Rum Glazed Ham,
8, **10–11**

artichokes, Warm Artichoke
Dip, **92**

asparagus
Asparagus with Pesto,
247, **248–49**
Greenest Green Salad,
244, **245**
One-Pan Lemon Chicken
with Asparagus and
Chives, **283**

avocados
Grilled Spicy Shrimp Tacos
with Avocado Butter and
Summer Cabbage, **280–81**
Quick Guacamole, **280**

bacon
"Confetti" Brussels with
Bacon and Raisins, **51**
World Cup Breakfast
Fry-Up, **266**

baked goods
heart-shaped cake,
24, 200
Homemade Biscuits,
197–98
My Grandma Catrino's
Biscotti, 16, 17, **19**
Popovers with Homemade
Strawberry Jam, **152**,
153, **154**
Rosa's Mud Cake, 24, 201,
202–3
Snickerdoodles, **26**
Sour Cream Chocolate Chip
Nut Loaf, 18, **19–20**
Tea Cup Brownie Sundaes,
95

Baked Polenta with
Feta, **242**

beans
Big World Event Super
Nacho Plate, 262–63,
264–65
Burrito Bowls, **277**,
279–80
Franks and Beans, xxvi, 35,
38, **40**

beef
Cranberry-Marinated
Beef Tenderloin, **86–87**
Interfaith Sliders
(Brisket & Ham),
70, 71, **72**

beets
Beet and Blood Orange
Salad with Pistachios, **94**
Quinoa Salad with Roast
Vegetables, Feta, and Herbs,
116, **117–18**

berries
Peach Berry Cobbler, **250**
Triple Berry Summer Pie
with Lattice Crust, xxvi,
xxvii, 118–20, **121**

beverages
Classic Negroni, **xxix**
Cold-Brewed Ice Coffee,
164, **165**
Strawberry-Almond
Milkshake, 112, **113**

biscotti, My Grandma
Catrino's Biscotti, 16, 17, **19**

biscuits, Homemade
Biscuits, **197–98**

bread, The $100 Challah, **6–7**

breakfast
Andy's birthday breakfasts,
196–98
Apple-Cinnamon Fritters,
154–55
Ham and Eggs with
Parm and Herbs, **11**
Homemade Sausage, Egg, and
Cheese on Homemade
Biscuits, **197–98**
Our Favorite Granola, **23**
Popovers with Homemade
Strawberry Jam, **152**, 153, **154**
Sleepover Chocolate Chip
Pancakes, **149**

World Cup Breakfast Fry-Up, **266**

Broccolini-Chickpea pizza, **180–81**, 182–83

Brown Butter Apple Pie, **193**

brownies, Tea Cup Brownie Sundaes, **95**

brussels sprouts, "Confetti" Brussels Sprouts with Bacon and Raisins, **51**

Burrito Bowls, **277**, **279–80**

"Bus Stop Social" ribs, **xxvi, xxviii**

butter
Avocado Butter, **281**
Champagne Butter, **93**

cabbage
Crowd-Pleaser Summer Slaw, xxvi, 31, **34**
Grilled Spicy Shrimp Tacos with Avocado Butter and Summer Cabbage, **280–81**

cakes
Doughnut Cake, **194**, 195
heart-shaped cake, 24, 200
Phoebe's Mint Chocolate Ice Cream Cake with Ganache, **208–10**
Rosa's Mud Cake, 24, 201, **202–3**
Sour Cream Chocolate Chip Nut Loaf, 18, **19–20**
See also brownies; pies

Caramelized Onion Mashed Potatoes, **175**

Carbonara, **xxviii–xxix**

carrots
Curried Carrots with Pecans, **87**
Quinoa Salad with Roast Vegetables, Feta, and Herbs, 116, **117–18**

Caviar on Potato Chips, 90, **92**

Champagne Butter, **93**

cheese
Abby's Homemade Gnocchi with Basil and Cheese, 126, 127, **129–30**
Baked Polenta with Feta, **242**
Big World Event Super Nacho Plate, 262–63, **264–65**
Broccolini-Chickpea pizza, **180–81**, 182–83
Foot Long Party Subs, 222, **223–24**
Grandma Jody's Lasagna, **252–53**
Grilled Halloumi and Asparagus with Pesto, 247, **248–49**
Ham and Eggs with Parm and Herbs, **11**
Homemade Sausage, Egg, and Cheese on Homemade Biscuits, **197–98**
Parm Mashed Potatoes, **175**
Pizza with Ramps and Taleggio, **114**
Post-Beach Grilled Cheddar and Apple Sandwich, **162**

Potato Gratin with Gruyère, **56**, 57
Quinoa Salad with Roast Vegetables, Feta, and Herbs, 116, **117–18**
Sybil's Salad, **88**

Cherry-Peach Relish, **105–6**

chicken
Big World Event Super Nacho Plate, 262–63, **264–65**
Burrito Bowls, **277**, **279–80**
Chicken Chorizo Chili, **40–41**
Harissa Roasted Chicken, **241–42**
One-Pan Lemon Chicken with Asparagus and Chives, **263**
Picnic Chicken, 30–31, **32–33**

chickpeas, Crispy Chickpeas with Yogurt Sauce and Naan, **274**, 275

chiles
Big World Event Super Nacho Plate, 262–63, **264–65**
Phoebe's Hatch Burgers, **130**

chives
Chive Croutons, **13**
One-Pan Lemon Chicken with Asparagus and Chives, **263**
Sliced Tomatoes with Sea Salt and Chives, **249**

chocolate
Chocolate Frosting, **203**
Ganache, **210**
Mom's Chocolate Pudding Pie, **45**

chocolate (*cont'd*):
  My Chocolate Pudding Pie,
    46, 47
  Rosa's Mud Cake, 24, 201,
    202–3
  Sleepover Chocolate Chip
    Pancakes, **149**
  Sour Cream Chocolate Chip
    Nut Loaf, 18, **19–20**
  Tea Cup Brownie Sundaes, **95**

chorizo, Chicken
  Chorizo Chili, **40–41**

Cider-Braised Pork
  Meatballs with Creamy
  Polenta, **178**, 179, **180**

Cilantro-Lime Rice, **240**

Classic Italian Foot Long
  Party Subs, 222, **223–24**

Classic Mashed Potatoes, 172,
  175

Classic Negroni, **xxix**

cobbler, Peach Berry
  Cobbler, **250**

cocktails, Classic Negroni, **xxix**

Cold-Brewed Ice Coffee,
  164, **165**

"Confetti" Brussels Sprouts
  with Bacon and Raisins, **51**

cookies
  Hubba's Christmas
    Cookies, 82, **83**, 84, 85

Star of David Christmas
  Cookies, 3
Snickerdoodles, **26**

corn
  Baked Polenta with Feta, **242**
  Creamy Polenta, 179, **180**

crab, Warm Artichoke Dip
  with Crab, **92**

cranberries
  Cranberry-Marinated Beef
    Tenderloin, **86–87**
  Cranberry Relish, **54**

Creamy Polenta, 179, **180**

Crispy Chickpeas with
  Yogurt Sauce and Naan,
  274, 275

croutons, Chive Croutons, **13**

Crowd-Pleaser Summer Slaw,
  xxvi, 31, **34**

Curried Carrots with
  Pecans, **87**

Curried Red Lentil Soup with
  Greens, **234**, 235

desserts
  Mom's Chocolate
    Pudding Pie, **45**
  My Chocolate
    Pudding Pie, **46**, 47
  Peach Berry Cobbler, **250**
  Phoebe's Mint Chocolate
    Ice Cream Cake with
    Ganache, **208–10**

Rosa's Mud Cake, 24, 201,
  202–3
Snickerdoodles, **26**
Tag-Team Whipped Cream,
  58, **59**
Tea Cup Brownie
  Sundaes, **95**
Triple Berry Summer Pie with
  Lattice Crust, xxvi, xxvii,
  118–20, **121**
See also cakes; chocolate;
  cookies; pie

Dill Pickled Vegetables,
  137, 138, 139, **140**

dips, Warm Artichoke Dip, **92**

Doughnut Cake, **194**, 195

duck, Grilled Duck Breast
  with Cherry-Peach Relish,
  105–6

eggs
  Ham and Eggs with Parm
    and Herbs, **11**
  Homemade Sausage, Egg,
    and Cheese on Homemade
    Biscuits, **197–98**

fennel, Quinoa Salad
  with Roast Vegetables,
  Feta, and Herbs, 116, **117–18**

finger foods, **92**

fish
  Grilled Fish Sandwiches with
    Salsa Fresca, **158–59**, 160
  Grilled Fish with Blender
    Sauce, **107**, **109**

Salmon and Potatoes with Yogurt Sauce, **271**, 272, 273

Foot Long Party Subs, 222, **223–24**

Franks and Beans, xxvi, 36, **38**, **40**

frosting
Chocolate Frosting, **203**
Chocolate Ganache, **210**

fruit
Apple-Cinnamon Fritters, **154–55**
Beet and Blood Orange Salad with Pistachios, **94**
Brown Butter Apple Pie, **193**
Cherry-Peach Relish, **105–6**
"Fruit First Thing" ritual, 133–34
Kale Salad with Pomegranates, **110**, 111, 178
Peach Berry Cobbler, **250**
Phoebe's Fried Pineapple, **92**
Shredded Pork Lettuce Wraps with Pomegranates, **238**, 239, **240**
Strawberry-Almond Milkshakes, 112, **113**
Triple Berry Summer Pie with Lattice Crust, xxvi, xxvii, 118–20, **121**

ganache, **210**

German Potato Salad, xxvi, 31, **35**

glazes
Apricot-Rum Glazed Ham, 8, **10–11**

Grilled Soy-Glazed Pork Chops, **246**, 247

gnocchi, Abby's Homemade Gnocchi with Basil and Cheese, 126, 127, **129–30**

Grandma Jody's Lasagna, **252–53**

Grandma Jody's Marinara, **255**

granola, Our Favorite Granola, **23**

gravies, Turkey Gravy, **50–51**

green chiles, Phoebe's Hatch Burgers, **130**

Greenest Green Salad, 244, **245**

grilled foods
Grilled Duck Breast with Cherry-Peach Relish, **105–6**
Grilled Fish Sandwiches with Salsa Fresca, **158–59**, 160
Grilled Fish with Blender Sauce, **107**, **109**
Grilled Halloumi and Asparagus with Pesto, 247, **248–49**
Grilled Smashed Potatoes with Chutney, **109**
Grilled Soy-Glazed Pork Chops, **246**, 247
Grilled Spicy Shrimp Tacos with Avocado Butter

and Summer Cabbage, **280–81**
Post-Beach Grilled Cheddar and Apple Sandwich, **162**

ham
Apricot-Rum Glazed Ham, 8, **10–11**
Ham and Eggs with Parm and Herbs, **11**
Ham Sandwiches (or Sliders) with Pickled Vegetables, **12**, 72
Interfaith Sliders (Brisket & Ham), **70**, 71, **72**
Split Pea Soup with Leftover Ham and Chive Croutons, **12–13**

hamburgers
Phoebe's Hatch Burgers, **130**
See also sliders

Harissa Roasted Chicken, **241–42**

Hatch chiles, Phoebe's Hatch Burgers, **130**

holiday recipes
Christmas, 3, 82–88
Easter, 8, **10–13**
Fourth of July, 30–35
Jewish holidays, 3, 70–75
New Year's Eve, 89, 92–95
Thanksgiving, **49–56**
Valentine's Day, 24
winter holiday parties, 3, 70–75

Horseradish Mashed Potatoes, **175**

hot dogs, Franks and
Beans, xxvi, 35, **38**, **40**

Hubba's Christmas
Cookies, 82, **83**, 84, 85

The $100 Challah, **6–7**

ice cream
Phoebe's Mint Chocolate
Ice Cream Cake with
Ganache, **208–10**
Tea Cup Brownie Sundaes, **95**

Ice Coffee, Cold-Brewed, 164, **165**

Interfaith Sliders
(Brisket & Ham), **70**, **71**, **72**

jam, Homemade Strawberry
Jam, **152**, 153, **154**

Jewish foods
Jewish Star of David
Christmas Cookies, 3, **6–7**
Potato Latkes With Fixin's,
73, 74–75
The $100 Challah, **6–7**

Kale Salad with
Pomegranates, **110**, 111, 178

lasagna
Grandma Jody's Lasagna,
252–53
Grandma Jody's Marinara, **255**

"Leaf" (salad), 256

lemons, One-Pan Lemon
Chicken with Asparagus
and Chives, **263**

lentils, Curried Red Lentil Soup
with Greens, **234**, 235

lettuce
Greenest Green Salad, 244, **245**
"Leaf," 256
Shredded Pork Lettuce
Wraps with Pomegranates,
238, 239, **240**
Sybil's Salad, **88**

lobster, New Year's Eve
Lobsters with Champagne
Butter, **93**

mayonnaise, Spicy Mayo,
159, 161

meatballs, Cider-Braised
Pork Meatballs with Creamy
Polenta, **178**, 179, **180**

Mexican cuisine
Big World Event Super Nacho
Plate, 262–63, **264–65**
Burrito Bowls, **277**, **279–80**
Grilled Spicy Shrimp Tacos
with Avocado Butter and
Summer Cabbage, **280–81**
Quick Guacamole, **280**

milkshakes, Strawberry-
Almond Milkshakes, 112, **113**

Mint Chocolate Ice Cream Cake
with Ganache, **208–10**

Mom's Chocolate Pudding
Pie, **45**

Mom's Herb-Roasted Turkey
with Gravy, 48, **49–51**

My Chocolate Pudding Pie,
46, 47

My Grandma Catrino's
Biscotti, **16**, 17, **19**

nachos, Big World Event Super
Nacho Plate, 262–63, **264–65**

Negroni, **xxix**

New Year's Eve Lobsters
with Champagne Butter, **93**

nuts
Beet and Blood Orange
Salad with Pistachios, **94**
Curried Carrots with
Pecans, **87**
My Grandma Catrino's
Biscotti, **16**, 17, **19**
Sour Cream Chocolate
Chip Nut Loaf, 18, **19–20**
Strawberry-Almond
Milkshakes, 112, **113**
Sybil's Salad, **88**

One-Pan Lemon Chicken
with Asparagus and Chives,
263

Orecchiette with Sweet
Sausage Bolognese, **270**

pancakes, Sleepover Chocolate
Chip Pancakes, **149**

Parm Mashed Potatoes, **175**

pasta
Grandma Jody's Lasagna,
252–53

Grandma Jody's Marinara, **255**
Orecchiette with Sweet
   Sausage Bolognese, **270**
Pasta Carbonara, **xxviii–xxix**

Peach Berry Cobbler, **250**

peas
   Greenest Green Salad,
     244, **245**
   Split Pea Soup with
     Leftover Ham and
     Chive Croutons, **12–13**

Pesto, **248–49**

Phoebe's Fried Pineapple, **92**

Phoebe's Hatch Burgers, **130**

Phoebe's Mint Chocolate
   Ice Cream Cake with
   Ganache, **208–10**

pickling
   Dill Pickled Vegetables,
     137, 138, 139, **140**
   Ham Sandwiches (or Sliders)
     with Pickled Vegetables,
     12, 72
   Quick Pickles, **141**
   uses for pickled vegetables,
     142

Picnic Chicken, 30–31, **32–33**

pies
   Brown Butter Apple Pie, **193**
   Mom's Chocolate Pudding
     Pie, **45**
   My Chocolate Pudding Pie,
     46, 47

Triple Berry Summer Pie with
   Lattice Crust, xxvi, xxvii,
   118–20, **121**

pineapple, Phoebe's Fried
   Pineapple, **92**

pistachios, Beet and
   Blood Orange Salad with
   Pistachios, **94**

pizza
   Broccolini-Chickpea pizza,
     180–81, 182–83
   Pizza with Ramps and
     Taleggio, **114**

polenta
   Baked Polenta with Feta, **242**
   Creamy Polenta, 179, **180**

pomegranates
   Kale Salad with Pomegranates,
     110, 111, 178
   Shredded Pork Lettuce Wraps
     with Pomegranates,
     238, 239, **240**

popcorn, Truffle Popcorn, **92**

Popovers with Homemade
   Strawberry Jam, **152**, 153,
   154

pork
   Apricot-Rum Glazed Ham,
     8, **10–11**
   "Bus Stop Social" ribs,
     xxvi, xxviii
   Cider-Braised Pork Meatballs
     with Creamy Polenta,
     178, 179, **180**

Grilled Soy-Glazed Pork
   Chops, **246**, 247
Shredded Pork Lettuce
   Wraps with Pomegranates,
   238, 239, **240**

Post-Beach Grilled
   Cheddar and Apple
   Sandwich, **162**

potatoes
   Abby's Homemade Gnocchi
     with Basil and Cheese,
     126, 127, **129–30**
   Classic Mashed Potatoes,
     172, **175**
   German Potato Salad,
     xxvi, 31, **35**
   Grilled Smashed Potatoes
     with Chutney, **109**
   Potato Gratin with Gruyère,
     56, 57
   Potato Latkes with Fixin's,
     73, 74–75
   Salmon and Potatoes with
     Yogurt Sauce, **271**, 272,
     273

Quick Guacamole, **280**

Quick Pickles, **141**

Quinoa Salad with Roast
   Vegetables, Feta, and Herbs,
   116, **117–18**

ramps, Pizza with Ramps
   and Taleggio, **114**

relish
   Cherry-Peach Relish, **105–6**
   Cranberry Relish, **54**

ribs, "Bus Stop Social" ribs, **xxvi, xxviii**

rice
Burrito Bowls, **277**, **279–80**
Cilantro-Lime Rice, **240**

Rosa's Mud Cake,
24, 201, **202–3**

salads
Beet and Blood Orange
Salad with Pistachios, **94**
Greenest Green Salad,
244, **245**
Kale Salad with Pomegranates,
110, 111, 178
"Leaf," 256
Quinoa Salad with Roast
Vegetables, Feta, and Herbs,
116, **117–18**
Sybil's Salad, **88**

Salmon and Potatoes
with Yogurt Sauce,
271, 272, 273

salsas and dressings
Basic Vinaigrette, **118**
Crowd-Pleaser Summer
Slaw, **34**
for Greenest Green Salad,
245
Pesto, **248–49**
Quick Guacamole, **280**
salsa for Burrito Bowls,
277, **279–80**
Salsa Fresca, **158–59**, 160
Salsa Verde, **107**, **109**
Spicy Mayo, **159**, 161
Tomato Coulis, **107**, **109**
Vinaigrette, **110**, **118**

sandwiches
Foot Long Party Subs,
222, **223–24**
Post-Beach Grilled Cheddar
and Apple Sandwich, **162**
The Tomato Sandwich,
104, **105**
Vegetarian Sub, **224–25**

sauces
Salsa Verde (Blender Sauce),
107
Tomato Coulis
(Blender Sauce), **107**
Yogurt Sauce, **271**, 273,
274, 275

sausage
Homemade Sausage, **198**
Orecchiette with Sweet
Sausage Bolognese, **270**
Sausage and Apple Stuffing,
53
World Cup Breakfast Fry-Up,
266

seafood
Grilled Spicy Shrimp Tacos
with Avocado Butter and
Summer Cabbage, **280–81**
News Year's Eve Lobsters
with Champagne Butter, **93**
Warm Artichoke Dip
with Crab, **92**

shakes, Strawberry-Almond
Milkshakes, 112, **113**

shrimp, Grilled Spicy Shrimp
Tacos with Avocado Butter
and Summer Cabbage,
280–81

slaw
Crowd-Pleaser Summer Slaw,
xxvi, 31, **34**
Grilled Spicy Shrimp Tacos
with Avocado Butter and
Summer Cabbage,
280–81

Sleepover Chocolate Chip
Pancakes, **149**

Sliced Tomatoes with Sea Salt
and Chives, **249**

sliders
Ham Sandwiches (or Sliders)
with Pickled Vegetables,
12, 72
Interfaith Sliders
(Brisket & Ham), **70**,
71, **72**

Snickerdoodles, **26**

soups
Curried Red Lentil Soup with
Greens, **234**, 235
Split Pea Soup with Leftover
Ham and Chive Croutons,
12–13

Sour Cream Chocolate Chip
Nut Loaf, 18, **19–20**

Spicy Mayo, **159**, 161

spinach, Grandma Jody's
Lasagna, **252–53**

Split Pea Soup with Leftover
Ham and Chive Croutons,
12–13

strawberries
Homemade Strawberry Jam,
152, 153, **154**
Peach Berry Cobbler, **250**
Strawberry-Almond
Milkshakes, 112, **113**

stuffing, Sausage and
Apple Stuffing, **53**

subs
Foot Long Party Subs,
222, **223–24**
Vegetarian Sub, **224–25**

swordfish, Grilled Fish
Sandwiches with Salsa
Fresca, **158–59**, 160

Sybil's Salad, **88**

tacos, Grilled Spicy Shrimp
Tacos with Avocado
Butter and Summer
Cabbage, **280–81**

Tag-Team Whipped Cream,
58, **59**

Tea Cup Brownie Sundaes, **95**

tomatoes
Grandma Jody's Marinara, **255**
Orecchiette with Sweet
Sausage Bolognese, **270**
Salsa Fresca, **158–59**, 160
Sliced Tomatoes with
Sea Salt and Chives, **249**
Tomato Coulis, **107**, **109**
The Tomato Sandwich,
104, **105**

tortilla chips, Big World Event
Super Nacho Plate, 262–63,
264–65

tortillas, Grilled Spicy Shrimp
Tacos with Avocado Butter
and Summer Cabbage,
280–81

Triple Berry Summer Pie
with Lattice Crust, xxvi,
xxvii, 118–20, **121**

Truffle Popcorn, **92**

tuna, Grilled Fish
Sandwiches with Salsa
Fresca, **158–59**, 160

turkey
Mom's Herb-Roasted
Turkey with Gravy, 48,
49–51
Sausage and Apple
Stuffing, **53**

Turkey Gravy, **50–51**

vegetables
Asparagus with Pesto, 247,
248–49
Beet and Blood Orange
Salad with Pistachios, **94**
Broccolini-Chickpea pizza,
180–81, 182–83
"Confetti" Brussels
Sprouts with Bacon
and Raisins, **51**
Crispy Chickpeas with
Yogurt Sauce and Naan,
274, 275

Curried Carrots with
Pecans, **87**
Dill Pickled Vegetables,
137, 138, 139, **140**
Ham Sandwiches (or Sliders)
with Pickled Vegetables, **12**
Kale Salad with Pomegranates,
110, 111, 178
Pizza with Ramps and
Taleggio, **114**
Quick Pickles, **141**
Quinoa Salad with Roast
Vegetables, Feta, and Herbs,
116, **117–18**
Salsa Fresca, **158–59**, 160
Salsa Verde, **107**, **109**
Sliced Tomatoes with
Sea Salt and Chives, **249**
Sybil's Salad, **88**
Tomato Coulis, **107**, **109**
The Tomato Sandwich,
104, **105**
Vegetarian Sub, **224–25**

Vegetarian Sub, **224–25**

Vinaigrette, **110**, **118**

Warm Artichoke Dip, **92**

Whipped Cream, 58, **59**

World Cup Breakfast Fry-Up,
266

wraps, Shredded Pork Lettuce
Wraps with Pomegranates,
238, 239, **240**

Yogurt Sauce, **271**, 273, **274**,
275

ABOUT THE AUTHOR

Jenny Rosenstrach writes the blog Dinner: A Love Story.
She is the author of Dinner: A Love Story *(Ecco, 2012)*
and Dinner: The Playbook *(Ballantine, 2014),*
a New York Times *bestseller. She and her husband,*
Andy Ward, co-write the column "The Providers"
for Bon Appétit *and live in Westchester County, New York,*
with their daughters, Phoebe and Abby.

dinneralovestory.com
Facebook.com/dinneralovestory
@DinnerLoveStory
Instagram.com/dinneralovestory

Let's do it again soon